Contrasts and Effect Sizes in Behavioral Research
A CORRELATIONAL APPROACH

Contrasts are statistical procedures for asking focused questions of data. Compared to diffuse or omnibus questions, focused questions are characterized by greater conceptual clarity and greater statistical power when examining those focused questions. If an effect truly exists, we are more likely to discover it and to believe it to be real when asking focused questions rather than omnibus ones. Researchers, teachers of research methods, and graduate students will be familiar with the principles and procedures of contrast analysis but will also be introduced to a series of newly developed concepts, measures, and indices that permit a wider and more useful application of contrast analysis. This volume takes on this new approach by introducing a family of correlational effect size estimates. By returning to these correlations throughout the book, the authors demonstrate special adaptations in a variety of contexts from two-group comparison to one-way analysis of variance contexts, to factorial designs, to repeated measures designs, and to the case of multiple contrasts.

Robert Rosenthal is Distinguished Professor of Psychology at the University of California, Riverside, and Edgar Pierce Professor of Psychology, Emeritus, at Harvard University. Dr. Rosenthal is also the coauthor, with Ralph L. Rosnow, of *Essentials of Behavioral Research, People Studying People, Beginning Behavioral Research*, and other books.

Ralph L. Rosnow is Thaddeus L. Bolton Professor of Psychology at Temple University. He is the author of *Paradigms in Transition: The Methodology of Social Inquiry* and other books.

Donald B. Rubin is Professor of Statistics at Harvard University. He is the author of *Multiple Imputation for Nonresponse in Sample Surveys* and the coauthor of *Bayesian Data Analysis, Statistical Analysis with Missing Data*, and other books.

Contrasts and Effect Sizes in Behavioral Research

A CORRELATIONAL APPROACH

ROBERT ROSENTHAL
Department of Psychology, University of California, Riverside, and Harvard University

RALPH L. ROSNOW
Department of Psychology, Temple University

DONALD B. RUBIN
Department of Statistics, Harvard University

PUBLISHED BY THE PRESS SYNDICATE OF THE UNIVERSITY OF CAMBRIDGE
The Pitt Building, Trumpington Street, Cambridge, United Kingdom

CAMBRIDGE UNIVERSITY PRESS
The Edinburgh Building, Cambridge CB2 2RU, UK   http://www.cup.cam.ac.uk
40 West 20th Street, New York, NY 10011-4211, USA   http://www.cup.org
10 Stamford Road, Oakleigh, Melbourne 3166, Australia
Ruiz de Alarcón 13, 28014 Madrid, Spain

© Cambridge University Press 2000

This book is in copyright. Subject to statutory exception
and to the provisions of relevant collective licensing agreements,
no reproduction of any part may take place without
the written permission of Cambridge University Press.

First published 2000

Printed in the United States of America

Typeface Stone Serif 9.5/13 pt.   *System* LaTeX 2_ε [TB]

A catalog record for this book is available from the British Library.

Library of Congress Cataloging in Publication data
Rosenthal, Robert, 1933 –
    Contrasts and effect sizes in behavioral research : a
    correlational approach / Robert Rosenthal, Ralph L. Rosnow, Donald
    B. Rubin.
        p.   cm.
    Includes bibliographical references and index.
    ISBN 0-521-65258-8 (hc). – ISBN 0-521-65980-9 (pb)
    1. Psychometrics.   2. Analysis of variance.   3. Psychology –
Statistical methods.   4. Social sciences – Statistical methods.
I. Rosnow, Ralph L.   II. Rubin, Donald B.   III. Title.
BF39.2.A52R67   1999
150′.7′27 – dc21   99-24199
                                                              CIP

ISBN 0 521 65258 8 hardback
ISBN 0 521 65980 9 paperback

Contents

	Preface	*page*	ix
1	**Basic Concepts of Focused Procedures**		1
	Focused versus Omnibus Questions		1
	An Example		1
	Effect Sizes and Significance Levels		4
	REVIEW QUESTIONS		6
2	**Basic Procedures for Two Groups**		8
	Comparing Two Groups		8
	Correlation Effect Size (r)		9
	Other Effect Sizes: Cohen's d and Hedges's g		11
	Transforming Between Effect Size Measures		12
	Counternull Value of an Effect Size		13
	Counternull Value of a Point-Biserial r		14
	Problems When Interpreting Effect Sizes		15
	Binomial Effect Size Display		17
	Relating BESD, r, and r^2		17
	Counternull Value of the BESD		20
	The BESD with Dichotomous Outcome Variables		21
	How Big an Effect Size Is "Important"?		25
	How Many Subjects? Considerations of Power		28
	Extension to Unequal Sample Sizes in Two Groups		30
	REVIEW QUESTIONS		35
3	**One-Way Contrast Analyses**		37
	Obtaining Significance Levels		37
	Effect Size Correlations		42
	The Four rs in the Meta-Analytic Context		61
	Extension to Unequal Sample Sizes in Three or More Groups		63
	REVIEW QUESTIONS		68

4	Contrasts in Factorial Designs	71
	Prologue	71
	$r_{alerting}$: A Preliminary Look at the Data	71
	Obtaining Significance Levels	73
	$r_{contrast}$: The Maximally Partialed Correlation	74
	Another Example of the Calculation of $r_{alerting}$, Significance Levels, and $r_{contrast}$	76
	$r_{alerting}$, Significance Levels, and $r_{contrast}$ in Multifactor Designs with Unequal Sample Sizes	79
	$r_{effect\ size}$	79
	A More Detailed Example of the Calculation of $r_{effect\ size}$ and $r_{effect\ size|NS}$	82
	A Three-Factor Example	84
	A Four-Factor Example	88
	r_{BESD}	92
	Effect Size Estimation When Contrast Weights of 0 Are Set Aside	102
	Extension to Unequal Sample Sizes in Factorial Designs	113
	Preview	121
	REVIEW QUESTIONS	122
5	**Contrasts in Repeated Measures**	125
	Intrinsically Repeated Measures Studies	125
	Introduction to Nonintrinsically Repeated Measures Studies	136
	Nonintrinsically Repeated Measures Studies: Significance Levels and $r_{contrast}$	137
	Nonintrinsically Repeated Measures Studies: Effect Size Correlations Other Than $r_{contrast}$	142
	REVIEW QUESTIONS	147
6	**Multiple Contrasts**	151
	Relationships among Contrasts	151
	Examining the Difference between Contrasts	159
	Unplanned Contrasts	170
	REVIEW QUESTIONS	178
Appendix A	**List of Equations**	185
	Chapter 2	185
	Chapter 3	187
	Chapter 4	189
	Chapter 5	190
	Chapter 6	190
Appendix B	**Statistical Tables**	191
	Table B.1 Table of Standard Normal Deviates (Z)	191
	Table B.2 Extended Table of t	192

Table B.3 Table of F 196
Table B.4 Table of χ^2 202

References 205
Index 209

Preface

There is a dual purpose to this book. First, we want to make available in a single volume an exposition of the principles and procedures of contrast analysis that have applications in a wide range of fields in the behavioral and social sciences. Second, we want to introduce to the community of researchers, teachers of research methods, and graduate students in these fields a series of newly developed concepts, measures, and indices that permit a wider and more useful application of contrast analysis. In short, this book is intended as both a text and a contribution to new knowledge in the area of contrast analysis.

Although one of us might be viewed as a mathematical statistician (DBR), our approach in this book is intuitive, concrete, and arithmetic rather than rigorously or formally mathematical. The statistical examples we employ are in all cases hypothetical, constructed specifically to illustrate the logical bases of the computational procedures. The numbers are neater than real-life examples tend to be, and there are fewer numbers in any single example than we would find in an actual data set. All of this material has been pretested in our own courses, with the objective of showing how practical, convenient, and inviting it is to use this approach to contrast analysis.

So why is contrast analysis not used all the time? As Robert Abelson noted in an unpublished paper prepared in 1962, the answer is not that the "method of contrasts" is brand-new:

> This method dates back virtually to the invention of the analysis of variance itself.... It is well-known to most statisticians and to some psychologists, but it has received only the most cursory and off-hand treatment in standard statistical reference works ... and presentations by psychologists of some of its uses have tended toward very specialized applications.... Actually the method of contrasts is extraordinary for its wide range of varied uses. That the method has not heretofore received a comprehensive, unified treatment is a matter of some mystery. One compelling line of explanation is that the statisticians do not regard the idea as mathematically very interesting (it is based on quite elementary statistical concepts) and that quantitative psychologists have never quite appreciated its generality of application.

Indeed, the fact of the matter is that tradition in the behavioral and social sciences has pretty much ignored contrast analysis, often in favor of omnibus significance tests and more complex techniques of data analysis. The problem is that omnibus tests, although they provide protection for some investigators from the danger of "data mining" when multiple tests are performed as if each were the only one considered, do not usually tell us anything we really want to know. As for more complex techniques (such as canonical correlation or multivariate analysis of variance), they have useful exploratory data-analytic applications, but the danger is that they are commonly used to test null hypotheses that are typically of doubtful scientific value (cf. Huberty & Morris, 1989). Thus it is our hope that the present volume will help foster that appreciation of the value of contrast analysis that Bob Abelson found missing all those years ago.

Although the basic idea of contrasts is quite old, as Abelson pointed out long ago, the approach taken in the present volume is almost entirely new. What makes our approach new is the introduction of a family of correlational effect size estimates including $r_{alerting}$, $r_{contrast}$, $r_{effect\ size}$, r_{BESD}, and $r_{counternull}$. We return to the application of these five correlations throughout the book, showing their special adaptations in a variety of contexts from two-group comparisons to one-way analysis of variance contexts, to factorial designs, to repeated measures designs, to the case of multiple contrasts.

Since the publication of an earlier book on contrasts (Rosenthal & Rosnow, 1985), we have been thinking, teaching, and writing about the ideas elaborated more fully in this book. We are very much indebted to the many colleagues and graduate students who provided critical commentary at various stages in the evolution of these ideas. In particular, we thank Professors Larry Hedges and Miron Zuckerman for their recent suggestions. We are also grateful for the support provided by a number of institutions, including the James McKeen Cattell Fund, Temple University, and the National Science Foundation. We are grateful to Blair Boudreau for her superb keyboarding of our oft-revised and sharpened manuscript, and to Julia Hough of Cambridge University Press for her patience as our additions and improvements pushed the date of publication further and further away. We thank the following for generously granting permission to adapt the statistical tables that appear in this volume: the American Statistical Association, Lawrence Erlbaum Associates, Houghton Mifflin, and McGraw-Hill. And finally, we thank MaryLu Rosenthal, Mimi Rosnow, and Kathryn Rubin for their forbearance and support of their abstracted and overcommitted friends Bob, Ralph, and Don.

CHAPTER 1

Basic Concepts of Focused Procedures

This chapter discusses the basic distinction between contrasts and omnibus tests of significance. Omnibus tests seldom address questions of real interest to researchers and are typically less powerful than focused procedures. Contrasts accompanied by effect size estimates address focused questions, and the effect size tells us something very different from the *p* value.

FOCUSED VERSUS OMNIBUS QUESTIONS

Contrasts are statistical procedures for asking focused questions of data. Compared to diffuse or omnibus questions, focused questions are characterized by greater conceptual clarity, and the statistical procedure by greater statistical power when examining those focused questions. That is, if an effect truly exists, we are more likely to discover it and to believe it to be real when asking focused questions rather than omnibus ones. Contrast analyses yield both estimates of the magnitude of the effects investigated and the associated significance levels.

AN EXAMPLE

Suppose developmental researchers interested in psychomotor skills had a total of fifty children at five age levels (11, 12, 13, 14, 15) play a new video game. The specific question of interest to the researchers was whether age is an effective predictor of proficiency in this game. The mean performance scores of ten children at each of the five age levels were 25, 30, 40, 50, and 55, respectively. These values are plotted in Figure 1.1, whereas Table 1.1 shows the overall analysis of variance (ANOVA) computed on the individual scores. Should the researchers conclude, on the basis of the omnibus F with $p = .40$ noted in Table 1.1, that age was not an effective predictor variable?

If they did so, they would be ignoring what we can see very plainly in Figure 1.1. We observe that the mean performance increased in a monotonic fashion from the lowest to the highest age. In fact, the product-moment correlation for the relation between the five age levels and five performance means is .99. We

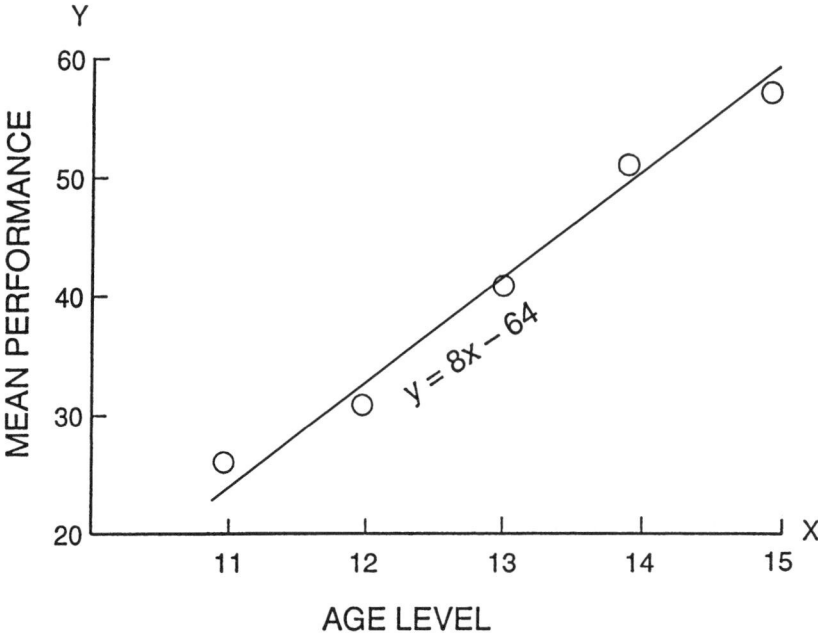

FIGURE 1.1
Graph of group performance data.

call this correlation between an indicator of the "treatment level" (e.g., age) and mean response (e.g., mean performance) an *alerting correlation* ($r_{alerting}$) because it can alert us to overall trends of interest. This alerting correlation is a poor estimate of the relation between *individual* children's ages and performances, because correlations based on aggregated date (e.g., group means) can be dramatically larger or smaller (even in the opposite direction) than correlations based on individual scores. Typically, however, in behavioral research, alerting correlations tend to be larger than correlations based on individual scores. Nonetheless, this correlation alerts us that, although the omnibus F for age levels was far from significant at the conventional .05 level, we should not simply dismiss the idea that age was an effective predictor variable. Notice also in Figure 1.1 that the circles signifying the group means coincide very closely with the straight-line graph with slope 8 and

TABLE 1.1
Summary of Overall ANOVA

Source	SS	df	MS	F	p
Age levels	6,500	4	1,625	1.03	.40
Within error	70,875	45	1,575		

Y value at the mean age, 13, equal to 40. Clearly the mean performance can be predicted with little error as a linear function of age level.

Common as omnibus significance tests are, this hypothetical case illustrates that they typically do not tell us anything we really want to know. The omnibus F addressed the diffuse question of whether there were any differences among the five age levels, disregarding entirely their ordinal arrangement. The number of possible permutations of the five age levels is 120. Any of these 120 orderings (e.g., 15, 14, 13, 12, 11 or 13, 12, 14, 15, 11) would have yielded the same F with the numerator degrees of freedom of 4. On the other hand, had the researchers performed a contrast analysis to address the specific question of interest, their finding would have been more illuminating. For example, had they performed a t test to assess the linear pattern between age and performance (using a contrast procedure described in Chapter 3), their finding would have been that $t(45) = 2.02$, $p = .025$ one-tailed. Not surprisingly (because squaring the value of a t statistic gives an F statistic with 1 df in the numerator), their finding, had they addressed the predicted linear trend by a focused F, would have been that $F(1, 45) = 4.06$, $p = .05$ (also described in Chapter 3).

Even though a linear pattern among the means was clearly evident to the naked eye, the researchers' omnibus F test was insufficiently focused to reject the null hypothesis that the five means were statistically identical. To be sure, this kind of dramatic change – in which the result of the omnibus F has an "insignificant" p value but the result of the contrast is clearly associated with a "significant" p – cannot be expected always, or perhaps even very often, to occur. But what we can usually expect is an increase both in the conceptual clarity concerning the question being asked and in statistical power when, instead of automatically employing omnibus tests of diffuse hypotheses, we formulate precise questions using planned contrasts with associated focused effect size estimates and p values. Because researchers generally want to use statistical tests that will lead to more significant p values when the null hypothesis is false, tests based on contrasts can be said to be more "useful" or more "successful" than omnibus tests.

As we will describe in Chapter 3, our focused procedures compared ("contrasted") the group means of 25, 30, 40, 50, 55 with fixed weights of $-2, -1, 0, +1, +2$ (called *lambda weights*) representing a linear increase in group means. In other words, contrasts are simply focused comparisons of actual group means with predicted lambda (λ) weights, with the predictions made on the basis of theory, hypothesis, or hunch. Such a comparison may include all the condition means or only some of the means (e.g., results at age 11 and age 15 using lambda weights of $-1, 0, 0, 0, +1$). The only formal stipulation for a contrast is that the lambda weights must sum to zero (i.e., $\Sigma\lambda = 0$). For example, suppose the hypothesis were that economic incentive improves the productivity of work groups but that a boomerang effect can result from excessive external reward. Because the predicted quadratic pattern is ∩-shaped (i.e., an upside-down ∪), we might select contrast weights of $-2, +1, +2, +1, -2$. Now that we have introduced the idea of contrast weights, we can more precisely define $r_{alerting}$ as the correlation between the means of the various conditions or groups investigated and the contrast weights with which the conditions or groups are associated.

EFFECT SIZES AND SIGNIFICANCE LEVELS

The basic lesson so far is that contrasts usually give us greater substantive interpretation of research results and greater power for tests of significance. Another advantage of contrasts is that effect sizes can often be easily computed from data in published reports as well as from raw data. Indeed, a maxim of data analysis is that when reporting results, we should give the sizes of the effects as well as the p values.

It is important to realize that the effect size tells us something very different from the p level. A result that is statistically significant at conventional levels is not necessarily "practically significant" as judged by the magnitude of the effect. Consequently, highly significant p values should not be interpreted as automatically reflecting large effects. In the case of F ratios, a numerator mean square (MS) may be large relative to a denominator MS because (a) the effect size is large, (b) the sample size per condition is large, or (c) both. On the other hand, even if the effect size were considered quantitatively unimpressive, it might still have important practical implications. In the next chapters, we will see why that is so, but for now, we will simply sketch some broad ideas about effect sizes and p levels.

Table 1.2 shows four possible outcomes of p levels and effect sizes as joint determinants of inferential evaluations (Rosnow & Rosenthal, 1988). The tag labels of "acceptable" and "unacceptable" simply imply that the notion that a particular value of an effect size or a significance level is large enough or sufficiently stringent to detect the presence of a "real" effect or "real" difference is not cut in stone. Unfortunately, many researchers operate as if the only proper significance-testing decision should automatically be antinull if p is not greater than .05 and pronull if p is greater than .05 (Nelson, Rosenthal, & Rosnow, 1986; Rosenthal & Gaito, 1963; Zuckerman, Hodgins, Zuckerman, & Rosenthal, 1993). It may not be

TABLE 1.2
Potential Problems of Inference as a Function of Obtained Effect Sizes and Significance Levels

Level of significance	Effect Size	
	"Acceptable" (large enough)	"Unacceptable" (too small)
"Acceptable" (low enough)	No inferential problem	Mistaking statistical significance for practical importance
"Unacceptable" (too high)	Failure to perceive practical importance of "nonsignificant" results	No inferential problem

an exaggeration to say that for many Ph.D. students, for whom the .05 alpha has acquired a kind of mystique, it can mean joy, doctoral degrees, and tenure track positions at major universities if their dissertation ps are less than .05. On the other hand, ps greater than .05 can mean ruin, despair, and their advisers' suddenly thinking of new control conditions that should be run. Logically, of course, there is no justification for a sharp line between a "significant" and a "nonsignificant" difference; the distressing implications of drawing a sharp line have been discussed (e.g., Bakan, 1966; Cohen, 1990; Meehl, 1978; Rosnow & Rosenthal, 1989, 1996b; Schmidt, 1996).

Interestingly, R. A. Fisher chose the 5%, 1%, and 0.1% levels for his tables simply because he regarded them as convenient points on a continuous scale (Yates, 1990, p. xviii). Because it was cumbersome to interpolate between tabulated levels of significance (in the days before powerful hand calculators and desktop computers), writers got into the habit of indicating rough interpolations by stars and asterisks. In behavioral science, it was the 5% (in some cases, the 1%) level that became entrenched in the minds of leading journal editors, textbook authors, and researchers themselves as a "fixed critical level" of significance (Gigerenzer, 1993). Nonetheless, significance in statistics, like the significance of a value in the universe of values, varies continuously between extremes (Boring, 1950; Gigerenzer & Murray, 1987).

Furthermore, as many, including Robert Abelson (1962), have wisely cautioned, significance tests should always be used "for guidance rather than for sanctification" (p. 9). We recommend the practice, endorsed by many statisticians, of reporting precise p values (e.g., $p = .06$ rather than $p > .05$). That effort, in turn, will make it easier for informed consumers and meta-analysts to evaluate the implications of a given p value or, more usefully, of that p value with its associated effect size.

Returning to Table 1.2, suppose we were confronted with a "nonsignificant" p and a "large" effect size – what should this tell us? Were we simply to conclude on the basis of the significance level that "nothing happened," we might be making a serious mistake. A small sample size may have led to failure to detect the true effect, in which case, we should continue this line of investigation with a larger sample size before embracing the null as approximately true.

On the other hand, suppose we obtain a "significant" p and a "small" effect size – what should this tell us? The answer depends both on the sample size and on what we consider the practical importance of the estimated effect size. With a large sample size, we may mistake a result that is merely "very significant" for one that is of practical importance. In the next chapter, we describe convenient formulas for computing informative effect sizes when comparing two groups. We also show how to calculate counternull values, that is, effect sizes that are just as well supported by the data as the null hypothesis. Chapter 3 describes extensions of the procedures in Chapter 2 for studies employing more than two groups. Chapter 4 presents procedures applicable when it is useful to conceptualize the data as made up of more than one factor. Chapter 5 describes repeated measures designs in which each subject contributes two or more measurements (e.g., under different experimental conditions). Chapter 6, the concluding chapter, describes procedures employed when multiple contrasts are computed, combined, and compared.

One aspect of our presentation is especially distinctive. Essentially all of our effect size measures are correlations of one kind or another. We feel that using correlations is particularly appropriate in the behavioral and social sciences, where the same conceptual outcome variable (e.g., improvement of mental health) can be measured in a wide variety of ways (e.g., test scores, ratings on a scale, rehospitalizations). In such situations, regression coefficients, for instance, are not directly comparable across different studies even in the same research area, whereas correlation coefficients can be sensibly compared. The outcome variables in much of the social sciences are typically not like those in medicine (e.g., death, blood pressure), chemistry (temperature, pressure), physics (acceleration, velocity), or even some of the social sciences (e.g., money in economics), where the outcome variables have intrinsic meaning.

In the area of interpersonal expectancy effects, for example, dozens of different outcome variables have been employed, including maze-learning and Skinner-box-learning scores earned by rats, pupils' intellectual performance, responses to inkblot tests, reaction times, psychophysical judgments, interview behavior, and person perception tasks. In each of these areas, many different specific measures can be employed, and yet all these measures, of all these outcome variables, are subsumed under the single conceptual outcome variable of interpersonal expectancy effects, the degree to which one person's expectation for another's behavior comes to serve as a self-fulfilling prophecy (Rosenthal, 1966, 1976, 1994; Rosenthal & Rubin, 1978; Rosnow & Rosenthal, 1997). Clearly, the enormous variety of specific measures employed by researchers points to the greater utility of correlation coefficients than of regression coefficients as general indices of effect size.

REVIEW QUESTIONS

1. A widely used publication manual for psychologists urged that effect sizes be routinely reported and added that "in most cases such measures are readily obtainable whenever the omnibus test statistics (e.g., t and F) ... are reported." What is wrong with the quoted statement?

    Answer: The t test is not an omnibus test but a focused test, and not all F tests are omnibus tests (only those with numerator $df > 1$). Furthermore, effect sizes reported for omnibus F tests are typically uninterpretable.

2. Computing the analysis of variance on results of a five-group randomized experiment in which the subjects have been assigned to one of five levels of the independent variable, the researchers find $F(4, 95) = 1.24$, $p = .30$, and report that there was "no effect" of the independent variable. What is wrong with their report?

    Answer: Their report is of an omnibus effect that is unlikely to be of any real scientific interest. In addition, an important contrast may be hidden within the omnibus test with p as low as .028.

3. Is it possible for a large effect to escape detection by a significance test, and for a small effect to be statistically significant?

Answer: The answer is yes to both questions. A large effect might escape detection if there were too few subjects. A small effect would be detectable if the sample were large enough.

4. In discussing our hypothetical example with group means of 25, 30, 40, 50, and 55, we noted an alternative prediction using lambda weights of −1, 0, 0, 0, +1. What does the alerting r on these data tell us, particularly in comparison with the alerting r of .99 with the weights of −2, −1, 0, +1, +2 that was discussed previously?

    Answer: Correlating the alternative lambda weights with the group means gives alerting $r = .83$, which is another strong signal of a predicted relationship of interest. Later, we will see that squaring the alerting r tells us the proportion of the between-conditions sum of squares accounted for by the set of lambda weights. In this case, squaring .83 tells us that the alternative prediction with weights of −1, 0, 0, 0, +1 accounts for over two thirds of the between-conditions sum of squares. Squaring $r = .99$, the original prediction using weights of −2, −1, 0, +1, +2 accounted for 98% of the between-conditions sum of squares. Both hypotheses fare well, but the original one is a better predictor of the children's performance.

5. Another hypothesis mentioned is that economic incentive improves the productivity of work groups but that a boomerang effect can result from excessive reward. Given five increasing levels of economic incentive, this hypothesis was described as an "upside-down ∪" with weights of −2, +1, +2, +1, −2. Imagine two alternative experiments, with condition means of 50, 53, 56, 56, 43 in Study A, and with condition means of 56, 49, 41, 47, 55 in Study B. What can alerting rs computed on these results tell us?

    Answer: The alerting rs are .86 for Study A and −.96 for Study B. Study A's hypothesis is a good predictor, as it can account for 74% of the between-conditions sum of squares. Study B's lambda weights, although they account for 92% of the between-conditions sum of squares, are in the opposite direction of the obtained pattern. That is, an upside-down ∪ was predicted, but the group means are ∪-shaped in Study B.

6. Researcher Smith assigns a total of forty subjects at random to either an experimental or a control condition. She hypothesizes that subjects in the experimental condition will score higher on the dependent variable than will subjects in the control condition. She reports $F(1, 38) = 4.71$, $p = .036$, and concludes that her hypothesis was statistically supported. Researcher Jones repeats Smith's study using a total of twenty subjects, finds the same direction of difference, but reports $F(1, 18) = 2.22$, $p = .15$. Disappointed by this result, he questions the validity of Smith's hypothesis, reporting that he failed to replicate her result. Is he correct?

    Answer: Readers who already know how to calculate an effect size based on a focused test (reviewed in the next chapter) will have figured out that Jones was confused. Had he calculated the effect size instead of fixating on the obtained p level, he would have immediately seen that his findings replicated Smith's almost perfectly. The reason why Jones failed to replicate Smith's p value was that he was operating with half as many subjects and therefore less power.

CHAPTER 2

Basic Procedures for Two Groups

This chapter describes the computation of three effect size indices (Pearson *r*, Cohen's *d*, and Hedges's *g*) for two-group designs. The counternull value of the effect size is introduced as is the null-counternull interval with its associated *p* value. The binomial effect size display (BESD) is discussed, as is its null-counternull interval. Sample size estimation is reviewed, and the power-loss index and correlation effect sizes are introduced in the context of designs with unequal *n*s.

COMPARING TWO GROUPS

Imagine an experiment in which the subjects were assigned at random to either an experimental or a control condition. The hypothesis is that the experimental group will score higher on the dependent variable than will the control group. This is the simplest type of contrast where one group is contrasted or compared with the other group. Given the findings shown in Table 2.1, the researcher decides to employ a *t* test to compare the results in the experimental condition with those in the control condition,

$$t = \left(\frac{M_1 - M_2}{S_{within}}\right)\left(\frac{\sqrt{N}}{2}\right), \qquad (2.1)$$

where M_1 and M_2 are the group means, N is the total number of sampling units with $n = N/2$ in each of the two groups, and S^2_{within} is the pooled estimate of the population variance computed as

$$S^2_{within} = \frac{(n-1)S_1^2 + (n-1)S_2^2}{df_{within}}, \qquad (2.2)$$

where $df_{within} = N - 2$, S_1^2 is the usual unbiased estimate of the variance within Group 1 (i.e., with denominator $n - 1$), and analogously for S_2^2. Substituting in Equation 2.1, the researcher reports $t(8) = 4.74$, $p = .001$ one-tailed.

TABLE 2.1
Basic Data for Computing t and Effect Sizes

	Experimental condition	Control condition
	S1 = 7	S2 = 4
	S3 = 7	S4 = 4
	S5 = 6	S6 = 3
	S7 = 5	S8 = 2
	S9 = 5	S10 = 2
Sum	30	15
Mean	6	3
Std. dev. $(S)^a$	1.00	1.00
Std. dev. $(\sigma)^b$	0.894	0.894

[a] With divisor $n-1$.
[b] With divisor n.

CORRELATION EFFECT SIZE (r)

One option for indexing the effect size is by means of the correlation r, which can be computed from the researcher's t statistic and df_{within} directly from:

$$r = \sqrt{\frac{t^2}{t^2 + df_{within}}} = \frac{t}{\sqrt{t^2 + df_{within}}}. \tag{2.3}$$

Substituting in Equation 2.3, we find

$$r = \sqrt{\frac{(4.74)^2}{(4.74)^2 + 8}} = .86,$$

which tells us the magnitude of the effect on subjects of having been assigned to the experimental or control condition. Whenever we report r, it is essential to give its sign, which, for convenience, is positive if the effect is in the predicted direction and negative if the effect is in the unpredicted direction.

As Table 2.2 shows, our r computed from Equation 2.3 is not just an "alerting r" based on aggregated scores (as described in Chapter 1) but is typically more informative because it is based on individual scores and has an associated valid test of significance. Because one of the variables is continuous (as are both variables employed for the usual case of r) whereas the other variable is dichotomous with arbitrarily coded numerical values (0 and 1, or 1 and −1), this correlation coefficient is called the *point-biserial r*. As this table illustrates, the point-biserial r is simply a

TABLE 2.2
Basic Data for Computing Point-Biserial *r*

Subject	Condition (E=1, C=0) X	Standardized X Z_x	Dependent variable Y	Standardized Y Z_y	$Z_x Z_y$
S1	1	1	7	1.43	1.43
S2	0	−1	4	−0.29	0.29
S3	1	1	7	1.43	1.43
S4	0	−1	4	−0.29	0.29
S5	1	1	6	0.86	0.86
S6	0	−1	3	−0.86	0.86
S7	1	1	5	0.29	0.29
S8	0	−1	2	−1.43	1.43
S9	1	1	5	0.29	0.29
S10	0	−1	2	−1.43	1.43
Sum	5	0	45	0	8.6
Mean	0.5	0	4.5	0	.86
Std. dev.[a]	0.5	1.0	1.75	1.0	—

[a] With divisor *n* rather than *n* − 1.

special case of the product-moment correlation, which can be defined as

$$r_{xy} = \frac{\Sigma Z_x Z_y}{N}, \qquad (2.4)$$

where the product-moment correlation between the two variables *X* and *Y* is equal to the sum of the products of the *Z* scores (standard scores or "moments") of *X* and *Y* divided by the number *(N)* of pairs of *X* and *Y* scores. Column 2 of Table 2.2 shows the dummy-coded independent variable, *X* (1 for experimental and 0 for control), and column 3 shows those 1s and 0s transformed into *Z* scores of +1 and −1; similarly, the next two columns show the results for the dependent variable *Y*. Noted at the bottom of the right-hand column is the effect size *r* obtained from Equation 2.4 (i.e., 8.6/10 = .86), which is, as it must be, the same value that we obtained from Equation 2.3.

Had the researcher reported *F* instead of *t* (i.e., *F* with numerator degrees of freedom = 1 and denominator degrees of freedom = df_{within}), we could find $t = \sqrt{F}$ and again employ Equation 2.3, or we could calculate *r* directly:

$$r = \sqrt{\frac{F}{F + df_{within}}}, \qquad (2.5)$$

which gives

$$r = \sqrt{\frac{22.47}{22.47 + 8}} = .86,$$

as before. The formula for calculating r from sums of squares directly is

$$r = \sqrt{\frac{SS_{contrast}}{SS_{contrast} + SS_{within}}}, \quad (2.6)$$

where $SS_{contrast}$ is the sum of squares for the effect of interest, and SS_{within} is the sum of squares for the error term.

OTHER EFFECT SIZES: COHEN'S d AND HEDGES'S g

An alternative to indexing the size of the effect by the product-moment correlation is to measure the standardized difference between the group means. The difference between the means is divided either by $\sqrt{SS_{within}/N}$, to give "Cohen's d," or by $\sqrt{SS_{within}/df_{within}}$, to give "Hedges's g." That is, both d and g transform the effect size into standard score units (i.e., Zs) derived from the samples themselves, but Cohen's measure uses N for the denominator of the estimated variance, whereas Hedges's uses the within-group degrees of freedom.

Cohen's measure of the standardized difference between group means is defined here as

$$d = \frac{M_1 - M_2}{\sigma_{within}}, \quad (2.7)$$

where σ_{within} is computed as

$$\sigma_{within} = S_{within}\sqrt{\frac{df_{within}}{N}}.$$

Substituting the values from Table 2.1 gives

$$d = \frac{6 - 3}{.894} = 3.35.$$

In the same way that we obtained r from t, we can also do so for d:

$$d = \frac{2t}{\sqrt{df_{within}}}, \quad (2.8)$$

which gives in the example

$$d = \frac{2(4.74)}{\sqrt{8}} = 3.35.$$

Hedges's measure of the standardized difference between groups is defined as

$$g = \frac{M_1 - M_2}{S_{within}}. \quad (2.9)$$

Substituting the values from Table 2.1 gives

$$g = \frac{6-3}{1.00} = 3.00.$$

When we compute this measure from t, we use

$$g = \frac{2t}{\sqrt{N}}, \tag{2.10}$$

which gives in the example

$$g = \frac{2(4.74)}{\sqrt{10}} = 3.00.$$

TRANSFORMING BETWEEN EFFECT SIZE MEASURES

All three effect size measures – r, d, and g – can be easily transformed back and forth in a two-group study with equal sample sizes. Thus we can transform Hedges's g into Cohen's d by

$$d = g\sqrt{\frac{N}{df_{within}}}, \tag{2.11}$$

which gives in the example

$$d = 3.00\sqrt{\frac{10}{8}} = 3.35,$$

and then transform Cohen's d into Hedges's g by

$$g = d\sqrt{\frac{df_{within}}{N}}, \tag{2.12}$$

which gives in the example

$$g = 3.35\sqrt{\frac{8}{10}} = 3.00.$$

Similarly, we can transform Hedges's g into r from

$$r = \frac{g}{\sqrt{g^2 + 4\left(\frac{df_{within}}{N}\right)}}, \tag{2.13}$$

which gives in the example

$$r = \frac{3.00}{\sqrt{(3.00)^2 + 4\left(\frac{8}{10}\right)}} = .86.$$

Basic Procedures for Two Groups

We can also transform Cohen's d into r by

$$r = \frac{d}{\sqrt{d^2 + 4}}. \tag{2.14}$$

COUNTERNULL VALUE OF AN EFFECT SIZE

Behavioral researchers often conclude (a) that failure to reject the null hypothesis implies an effect size of zero, and (b) that finding a statistically significant p value implies an effect size of important magnitude. To address these two problems, a new statistic was recently proposed: the counternull value of an obtained effect size (Rosenthal & Rubin, 1994). The counternull value is the nonnull magnitude of effect size that is supported by exactly the same amount of evidence as is the null value of the effect size. That is, if the counternull value were taken as the null hypothesis, the resulting p value would be the same as the obtained p value for the actual null hypothesis.

The counternull, with its associated p value, is conceptually related to confidence intervals, which provide limits for such fixed coverage probabilities as, for example, 95% and 99% but do not involve the null hypothesis or the obtained p value. The counternull, however, is tied directly to the null and the obtained effect size, and our discussion focuses on null-counternull intervals with their associated p values rather than on confidence intervals with their a priori fixed confidence coverages. A detailed discussion of confidence intervals for effect sizes can be found in many places, for example, Hedges and Olkin (1985). Although confidence intervals can be very valuable, we can convey much the same type of information using counternull values of effect sizes and associated p values, and we can do this very simply for almost any effect size. Thorough presentation of standard errors and confidence intervals for all of our various effect sizes, although valuable, would involve complexities beyond the scope of our intended discussion.

The obtained effect size estimate always falls between the null value of the effect size and the counternull value. In addition, for effect size estimates that are based on symmetric reference distributions, such as the normal or t distributions (e.g., g or d), the obtained effect size falls exactly halfway between the null value of the effect size and the counternull value. The following equation gives the counternull value of the effect size for any effect size with a symmetric reference distribution (e.g., the normal or t distribution) no matter what the magnitude of the effect size (ES) is under the null:

$$ES_{counternull} = 2ES_{obtained} - ES_{null} \tag{2.15}$$

Because the effect size expected under the null is zero in so many applications, the value of the counternull is often simply twice the obtained effect size, or $2ES_{obtained}$.

When dealing with effect sizes with asymmetric distributions (e.g., the correlation between two continuous variables or a proportion of successes, π), it is best to (a) transform the effect size so as to have a symmetric distribution (e.g., correlations should be transformed to Fisher's $z_r = \log_e \frac{(1+r)}{(1-r)}$, and the proportion of successes, π, to $\log_e \pi/(1-\pi)$; Rosenthal & Rubin, 1989, 1991, 1992-1993); (b) calculate the counternull on the symmetric scale; and then (c) transform back to obtain the counternull on the original scale.

Suppose we have a study with a g of .30 that differs from the null value of 0.00 at $p = .15$. The counternull value is .60 in this example and reminds us that the true effect size g could as readily be as large as .60 as it could be as small as 0.00, despite the modest p value of .15. This example illustrates that we should not treat a nonsignificant result as indicating a null value of the effect size (0.00 in our example). The next example illustrates that we should not necessarily treat a significant nonnull value of an effect size as scientifically important.

Suppose a very large clinical trial is designed to test a very expensive new medication intended to lower excessive body temperature more effectively than aspirin, which is used as the control medication. Because the clinical trial is so large, we find a clearly significant effect of the new medication, $p = .013$, one-tailed, but with an effect size (g) of only .03. In this example, the null value of the effect size is again 0.00, so the counternull value is 0.06. The null-counternull interval (0.00, 0.06) has an associated p value of .013, one-tailed, and thus has $1 - 2(.013) = .974$, or 97.4%, associated with it. In general, the coverage of the null-counternull interval is given by subtracting the two-tailed p from 1.00. Despite the fact that the effectiveness of the new medication is statistically significant, clinical scientists might decide that the decrease in temperature associated with the new medication, compared with the old, even if as large as the counternull value, is just too small to warrant the use of a substantially more expensive treatment.

An example in which the null value of the effect size is not zero might be the case of a study testing a new treatment against a placebo control. An earlier developed treatment is believed to have an average effect size d of .40. The null hypothesis is that the new treatment is not different from the earlier developed treatment. The d obtained for the new treatment is .60, but with the size of the study, that d attains only $p = .105$, one-tailed, for being greater than the standard d of .40. The counternull value of the effect size in this example, however, is $2ES_{obtained} - ES_{null} = 2(0.60) - 0.40 = 0.80$. The evidence for a d of .80, therefore, is as strong as it is for a d of .40. The null-counternull interval (0.40, 0.80) is a 79% interval because one minus two-tailed p equals $1 - 2(.105) = .79$, where .105 is the one-tailed p value.

COUNTERNULL VALUE OF A POINT-BISERIAL r

To calculate the counternull value of the point-biserial r, we find

$$r_{counternull} = \sqrt{\frac{4r^2}{1 + 3r^2}}. \tag{2.16}$$

For an example, suppose an investigator has found an effect size point-biserial r to be .33. However, because the experiment was of modest size, this effect size had

$p = .12$. We find the $r_{counternull}$ from Equation 2.16 to be

$$r_{counternull} = \sqrt{\frac{4r^2}{1+3r^2}} = \sqrt{\frac{4(.33)^2}{1+3(.33)^2}} = .57.$$

This example shows that, although an obtained effect size may not attain a significant p value, it would be an error to assume that the effect size obtained supported a conclusion of a null value of r (.00 in this case). Indeed, the value of $r_{counternull}$ in this example shows that the true value of the effect size could just as likely be .57 as .00.

The rationale for Equation 2.16 is the following: The effect size estimates, d and g, both have symmetric sampling distributions. Therefore, when their null values are .00, as is ordinarily the case, their counternull values are simply twice their observed values. The corresponding counternull value of r, which has a more complicated asymmetric sampling distribution, is found by substituting the counternull value of d (or g) into Equation 2.14 (or Equation 2.13 for g). Therefore,

$$r_{counternull} = \frac{d_{counternull}}{\sqrt{d_{counternull}^2 + 4}}.$$

But $d_{counternull} = 2d$, so

$$r_{counternull} = \frac{2d}{\sqrt{4d^2 + 4}} = \sqrt{\frac{d^2}{d^2 + 1}}.$$

Now, from Equation 2.14, the observed d^2 can be written in terms of the observed r^2 as

$$d^2 = \frac{4r^2}{1-r^2}.$$

Thus

$$r_{counternull} = \sqrt{\frac{\frac{4r^2}{1-r^2}}{\frac{4r^2}{1-r^2}+1}} = \sqrt{\frac{4r^2}{1+3r^2}} = \frac{2r}{\sqrt{1+3r^2}}.$$

PROBLEMS WHEN INTERPRETING EFFECT SIZES

Despite the growing awareness of the importance of estimating sizes of effects along with obtaining levels of significance, problems of interpretation remain. For example, one problem stems from the practice of some researchers of mechanically defining "small" effects *strictly* as rs of .1 and ds of .2, "medium" as rs of .3 and ds of .5, and "large" as rs of .5 and ds of .8. Those are convenient guidelines as suggested by Cohen (1977) (in the way that p values of .05, .01, and .001 are convenient points for tables of test statistics), but mechanically labeling such rs and ds automatically as "small," "medium," and "large" can lead to later difficulties.

TABLE 2.3
Relation between r and Cohen's d for the Case in Which Two Conditions of Equal Sample Size Are Compared

r	Cohen's d	d/r
.01	.02	2.0
.02	.04	2.0
.03	.06	2.0
.04	.08	2.0
.05	.10	2.0
.10	.20	2.0
.15	.30	2.0
.20	.41	2.1
.25	.52	2.1
.30	.63	2.1
.35	.75	2.1
.40	.87	2.2
.45	1.01	2.2
.50	1.15	2.3
.55	1.32	2.4
.60	1.50	2.5
.70	1.96	2.8
.80	2.67	3.3
.90	4.13	4.6
1.00	∞	∞

The reason is that even "small" effects can turn out to be practically important (as we will illustrate later in this chapter). A related problem is illustrated in Table 2.3, which shows the equivalents of different values of r and d. Although "small" rs and ds do not run afoul of these labeling conventions, we see that an r of .3 (a "medium" effect) actually corresponds to a d of .63, whereas an r of .5 (a "large" effect) actually corresponds to a d of 1.15 (a "jumbo" effect?). As the third column in this table reveals, the relation between d and r is clearly not a straight line.

An older convention, more problematic, is employing the coefficient of determination (defined as r^2) as the measure of effect size. As traditional as r^2 is as an index of the goodness of prediction (i.e., the proportion of variation among outcome scores that is attributable to variation in predictor scores), it suffers from the expository problem that important effects can appear to be smaller than they actually are in terms of practical importance (Abelson, 1985; Ozer, 1985; Rosenthal, 1990: Rosenthal & Rubin, 1979; Rosnow & Rosenthal, 1988, 1996a).

TABLE 2.4
BESD for $r = .32$

Condition	Treatment outcome		Totals
	Improved	Not improved	
Psychotherapy	66	34	100
Control	34	66	100
Totals	100	100	200

BINOMIAL EFFECT SIZE DISPLAY

Instead of concentrating on r^2, we recommend using the point-biserial r itself to create a display of the practical importance of the particular magnitude of effect (Rosenthal & Rubin, 1982). This is done simply by recasting r as a 2×2 contingency table, in which the rows correspond to the independent variable displayed as a dichotomous predictor (e.g., experimental vs. control) and the columns correspond to the dependent variable displayed as a dichotomous outcome (e.g., improved vs. not improved): The correlation between these two dichotomous variables is set to equal the obtained point-biserial correlation, r. The specific question addressed by this *binomial effect size display* (BESD) is: What is the effect on the success rate of the implementation of a certain treatment procedure?

Table 2.4 illustrates the BESD based on an r of .32, which was reported to be the average size of the effect of psychotherapy in an early report of a meta-analysis (Glass, 1976). To find the psychotherapy success rate of 66%, we computed $.50 + r/2$, and to find the control success rate of 34%, we computed $.50 - r/2$. In other words, $r = .32$ is equivalent to increasing the success rate from 34% to 66% (which in another case might mean, for example, reducing an illness rate or a death rate from 66% to 34%). Notice that the difference between the rate of improvement in the psychotherapy group and that in the control group (i.e., 66% − 34% = 32%) corresponds to the value of r times 100. These percentages should not, of course, be mistaken for the raw percentages in the actual data, but they can be interpreted as "standardized" percentages in order for all the margins to be equal. Another way of saying this is that an r of .32 (or an r^2 of .10) will amount to a difference between rates of improvement of 34% and 66% if half the population received psychotherapy and half did not, and if half the population improved and half did not.

RELATING BESD, r, AND r^2

Table 2.5 provides a general summary of the relation between increases in success rates (BESDs) and various values of r^2 and r. The first and second columns show that, except in the most extreme cases (rs of 0 or ±1), r^2 is always less than r. Columns 3 and 4 show that even so small an r as .10, accounting for a mere .01

TABLE 2.5
Success Rates Corresponding to Values of r^2 and r

r^2	r	Success rate increased		Difference in success rates
		From	To	
.00	.00	.00	.00	.00
.01	.10	.45	.55	.10
.04	.20	.40	.60	.20
.09	.30	.35	.65	.30
.16	.40	.30	.70	.40
.25	.50	.25	.75	.50
.36	.60	.20	.80	.60
.49	.70	.15	.85	.70
.64	.80	.10	.90	.80
.81	.90	.05	.95	.90
1.00	1.00	.00	1.00	1.00

(i.e., 1%) of the variance, is associated with an increase in success rate from .45 to .55. This increase would be very important if the dependent variable implied, say, an increase in cure rate or survival rate from 45% to 55%. An especially useful feature of the BESD is how easily we can go from the display to an r (just take the difference between the success rates of the experimental vs. the control group) and how easily we can go from an effect size r to the display (just compute the treatment success rate as .50 plus one-half of r and the control success rate as .50 minus one-half of r). It can be shown that the BESD is most appropriate when the variances within the two conditions are similar, as they are assumed to be whenever we compute the usual t statistic and its associated p value (Rosenthal & Rubin, 1982).

Table 2.6 brings our discussion of the BESD full circle by clarifying what is meant by "proportion of variance accounted for" within the context of the BESD (Rosenthal, 1986). The first four columns show the cell values for a range of BESDs, where A denotes the value in the upper left cell, B the upper right cell, C the lower left cell, and D the lower right cell. The column headed SS shows the sum of the squared deviations around the mean (50) of the four values of each BESD. Notice that the largest possible SS occurs when Cells A and D are 100 and Cells B and C are 0, which simply indicates that all the variation in the dependent variable is predictable from a knowledge of status on the independent variable (e.g., experimental vs. control treatment). The maximum value of a sum of squares for the BESD (10,000) is associated with an r^2 of 1.00 (i.e., a "proportion of variance accounted for" of 1.00). For any BESD, the associated sum of squares divided by the

TABLE 2.6
Values of r and r^2 Associated with Sums of Squares (SS) for Various BESDs

BESD cells				SS	r^2	$\sqrt{SS}$	r	$\chi^2(1)$	Z
A	B	C	D						
100	0	0	100	10,000	1.00	100	1.00	200	14.14
95	5	5	95	8,100	.81	90	.90	162	12.73
90	10	10	90	6,400	.64	80	.80	128	11.31
85	15	15	85	4,900	.49	70	.70	98	9.90
80	20	20	80	3,600	.36	60	.60	72	8.49
75	25	25	75	2,500	.25	50	.50	50	7.07
70	30	30	70	1,600	.16	40	.40	32	5.66
65	35	35	65	900	.09	30	.30	18	4.24
60	40	40	60	400	.04	20	.20	8	2.83
55	45	45	55	100	.01	10	.10	2	1.41
52	48	48	52	16	.0016	4	.04	0.32	0.57
50	50	50	50	0	.00	0	.00	0	0

maximum possible sum of squares (10,000) yields r^2, or the proportion of variance accounted for. Analogously, for any BESD, the square root of the ratio of the sum of squares divided by the maximum possible sum of squares yields r immediately.

For the BESD, r gives the difference between success rates, whereas r^2 gives the square of that difference (a metric that does not have a very useful real-life interpretation). The last two columns of Table 2.6 speak to those readers who prefer to think in terms of $\chi^2(1)$ and $\sqrt{\chi^2(1)}$ (i.e., Z) instead of SS and $\sqrt{SS}$. Any chi-square associated with any BESD can be divided by the maximum possible value of chi-square (which is N, or 200 for the BESD) to yield r^2. Any Z associated with any BESD can be divided by the maximum possible Z (which is $\sqrt{N}$, or 14.1421 for the BESD) to yield r.

The $\chi^2(1)$ values of Table 2.6 are computed in the usual way from the basic equation for χ^2:

$$\chi^2(1) = \Sigma \frac{(Obs - Exp)^2}{Exp}, \tag{2.17}$$

where Obs is the observed frequency in each cell, and Exp is the frequency expected in each cell if the null hypothesis of no relationship between rows and columns is true. In the special case of the BESD where row and column counts all equal 100, the expected frequencies are all 50. Therefore, the general equation for χ^2 given by (2.17) can be written as

$$\chi^2(1) = \frac{4(Obs - 50)^2}{50}.$$

The numerator $4(Obs - 50)^2$ will be recognized as the sum of squares for any particular BESD. As is always the case for $\chi^2(1)$, the square root is the standard normal deviate, Z, so

$$Z = \frac{\sqrt{2}(Obs - 50)}{5}.$$

COUNTERNULL VALUE OF THE BESD

Earlier, we saw the benefits of computing and evaluating the counternull value of an obtained effect size. We further recommend that the counternull be employed whenever we display an effect size by means of the BESD.

Computation of the counternull value is readily accomplished by means of Equation 2.16, which can also be written as

$$r_{counternull} = \frac{2r}{\sqrt{1 + 3r^2}}. \tag{2.18}$$

Table 2.7 shows the relation between r and $r_{counternull}$.

After $r_{counternull}$ is computed, it can be displayed as a BESD in the usual manner. To illustrate, imagine a small experiment ($N = 12$) that does not find a significant effect of the treatment ($p = .20$, two-tailed) but for which the effect size, r, is .40. The BESD for this r would be the following table:

	Improved	Not improved	Σ
Treatment	70	30	100
Control	30	70	100
Σ	100	100	200

If we continue to assume that the null value of r is .00, the BESD for the null value is, of course,

	Improved	Not improved	Σ
Treatment	50	50	100
Control	50	50	100
Σ	100	100	200

The counternull value of the obtained r of .40 is obtained from Equation 2.16 (or Equation 2.18):

$$r_{counternull} = \sqrt{\frac{4(.40)^2}{1 + 3(.40)^2}} = \frac{2(.40)}{\sqrt{1 + 3(.40)^2}} = .66.$$

The BESD for this r, then, is the BESD-displayed counternull

	Improved	Not improved	Σ
Treatment	83	17	100
Control	17	83	100
Σ	100	100	200

TABLE 2.7
Relation between r and $r_{counternull}$

r	$r_{counternull}$ [a]	Ratio: $\dfrac{r_{counternull}}{r}$	Difference: $r_{counternull} - r$
.01	.02	2.00	.01
.05	.10	2.00	.05
.10	.20	2.00	.10
.15	.29	1.93	.14
.20	.38	1.90	.18
.25	.46	1.84	.21
.30	.53	1.77	.23
.35	.60	1.71	.25
.40	.66	1.65	.26
.45	.71	1.58	.26
.50	.76	1.52	.26
.55	.80	1.45	.25
.60	.83	1.38	.23
.65	.86	1.32	.21
.70	.89	1.27	.19
.75	.91	1.21	.16
.80	.94	1.18	.14
.85	.96	1.13	.11
.90	.97	1.08	.07
.95	.99	1.04	.04
.99	.997	1.01	.01

[a] $r_{counternull} = \sqrt{\dfrac{4r^2}{1+3r^2}} = \dfrac{2r}{\sqrt{1+3r^2}}$.

Although the obtained p value of this study ($p = .20$) might lead some investigators to conclude that there is probably "no effect" of treatment, the counternull reminds us that a true effect of 83% versus 17% (the counternull) is just as likely as a true effect of 50% versus 50% (the null). Table 2.8 summarizes the BESDs based on the results actually obtained, the null results, the counternull results, and the 80% null-counternull interval.

THE BESD WITH DICHOTOMOUS OUTCOME VARIABLES

Typically, the outcome data in behavioral research are more-or-less continuous rather than dichotomous. It is not unusual, however, for our data to be

TABLE 2.8
BESD Based on the Obtained Result, the Null Result, and the Counternull Result

Null result ($r = .00$)			Obtained result ($r = .40, p = .20$, two tailed)				Counternull result ($r = .66$)		
	I	NI		I	NI	Σ		I	NI
T	50	50	T	70	30	100	T	83	17
C	50	50	C	30	70	100	C	17	83
			Σ	100	100	200			

80% Null-counternull interval

$r = .00$ ⟵⎯⎯⎯⎯⎯⎯⎯⎯⎯⎯⎯⎯⎯⎯⎯⎯⎯⎯⎯⟶ $r = .66$

Note: I, NI, T, and C refer to Improved, Not improved, Treatment, and Control, respectively.

dichotomous, for example, improved–not improved, passed the test–did not pass the test, volunteered–did not volunteer, agreed with the question–did not agree.

Obtaining Significance Levels

When both the independent and the dependent variable are dichotomous, perhaps the most common test of significance is $\chi^2(1)$ based on the 2 × 2 table of counts and computed from Equation 2.17. For example, consider the following data from a large clinical study:

		Dependent variable		
		Improved	Not improved	Σ
Independent variable	Treatment	200	800	1,000
	Control	10	990	1,000
	Σ	210	1,790	2,000

We obtain $\chi^2(1)$ from

$$\Sigma \frac{(Obs - Exp)^2}{Exp} = \frac{(200 - 105)^2}{105} + \frac{(800 - 895)^2}{895} + \frac{(10 - 105)^2}{105}$$

$$+ \frac{(990 - 895)^2}{895} = 192.07.$$

If we wanted a Z test we could simply take the square root of this (or any) 1-degree-of-freedom χ^2 and obtain the corresponding Z.

We could also compute F or t tests to compare the results of the treatment and control conditions. We could, for example, score each improved patient as 1 and each not-improved patient as 0. For the data above, $F(1,1998) = 212.27$, and t (i.e., the square root of $F[1,1998]) = 14.57$. The p values for the $\chi^2(1)$ (and Z) tests are essentially the same as the p values for the $F(1,1998)$ (and t) tests, both $p < 1/10^{40}$.

Effect Size Estimation

To compute the effect size r for the situation in which both the independent and the dependent variables are dichotomous (often referred to as r_ϕ or *phi*), and sample sizes are large, we can employ Equation 2.4 or, equivalently in this case, Equation 2.19:

$$r_\phi = \sqrt{\frac{\chi^2(1)}{N}}. \tag{2.19}$$

Had we preferred to do so, we could also have computed r from t or F by employing Equation 2.3 or 2.5. Using any of these equations for the present example would have yielded the same result to four decimal places:

$$r_\phi = \sqrt{\frac{192.07}{2,000}} = \sqrt{\frac{212.27}{212.27 + 1,998}} = .3099.$$

This r can be displayed directly as a BESD:

	Effect size r ($p < 1/10^{40}$)		
	Improved	Not improved	Σ
Treatment	65	35	100
Control	35	65	100
Σ	100	100	200

as can its counternull value of $r = .54$, obtained via Equation 2.16:

	Counternull r ($p < 1/10^{40}$)		
	Improved	Not improved	Σ
Treatment	77	23	100
Control	23	77	100
Σ	100	100	200

Other Routes to a BESD

Computing r from a 2 × 2 table in order to go to a BESD is not the only method that could be employed to obtain a BESD. Notice that the original 2 × 2 table and the BESD based on r have the same value of the correlation (i.e., .31). There are other ways of constructing a BESD that do not make the *correlations* identical but make some other property of the 2 × 2 tables identical. Three standard alternatives to r are the risk difference (*RD*), relative risk (*RR*), and the odds ratio (*OR*).

Table 2.9 gives the definition of each of the four indices in terms of the four cells of a 2 × 2 table with cells labeled A, B, C, and D. The final column of this table shows

TABLE 2.9
Four Routes to a BESD from a 2 × 2 Table

Cell definitions		Improved	Not improved	
	Treatment	A	B	(A + B)
	Control	C	D	(C + D)
		(A + C)	(B + D)	

Index[a]	Definition	Computation of upper left cell, A_{BESD}, of the BESD with same index as original table[b]
Risk difference (RD)	$\dfrac{A}{A+B} - \dfrac{C}{C+D}$	$100(.50 \pm RD/2)$
Relative risk (RR)	$\dfrac{A}{A+B} \Big/ \dfrac{C}{C+D}$	$100[RR/(1+RR)]$
Odds ratio (OR)	$\dfrac{A}{B} \Big/ \dfrac{C}{D}$	$100[\sqrt{OR}/(1+\sqrt{OR})]$
Pearson correlation (r)	$\dfrac{AD - BC}{\sqrt{(A+B)(C+D)(A+C)(B+D)}}$	$100(.50 \pm r/2)$

[a] The values of RD, RR, OR, and r for the present example are 0.19, 20.0, 24.75, and .31, respectively.
[b] These values for RD, RR, OR, and r for the present example are 60, 95, 83, and 65, respectively.

how to get A_{BESD} (the upper left cell of a BESD) from each of the four indices of effect size in a 2 × 2 table. It follows that $B_{BESD} = 100 - A_{BESD}$; $C_{BESD} = 100 - A_{BESD}$; and $D_{BESD} = A_{BESD}$. In our continuing example (in which, for simplicity, we rounded the effect size correlation of .3099 to the nearest even value [.30] for the BESD), we saw that $A_{BESD} = D_{BESD} = 65$, and that $B_{BESD} = C_{BESD} = 35$.

Although risk differences, relative risks, and odds ratios can all be useful indices of effect size with dichotomous outcomes, we feel that using r to create the BESD usually better captures the implications of the data for the population as a whole (Rosenthal, 1991a, 1991b; Rosenthal & Rubin, 1998). Indeed, we feel that it can be useful to compute r, display it by means of the BESD, and then compute "standardized" risk differences, relative risks, and odds ratios from these r-based BESDs. When this is done, $RD = r$ and $OR = (RR)^2$. In our example with $r = .30$, we find

$$RD = \left(\dfrac{A}{A+B}\right) - \left(\dfrac{C}{C+D}\right) = \left(\dfrac{65}{100}\right) - \left(\dfrac{35}{100}\right) = .30,$$

which is the same as the value of r. We find

$$RR = \frac{\left(\dfrac{A}{A+B}\right)}{\left(\dfrac{C}{C+D}\right)} = \frac{\left(\dfrac{65}{100}\right)}{\left(\dfrac{35}{100}\right)} = 1.8571$$

and

$$OR = \frac{\left(\dfrac{A}{B}\right)}{\left(\dfrac{C}{D}\right)} = \frac{\left(\dfrac{65}{35}\right)}{\left(\dfrac{35}{65}\right)} = 3.4490,$$

so we see that $OR = (RR)^2$. In the case of a BESD, it follows that $RR = A_{BESD}/C_{BESD}$, which in this example gives $65/35 = 1.8571$, and that $OR = (A_{BESD}/C_{BESD})^2$, which in this example gives 3.4490.

HOW BIG AN EFFECT SIZE IS "IMPORTANT"?

Before continuing our discussion of specific procedures, we should say something more about how large an effect must be in order to be considered "important." The answer to this question will be of particular interest to those researchers who work in the "softer, wilder" areas of the social and behavioral sciences – the areas where the results often seem ephemeral and unreplicable, and where r^2 seems always to be too small: clinical, developmental, educational, organizational, personality, social, and health psychology and parts of psychobiology and cognitive psychology. Our message to those toiling in these muddy vineyards is that they are doing better than they might have thought. To explain what we mean, we will examine the BESDs corresponding to some "important" effects in human subjects research outside social and behavioral science.

Our first example concerns a major biomedical study that, in 1988, reported that heart attack risk in the U.S. population may be reduced by regular use of aspirin (Steering Committee of the Physicians' Health Study Research Group, 1988). This conclusion was based on the results of a five-year randomized investigation of a sample of 22,071 male physicians, approximately half of whom (11,037) were given an ordinary aspirin tablet (325 mg) every other day, while the remainder (11,034) were given a placebo. Presumably, the way that aspirin works to reduce mortality from heart attacks is to promote circulation even when fatty deposits have collected along the walls of the coronary arteries. That is, aspirin does not reduce the chances of clotting but eases transportation of blood as the arteries get narrower. At a special meeting held in December 1987, it was decided to end the study early because it had become so clear that aspirin prevented heart attacks (and deaths from heart attacks) that it would be unethical to continue to give half the subjects a placebo.

What was the magnitude of the experimental effect that was so dramatic as to call for the termination of this experiment and the prompt recommendation to use aspirin? We can get the answer to our question from Table 2.10, in which Parts I and II show the heart attack results in each condition. We see that 1.33% experienced an

TABLE 2.10
Aspirin's Effect on Heart Attack

Condition		Heart attack	No heart attack	Total
I.	Raw counts			
	Aspirin	104	10,933	11,037
	Placebo	189	10,845	11,034
	Total	293	21,778	22,071
II.	Percentages			
	Aspirin	0.94	99.06	100
	Placebo	1.71	98.29	100
	Total	1.33	98.67	100
III.	Binomial effect size display ($r = .034$, $p = .000001$)			
	Aspirin	48.3	51.7	100
	Placebo	51.7	48.3	100
	Total	100	100	200
IV.	BESD of counternull ($r = .068$, $p = .000001$)			
	Aspirin	46.6	53.4	100
	Placebo	53.4	46.6	100
	Total	100	100	200

attack, and this event occurred more frequently in the placebo condition (1.71%) than in the aspirin condition (0.94%). The statistical significance of the difference is $\chi^2(1, N = 22,071) = 25.01$, $p < .000001$, which tells us that the results were very unlikely to be a fluke or a lucky coincidence. (We could equally well have employed F or t tests on the dichotomous outcome; they would have yielded very similar p values.)

Computing r by means of Equation 2.19, we find the result to be so small ($r = .034$, $r^2 = .001$) as to be considered quantitatively unimpressive by methodological convention in our field. (We could equally well have employed Equations 2.3 or 2.5 based on t or F tests and would have obtained essentially identical effect sizes.) Nevertheless, the implications are far from unimpressive, and we see more clearly how impressive they are when we recast this magnitude of effect into the language of a BESD. As Part III in Table 2.10 shows, given the particular situation where population percentages in the marginals are equal, so that one-half received aspirin and one-half received placebo while one-half had heart attacks and one-half did not (i.e., a truly at-risk population as opposed to the raw data percentages in Part II), approximately 3.4% fewer persons who would probably experience a heart attack without aspirin would not experience it if they followed the regimen prescribed in the aspirin condition. This sort of subpopulation is actually the one we would most like to be able to study because it would yield the clearest information about the effects of the treatment.

A word of caution is in order: The sample in this study consisted entirely of male physicians, and the statistical results might not generalize to the population at large. Further, in prescribing aspirin, the physician would want to know about the medical history of the patient because the effects of aspirin can be dangerous to persons who have ulcers, high blood pressure, kidney problems, or allergies to aspirin or who are about to undergo surgery. Thus a further lesson is that it is important not to strip away the context from the content of a BESD. When considering the question of "practical importance," we need to weigh relevant aspects of the situation in addition to the size of the effect alone. That qualification notwithstanding, it can be noted that this magnitude of effect is not at all unusual in biomedical research.

Some years earlier, for example, the National Heart, Lung, and Blood Institute discontinued its placebo-controlled study of propranolol (a beta-blocker used to increase heart attack survival) because results were again so favorable to the treatment that it was considered unethical to continue withholding the lifesaving drug from the control patients (Kolata, 1981). The two-year data for this study were based on 2,108 patients, and the chi-square (1 df) was approximately 4.2. Thus, once again, the effect size was .04, and the leading decimal digits of the r^2 were double zero! As behavioral researchers, we are not used to thinking of rs of .04 as reflecting effect sizes of practical importance. But when we think of an r of .04 as reflecting a 4% decrease in further heart attacks for a subpopulation at risk – the interpretation given r in a BESD – the r does not appear to be quite so small, especially if we can count ourselves among the 4 per 100 at risk who manage to survive.

Table 2.11 gives three further examples of BESDs based on actual studies. Part I shows the display corresponding to a study of 4,462 U.S. Army veterans of the Vietnam War era (1965–1971). The correlation between having served in Vietnam (rather than elsewhere) and having suffered from alcohol abuse or dependence is .07 (Centers for Disease Control Vietnam Experience Study, 1988). The display shows that the difference between the problem rates of 53.5 and 46.5 per 100 implies a correlation of .07, with an associated p value of .0000015.

In 1989, one of us had occasion to take a small informal poll of some physicians spending the year at the Center for Advanced Study in the Behavioral Sciences (Rosenthal, 1990). They were asked to tell of some medical breakthrough that was of very great practical importance. The consensus was that the breakthrough was the effect of cyclosporine in increasing the probability that the body would not reject an organ transplant and that the recipient patient would not die. The results of a multicenter randomized experiment (Canadian Multicentre Transplant Study Group, 1983) are shown in Part II of Table 2.11. For the dependent variable of organ rejection, the effect size was $r = .19$ ($r^2 = .036$); for the dependent variable of patient survival, the effect size was $r = .15$ ($r^2 = .022$). The associated p values were .0033 and .016, respectively.

The display in Part III of Table 2.11 shows the results of the meta-analysis of psychotherapy outcome studies mentioned previously (Smith & Glass, 1977). An eminent critic insisted that those results sounded the "death knell" for psychotherapy because of the modest size of the effect: $r = .32$! Examination of this display shows that it is not very realistic to label as "modest indeed" an effect size

TABLE 2.11
Other Examples of Binomial Effect Size Displays

I. Vietnam service and alcohol problems ($r = .07$, $p = .0000015$)

	Problem	No problem	Total
Vietnam veteran	53.5	46.5	100.0
Non-Vietnam veteran	46.5	53.5	100.0
Total	100.0	100.0	200.0

II. Cyclosporine in the prevention of organ rejection ($r = .19$, $p = .0033$)

	Organ rejection	Nonrejection	
Cyclosporine	40.5	59.5	100.0
Control	59.5	40.5	100.0
Total	100.0	100.0	200.0

III. Benefits of psychotherapy ($r = .32$, $p < 1/10^{100}$)

	Less benefit	Greater benefit	
Psychotherapy	34.0	66.0	100.0
Control	66.0	34.0	100.0
Total	100.0	100.0	200.0

IV. BESDs of counternull values for the studies above (counternull r, original p)

	I ($r = .14$, $p = .0000015$)		II ($r = .36$, $p = .0033$)		III ($r = .56$, $p < 1/10^{100}$)	
	Problem	No prob.	Rejection	Nonrej.	Less	Greater
Treatment	57	43	32	68	22	78
Control	43	57	68	32	78	22
Total	100	100	100	100	100	100

equivalent to increasing a success rate from 34% to 66%. As we have seen, the "breakthrough" effects of cyclosporine were smaller ($r = .19$), not to mention the "minuscule" effect sizes for aspirin or propranolol. Incidentally, because the effect size correlation for psychotherapy outcome was based on hundreds of studies and thousands of subjects, the associated p was far smaller than $1/10^{100}$.

HOW MANY SUBJECTS? CONSIDERATIONS OF POWER

Too often, it seems that, when employing a particular size of sample, behavioral researchers ignore the extent to which they are stacking the odds against reaching a given p value for the expected size of effect. Indeed, even though the importance of power analysis for practice was recognized long ago by influential textbook writers, they often treated the mechanics of power analysis as too complex to present except in very broad terms (e.g., Guilford, 1956, p. 217). However, partly as a consequence of a series of influential works by Jacob Cohen beginning in the 1960s (e.g., Cohen, 1962, 1965), the concept of power resurfaced dramatically in the social and behavioral sciences. In this section, we describe the use of a compact power table to plan the conduct of research and to help us better interpret the failure to obtain statistically significant results in studies already conducted.

TABLE 2.12
Rounded Sample Sizes (Total N) Required to Detect Various Effects (for r and d) at .05, Two-Tailed Test, with a Null Value for r and d of Zero (assumes Equal Sample Sizes for the Two Conditions Being Compared)

		Effect size							
	d	.20	.40	.50	.60	.80	1.00	1.20	1.40
Power	r^a	.10	.20	.24	.29	.37	.45	.51	.57
.15		85	25	15	10	10	10	10	10
.20		130	35	20	15	10	10	10	10
.30		210	55	35	25	15	10	10	10
.40		300	75	50	35	20	15	10	10
.50		390	100	65	45	25	20	10	10
.60		500	125	80	55	30	20	15	10
.70		600	155	100	70	40	25	20	15
.80		800	200	130	90	50	35	25	20
.90		1100	260	170	120	70	45	30	25

[a] This is a point-biserial r in which one variable is continuous and the other variable is dichotomous.

Note: Based on *Statistical Power Analysis for the Behavioral Sciences* (2nd ed., pp. 36–37) by J. Cohen, 1988, Hillsdale, NJ: Erlbaum, used by permission of the author and the publisher.

We will concentrate on the sample size needed to reach the .05 level (two-tailed); more extensive tables are readily accessible (see Cohen, 1988). Equations 2.13 and 2.14 show that we can easily transform Hedges's g and Cohen's d into r. Table 2.12 shows, in rounded sample sizes, the total number of sampling units needed to detect a statistically significant effect of r and d against a theoretical value of zero at a two-tailed p of .05, for levels of power ranging from .15 to .90 – Cohen (1965) recommended .8 as a convention for a desirable level of power. Suppose we expect to see an average experimental effect of $r = .30$ – which, incidentally, seems to be the typical magnitude of effect reported in much of behavioral science (Brewer, 1972; Chase & Chase, 1976; Cohen, 1962, 1973; Haase, Waechter, & Solomon, 1982; Sedlmeier & Gigerenzer, 1989). Table 2.12 reveals (by interpolation between an r of .29 and an r of .37) that a total N of approximately 85 (split evenly into two groups) will be needed to reject the hypothesis of no relation between the independent and dependent variables with power = .80 at the 5% level of significance (two-tailed).

Suppose, however, a much smaller effect really exists. Given an r of .10, for example, we see in Table 2.12 that a total N of approximately 800 (split evenly into two groups) will be needed to detect this magnitude of effect at the same power level of .80 and at the same p level. But what if it were not feasible to achieve this sample size? One option is to sacrifice some power, although reducing it by even

10% still yields a call for approximately 600 sampling units. Another option is to use a higher value of alpha, for example, $p = .10$ or $p = .20$ (cf. Nelson et al., 1986). Still other options are implicit in Equations 2.7 and 2.9, which remind us that we can maximize d and g by driving the two means further apart and by decreasing the variability within groups. Suppose our hypothesis is that longer psychotherapy treatment sessions are more beneficial than shorter treatment sessions. In that case, we should be more apt to find a significant difference if we compare sessions lasting 15 minutes with sessions lasting 45 minutes than if we compare sessions lasting 30 minutes with sessions lasting 35 minutes (Hallahan & Rosenthal, 1996). To decrease the variability of response within groups, we might employ subject samples that are fairly homogeneous in those characteristics that are substantially correlated with the dependent variable. Finally, depending on the purposes of the study, we may decide to ignore issues of significance testing altogether and employ our modest sample size simply to obtain a reasonable, though noisy, estimate of the effect size in which we are interested.

EXTENSION TO UNEQUAL SAMPLE SIZES IN TWO GROUPS

The equations presented so far are for the simple situation of a two-group study with equal sample sizes in the two groups and an approximately normally distributed outcome. Here we extend these equations to the case of two groups of unequal size with an approximately normally distributed outcome.

t Test

The *t* test to compare the results in two conditions is a simple modification of the *t* test with equal *n* given by Equation 2.1:

$$t = \left(\frac{M_1 - M_2}{S_{within}}\right)\left(\frac{\sqrt{N}}{2}\right)\sqrt{\frac{n_h}{\bar{n}}}; \qquad (2.20)$$

in this expression, $\bar{n} = N/2$ is the average sample size per condition, and n_h is the harmonic mean sample size defined by

$$n_h = \frac{1}{\frac{1}{2}\left(\frac{1}{n_1} + \frac{1}{n_2}\right)}, \qquad (2.21)$$

where n_1 and n_2 are the sample sizes within each condition. Since n_h is always less than $\bar{n}$, the ratio $n_h/\bar{n}$ indexes the loss of power (i.e., the effective loss of sample size) in the unequal design relative to the equal *n* design. The nature of the $n_h/\bar{n}$ index will be illustrated shortly when we discuss Table 2.13.

Cohen's *d* and Hedges's *g*

Cohen's measure of the standardized difference between group means is still given by (2.7), and Hedge's *g* is still given by (2.9). The transformations between

TABLE 2.13
Effects of Unequal Sample Sizes on the Power-Loss Index $n_h/\bar{n}$ and on the Effective Loss of Fractional and Total N

n_1	n_2	Arithmetic mean $(\bar{n})^a$	Harmonic mean $(n_h)^b$	Power-loss index $(n_h/\bar{n})$	Effective fractional loss of N^c	Effective loss of total N^d
50	50	50	50	1.00	.00	0
60	40	50	48	.96	.04	4
70	30	50	42	.84	.16	16
80	20	50	32	.64	.36	36
90	10	50	18	.36	.64	64
95	5	50	9.50	.19	.81	81
98	2	50	3.92	.0784	.9216	92.16
99	1	50	1.98	.0396	.9604	96.04

[a] $(n_1 + n_2)/2$.
[b] $1 / \frac{1}{2}\left(\frac{1}{n_1} + \frac{1}{n_2}\right)$.
[c] $1 - (n_h/\bar{n})$.
[d] $N[1 - (n_h/\bar{n})]$.

each and the other are still given by (2.11) and (2.12). The expressions to obtain g or d from the t calculated from (2.20) need modifications from their equal n expressions. From (2.20) it follows that, to obtain g from t, we use

$$g = \frac{2t}{\sqrt{N}} \sqrt{\frac{\bar{n}}{n_h}}, \qquad (2.22)$$

and therefore d from t by

$$d = \frac{2t}{\sqrt{df_{within}}} \sqrt{\frac{\bar{n}}{n_h}}. \qquad (2.23)$$

Notice that since $\bar{n}/n_h$ is at least 1, obtaining d or g from t by using the correct expressions, (2.22) or (2.23), results in larger values for g or d than if the equal-n expressions were used.

In the context of many meta-analyses, only N (or df) and t values are available from all studies. It is then common to obtain d or g from the equal-n expressions (2.8) or (2.10), thus effectively setting $n_h/\bar{n}$ equal to 1 even though it is at most equal to 1. We see from (2.22) and (2.23) that this practice is conservative in that it underestimates the g or d for that study or the g or d that would be expected in a replication of the study with the same sample sizes.

If, on the other hand, we had N and valid d or g values and wished to calculate t without knowing $n_h/\bar{n}$, it would be risky to set $n_h/\bar{n}$ equal to 1 and use the equal-n

expression for t, because the actual p value would always be less significant than that obtained by assuming equal n. In practice, it is a good idea for studies using unequal n to report the power-loss index $n_h/\bar{n}$.

Power-Loss Index $n_h/\bar{n}$

Table 2.13 illustrates the nature of the power-loss index. The table shows for various values of n_1 and n_2 (when $N = n_1 + n_2$ is fixed, e.g., $N = 100$):

1. the arithmetic mean of the two sample sizes;
2. the harmonic mean of the two sample sizes;
3. the power-loss index $n_h/\bar{n}$, which gives the proportion of the total N that is effectively available, given the degree of inequality of the two sample sizes n_1 and n_2;
4. the effective loss of fractional N given by $1 - (n_h/\bar{n})$; and
5. the effective loss of total N, which is relevant to considerations of cost when cost per subject is constant.

This table shows that relative to the equal-n situation, an 80:20 split of the 100 subjects is equivalent to losing 36 of 100 subjects, while a 99:1 split is equivalent to losing 96 of 100 subjects.

Correlation Effect Size r

Expressions for the correlation effect size, r, need more careful interpretation than in the equal-n case. The point-biserial effect size r can still be obtained from t via (2.3) or from F via (2.5), but this effect size measure now changes with the power loss index $n_h/\bar{n}$ even with the same M_1, M_2, S_{within}, and N. To clarify this relationship, consider two very large studies with the same N and same experimental conditions (same population values of M_1, M_2, and S^2_{within}). But suppose one study has $n_h/\bar{n} = 1$ and the other study has $n_h/\bar{n} = 1/100$. Both studies will have approximately the same effect size values g and d because of the large N and identical population conditions. However, they will obtain very different t and r values. The equal-n study's t will be approximately ten times the unequal-n study's t value. Also, the value of r from the equal-n study will be larger: The equal-n r can be obtained from d by (2.14), whereas the r from the unequal-n study is obtained from d or g by using

$$r = \frac{d}{\sqrt{d^2 + 4\left(\dfrac{\bar{n}}{n_h}\right)}} \tag{2.24}$$

or

$$r = \frac{g}{\sqrt{g^2 + 4\left(\dfrac{\bar{n}}{n_h}\right)\left(\dfrac{df}{N}\right)}}. \tag{2.25}$$

In our illustration with $n_h/\bar{n} = .01$, r will be approximately $d/\sqrt{d^2 + 400}$ rather than $d/\sqrt{d^2 + 4}$ as with the equal-n study!

Obtaining r from valid g or d values by using the equal-n expressions (2.13) or (2.14) overstates the value of r in this study, or in a replication of this study with the same power loss index $n_h/\bar{n}$.

However, obtaining r from valid g or d values by using the equal-n expressions (Equations 2.13 or 2.14) does estimate something of substantial interest: It estimates the correlation effect size, r, that would be expected in a replication of the current study but with equal n, and this situation of equal n is relevant for the BESD. We label this correlation as $r_{effect\ size}$ in a notation consistent with later chapters.

BESD

The BESD effect size for two groups is defined for a situation with equal n. Computing the BESD in studies with unequal sample sizes should be done by the use of expressions for the correlation that would be expected in equal-n replications, $r_{effect\ size}$. From valid g or d values, r_{BESD} should be calculated from (2.13) or (2.14), or directly from t as

$$r_{BESD} = \sqrt{\frac{t^2}{t^2 + df_{within}\left(\frac{n_h}{\bar{n}}\right)}}, \tag{2.26}$$

which is always at least as large as the r obtained in the study. Using the equal-n expression for r_{BESD} (i.e., Equation 2.26 with $n_h/\bar{n} = 1$) is conservative when the sample sizes are unequal. The r_{BESD} of Equation 2.26 is for a hypothetical equal-n replication with $n_1 = n_2 = \bar{n}$. It is important to remember that the sign of r_{BESD} is reported as positive if the effect is in the predicted direction and negative if in the opposite direction. Finally, because the sampling distribution of d is still symmetric even with unequal n_1 and n_2, the counternull BESD with unequal n is obtained from the same equation as for the counternull BESD with equal n (i.e., either Equation 2.16 or Equation 2.18).

Extension to Unequal Variances in Two Samples

One of the assumptions underlying the use of the t test comparing two means is that the variances of the populations from which the two samples were drawn are equal. The t test still works quite well even if the variances are fairly different and especially so if sample sizes are equal or nearly so. However, if the population variances are very different *and* if the two sample sizes are quite different, the t computed from the expressions presented so far will not follow the t distribution very well.

One approach to this problem is to transform the data to make the variances in the two samples more nearly equal. The most commonly used transformations involve taking square roots, logs, reciprocal square roots, and reciprocals of the original data. Details are given, for example, in Box, Hunter, and Hunter (1978) and Tukey (1977).

When suitable transformations are not available or are ineffective, a serviceable procedure to make our t tests more accurate is available using Satterthwaite's approximate method (Snedecor & Cochran, 1989). This method can be employed either for continuous data or for dichotomous (0, 1) data as found in 2 × 2 tables of counts and employs (a) a modified computational procedure for t and (b) an estimate of the adjusted df with which to enter the t table along with the modified t.

We first compute t from

$$t = \frac{M_1 - M_2}{\sqrt{\frac{S_1^2}{n_1} + \frac{S_2^2}{n_2}}}, \tag{2.27}$$

where S_1^2 and S_2^2 are the within-group sample variances based on $n_1 - 1$ and $n_2 - 1$ degrees of freedom, respectively. We then enter a t table with this value and with the Satterthwaite-adjusted df obtained as follows:

$$df_{Satterthwaite} = \left[\frac{S_1^2}{n_1} + \frac{S_2^2}{n_2}\right]^2 \bigg/ \left[\frac{(S_1^2/n_1)^2}{n_1 - 1} + \frac{(S_2^2/n_2)^2}{n_2 - 1}\right]. \tag{2.28}$$

For an illustration, consider an experiment in which ten patients are assigned at random to a treatment condition, and the remaining twenty patients are assigned to a control condition. Suppose that five of the treated patients improve, whereas only one of the control patients improves, as displayed in the following table of counts.

	Improved	Not improved	Σ	M	S^2
Treated	5	5	10	.50	.2778
Controls	1	19	20	.05	.0500
Σ	6	24	30		

Patients who improve are scored as 1, and those who do not improve are scored as 0. The means (M_i) of the two groups, then, are $5/10 = .50$ and $1/20 = .05$; the S^2s of the two groups are .2778 and .0500, respectively, and the ns are 10 and 20, so that

$$t = \frac{.50 - .05}{\sqrt{\frac{.2778}{10} + \frac{.0500}{20}}} = 2.59.$$

Before entering a table of t, however, we must compute the adjusted degrees of freedom from

$$df_{Satterthwaite} = \left[\frac{.2778}{10} + \frac{.0500}{20}\right]^2 \bigg/ \left[\frac{(.2778/10)^2}{10 - 1} + \frac{(.0500/20)^2}{20 - 1}\right]$$

$$= .000917/[.0000857 + .000000329]$$

$$= 10.6,$$

which we truncate to the next lower integer, 10. We now enter our t table with $t = 2.59$ and $df = 10$ to find $p = .013$ (one-tailed). If instead of employing this t with $df_{Satterthwaite}$, we had used an overall S^2_{within} of .1232, we would have found t to be

$$t_{(28)} = \frac{.50 - .05}{\sqrt{\left(\frac{1}{10} + \frac{1}{20}\right).1232}} = 3.31, p = .0013 \text{ one-tailed,}$$

a substantially more significant value but inappropriately so.

Had we computed $\chi^2(1)$ for the data of this experiment, we would have found it to be 8.44, $p = .0037$, too significant because we had to base the $\chi^2(1)$ on an expected value of only 2 in one of the cells and 4 in another (for a review of work on $\chi^2(1)$ tests with small expected frequencies see, e.g., Rosenthal & Rosnow, 1991). Alternatively, computing Fisher's exact test for these data yields a p of .0088, a value closer to the Satterthwaite result of .013 than the ps based either on the $\chi^2(1)$ or the original, unadjusted t.

REVIEW QUESTIONS

1. Given $t(60) = 1.66$, (a) compute the effect size r and its counternull value; (b) estimate the power, assuming the obtained effect size is the true effect size; and (c) figure out how many subjects will be needed to increase the power to .80 for a two-tailed $p = .05$.

    Answer: (a) $r = .21$ from Equation 2.3, and the counternull value is an $r_{counternull}$ of .39 (employing Equations 2.16 or 2.18); (b) Table 2.12 tells us that that power is between .30 and .40 for this effect size and study size (say, approximately .35); (c) referring again to Table 2.12, we see that with $r = .20$ and $p = .05$ two-tailed, we will need a total N of 200 subjects to achieve .80 power.

2. Set up a BESD to display an effect size d of .45, and indicate the success rate.

    Answer: From Equation 2.14, we find Cohen's d is transformed into an r of .22. Cells A and D of the BESD are computed as .50 plus one-half of r (or .61), and cells B and C are computed as .50 minus one-half of r (or .39). Multiplying these proportions by 100 converts the values into percentages and thus tells us that the success rate increased from 39% in the control condition to 61% in the experimental condition.

3. The results of an experiment were as follows: $M_1 = 6.0$, $n_1 = 85$; $M_2 = 4.8$, $n_2 = 15$; $S_{within} = 2.0$. Compute (a) the power-loss index $n_h/\bar{n}$; (b) t; (c) d from t; (d) r from d; (e) r from t; and (f) r_{BESD} from t.

    Answer: (a) $n_h/\bar{n} = 25.5/50 = .51$; (b) from Equation 2.20, we find $t(98) = (.6)(5)\sqrt{.51} = 2.14$; (c) from Equation 2.23, we find $d = .61$ – had we used the equal-n equation (2.8) to compute d from t, we would have found $d = .43$, a conservative value that is about 30% too low; (d) to compute r from the correct d, we employ Equation 2.24 and find $r = .21$; (e) employing Equation 2.3 to find r from t, we also find $r = .21$; and (f) finally, we find r_{BESD} from Equation 2.26 to be .29, the same value we obtain for r from Equation 2.14 employing the proper value of $d = .61$.

4. Answer Question 3 with only the following change in the sample sizes: $n_1 = n_2 = 50$.

   Answer: (a) $n_h/\bar{n} = 50/50 = 1.00$; (b) from Equation 2.20, or from Equation 2.1, we find $t(98) = (.6)(5) = 3.00$, a value about 40% larger than in Question 3; (c) from Equation 2.23, or from Equation 2.8, we find $d = .61$, the same result as in Question 3; (d) from Equation 2.24, or from Equation 2.14, we find $r = .29$, a value nearly 40% larger than that obtained when $n_h/\bar{n}$ was .51 rather than 1.00; (e) from Equation 2.3, we find $r = .29$; and (f) we find r_{BESD} from Equation 2.26, or from Equation 2.3, to be .29, the same value as in Question 3.

5. In a randomized clinical trial, a new treatment was found to be more effective than a placebo control, with $t(128) = 2.10$, $p = .019$, one-tailed. A previously developed treatment for the same condition, based on 450 df, has an effect size of $d = .06$. In a statistical comparison of the effect size of the new versus the old treatment, the two-tailed p was found to be about .13. Examine the counternull value of the effect size and the null-counternull interval.

   Answer: From Equation 2.8, we find $d = .37$ for the new treatment. From Equation 2.15 (the obtained effect size of $d = .37$ is the effect size of the new treatment, and the null value of the effect size is the effect size of the old treatment, $d = .06$), we find the counternull value to be $2(.37) - .06 = .68$. Therefore, it is just as likely that the true effect size is .68 as that it is .06 (the null value). Subtracting the two-tailed p of .13 from 1.0 gives .87, which defines the null-counternull interval. That is, we can say roughly that there is a .87 chance that the magnitude of the new effect falls between $d = .06$ and $d = .68$.

CHAPTER 3

One-Way Contrast Analyses

In this chapter, basic computations of contrast t tests and F tests are presented for one-dimensional ("one-way") designs. Examples of dimensions include age, dosage levels of medication, intensity or type of psychotherapy, and levels of pretest scores. We deal with two-way and higher-order designs in Chapter 4. The contrast correlation, $r_{contrast}$, is defined and distinguished from the effect size correlation, $r_{effect\ size}$. Displaying an effect size as a BESD is described in this expanded framework, where r_{BESD} is distinguished from both $r_{contrast}$ and $r_{effect\ size}$. Procedures for handling unequal sample sizes are described.

OBTAINING SIGNIFICANCE LEVELS

Contrast F Tests

Table 3.1 lists the individual scores of $N = 20$ subjects in four groups (A, B, C, D). The bottom rows give for each of the k groups $(i = 1, \ldots k)$ the total (T_i), the sample mean (M_i), the sample variance (S_i^2), and the lambda weights used to define the contrast (λ_i). From Table 3.1, we see that the sample variance within each condition and for the entire table (mean square within) is 10.0; the pooled mean square within, MS_{within}, is the error term. Suppose that the researcher has hypothesized a regular increase in scores as we go from Conditions A to B to C to D. The overall F of the four condition means would tell us nothing about the researcher's very specific prediction. Instead of the overall, diffuse F, we want to compute a focused F that directly evaluates the specific question we have put to the data. To compute the mean square or the sum of squares attributable to our contrast, we employ a basic formula for equal sample size, n, per condition:

$$MS_{contrast} = SS_{contrast} = \frac{nL^2}{\Sigma \lambda_i^2}, \tag{3.1}$$

where L = the weighted sum of all condition means (M_i), and the weights are the corresponding lambda weights (λ_i); that is,

$$L = \Sigma[M_i \lambda_i] = M_1 \lambda_1 + M_2 \lambda_2 + \cdots + M_k \lambda_k$$

TABLE 3.1
Information for Computing Linear Trend from "Original" Data

	A	B	C	D	
	2	6	8	12	
	6	8	16	18	
	8	10	10	14	
	4	4	14	20	
	10	12	12	16	Means
T_i	30	40	60	80	52.5
M_i	6	8	12	16	10.5
S_i^2	10	10	10	10	10.0
λ_i	−3	−1	+1	+3	0

where k = number of conditions (or groups), and λ_is = weights, so that $\Sigma\lambda_i = 0$. To obtain the F test of the contrast, we will simply divide $MS_{contrast}$ by MS_{within}. Contrasts are based on only 1 degree of freedom with $SS_{contrast}$ identical to $MS_{contrast}$.

Substituting the data in Table 3.1 in Equation 3.1 gives

$$MS_{contrast} = \frac{5[(6)(-3) + (8)(-1) + (12)(+1) + (16)(+3)]^2}{(-3)^2 + (-1)^2 + (+1)^2 + (+3)^2}$$

$$= \frac{5(34)^2}{20} = 289,$$

which, when divided by the appropriate error term, gives

$$F_{contrast} = \frac{MS_{contrast}}{MS_{within}} = \frac{289}{10} = 28.90.$$

This value of $F_{contrast}$, with degrees of freedom equal to 1 and 16, has $p < .0001$.

When $F_{contrast}$ is substituted in Equation 2.5, we obtain a correlation of .80. We will call the correlation obtained from Equation 2.5 the *contrast correlation*, $r_{contrast}$:

$$r_{contrast} = \sqrt{\frac{F_{contrast}}{F_{contrast} + df_{within}}}. \tag{3.2}$$

The sign of the $r_{contrast}$ is positive when the sign of L is positive and negative when the sign of L is negative. The interpretation of $r_{contrast}$ based on three or more means will be discussed in more detail a little later. For now, we should think of $r_{contrast}$ as the partial correlation between each score (Y) and its associated contrast weight (λ) *after we have adjusted for any noncontrast differences among treatment conditions*. Later, we discuss distinctions between $r_{contrast}$ and the effect size correlation, $r_{effect\ size}$, and between these and r_{BESD}, which can be converted into a BESD.

TABLE 3.2
Information for Computing Linear Trend from "Published" Data in Chapter 1

Age level	11	12	13	14	15
M_i	25	30	40	50	55
λ_i	−2	−1	0	+1	+2

	Analysis of Variance			
Source	SS	df	MS	F
Age levels	6,500	4	1625	1.03
Contrast	6,400	1	6400	4.06
Noncontrast	100	3	33.33	0.02
Within	70,875	45	1575	
Total	77,375			

Having seen how to compute $F_{contrast}$ from original data, let us compute it on the example of "published" data that began Chapter 1. Table 3.2 shows the group means and the lambda weights, which again reflect a linear prediction, that is, a regular increment of performance on the video game for every regular increment of age level. In fact, the "alerting" r, the correlation between the five age levels and five performance means, was $r_{alerting} = .99$. Could we have used age levels as our λs (i.e., 11, 12, 13, 14, 15) inasmuch as they also reflect a linear pattern? The answer is no, not directly, because using age levels does not satisfy the criterion that $\Sigma \lambda = 0$. However, we can think of the selected weights as the age levels minus the mean age level (13), so that we have a set of lambdas that does sum to zero. Substitution in Equation 3.1 now gives

$$MS_{contrast} = \frac{10[(25)(-2) + (30)(-1) + (40)(0) + (50)(+1) + (55)(+2)]^2}{(-2)^2 + (-1)^2 + (0)^2 + (+1)^2 + (+2)^2}$$

$$= \frac{10(80)^2}{10} = 6,400.$$

We compute our F test for this contrast by dividing $MS_{contrast}$ by MS_{within}, the mean square for error of the overall ANOVA (previously noted in Table 1.1), which gives

$$F_{contrast} = \frac{MS_{contrast}}{MS_{within}} = \frac{6400}{1575} = 4.06.$$

This $F_{contrast}$, with degrees of freedom = 1 and 45, is significant at $p = .05$. Finally, by Equation 2.5, $r_{contrast} = .29$ for the data of Table 3.2.

$F_{contrast}$ from $r_{alerting}$

An alternative method of computing $F_{contrast}$ employs $r_{alerting}$, the correlation between the group means and their corresponding λ weights. In this approach, the denominator remains the same (i.e., MS_{within}), but the numerator is now written as

$$MS_{contrast} = r^2_{alerting} \times SS_{between}, \tag{3.3}$$

where $SS_{between}$ is the between-conditions sum of squares defined as

$$SS_{between} = \Sigma[n(M_i - \bar{M})^2], \tag{3.4}$$

$\bar{M}$ is the mean of the condition means, and $r_{alerting}$ is simply the correlation between the means of the k conditions, M_i, and the weights associated with the k conditions, the λ_i.

Thus, for Table 3.1, with this approach the first step is to calculate $r_{alerting}$, the correlation between the four group means of 6, 8, 12, and 16 and their corresponding λs of −3, −1, +1, and +3, which gives $r_{alerting} = .9898$ and $r^2_{alerting} = .9797$. Step 2 is to compute the between-conditions sum of squares. Substituting in Equation 3.4, with $\bar{M} = (6 + 8 + 12 + 16)/4 = 10.5$, gives

$$SS_{between} = 5(6 - 10.5)^2 + 5(8 - 10.5)^2 + 5(12 - 10.5)^2 + 5(16 - 10.5)^2$$
$$= 101.25 + 31.25 + 11.25 + 151.25$$
$$= 295.$$

We obtain our F test for this contrast by dividing the right-hand side of Equation 3.3 by the appropriate error term, or

$$F_{contrast} = \frac{r^2_{alerting} \times SS_{between}}{MS_{within}} = \frac{(.9797)(295)}{10} = 28.90.$$

The squared correlation between the means of the conditions and their λ weights can also be computed from

$$r^2_{alerting} = \frac{F_{contrast}}{F_{contrast} + F_{noncontrast}(df_{noncontrast})}, \tag{3.5}$$

where $F_{noncontrast}$ is the noncontrast F for all sources of variation other than the contrast, and $df_{noncontrast}$ is the noncontrast degrees of freedom associated with it. We find $F_{noncontrast}$ from

$$F_{noncontrast} = \frac{(SS_{between} - MS_{contrast})/df_{noncontrast}}{MS_{within}}, \tag{3.6}$$

or

$$F_{noncontrast} = \frac{F_{between}(df_{between}) - F_{contrast}}{df_{noncontrast}}. \tag{3.7}$$

Equation 3.6 is more convenient when we have access to all the sums of squares. Equation 3.7 is more appropriate when we have access only to various Fs, a situation frequently encountered when we reanalyze other investigators' results (e.g., in meta-analytic applications). The degrees of freedom for noncontrast sources of variation are obtained from

$$df_{noncontrast} = df_{between} - 1. \tag{3.8}$$

An alternative procedure for computing $r^2_{alerting}$ is

$$r^2_{alerting} = \frac{SS_{contrast}}{SS_{between}}. \tag{3.9}$$

In this book, we typically use the "F-test" version (Equation 3.5) rather than the "SS" version (Equation 3.6) for two reasons. First, the F-test version is more consistent with the expressions we will employ for other correlations conceptually related to the magnitudes of experimental effects. Second, when we are analyzing other investigators' data, as in meta-analytic work, we are likely to find that the F quantities, rather than the SS quantities, have been reported.

Contrast t tests

We could, if we wished, take the square root of our 1 degree of freedom F to find t. The general expression for a contrast t is

$$t_{contrast} = \frac{\Sigma(M_i \lambda_i)}{\sqrt{MS_{within}\left[\Sigma\frac{\lambda_i^2}{n}\right]}} = \frac{L}{\sqrt{MS_{within}\left[\Sigma\frac{\lambda_i^2}{n}\right]}}, \tag{3.10}$$

where $L = \Sigma(M_i \lambda_i)$, as defined following Equation 3.1. The degrees of freedom for $t_{contrast}$ are the degrees of freedom in MS_{within}.

Employing Equation 3.10 with the data in Table 3.1 gives

$$t_{contrast} = \frac{(6)(-3) + (8)(-1) + (12)(+1) + (16)(+3)}{\sqrt{10\left[\frac{(-3)^2}{5} + \frac{(-1)^2}{5} + \frac{(+1)^2}{5} + \frac{(+3)^2}{5}\right]}}$$

$$= \frac{34}{\sqrt{40}} = 5.38,$$

which is equal to the square root of $F = 28.90$, as it must be. Substituting in Equation 2.3 gives us $r_{contrast} = .80$.

Applying this method to the "published data" in Tables 1.1 and 3.2 gives

$$t_{contrast} = \frac{(25)(-2) + (30)(-1) + (40)(0) + (50)(+1) + (55)(+2)}{\sqrt{1575\left[\frac{(-2)^2}{10} + \frac{(-1)^2}{10} + \frac{(0)^2}{10} + \frac{(+1)^2}{10} + \frac{(+2)^2}{10}\right]}}$$

$$= \frac{80}{\sqrt{1575}} = 2.02,$$

which also turns out (as it must) to be the square root of $F_{contrast} = 4.06$, with an associated $r_{contrast} = .29$.

EFFECT SIZE CORRELATIONS

Contrast *r* as a Partial *r*

In Chapter 2, we stated that when the contrast is a simple comparison between two groups, the $r_{contrast}$ is the point-biserial correlation between the subjects' group membership (coded as 0 or 1) and their score on the outcome variable as shown in Table 2.2. When contrasts are computed on three or more groups or conditions, however, the associated $r_{contrast}$ is no longer a point-biserial correlation. Instead, the $r_{contrast}$ is a *partial* correlation, that is, a correlation between subjects' scores on the outcome variable and the λs associated with their groups *after the elimination of all between-group sources of variation other than the contrast in question*. In what follows, we provide a more concrete description of these partial correlations.

Adjusted Observations. Each observation has (a) a value predicted from the contrast (whose computation will be described shortly) and (b) a residual from its group mean (i.e., the observation minus its group's mean). The group mean will exactly equal the predicted value for that group when the $r_{alerting}$ is 1.00. Suppose we replace each observation by an adjusted observation: its value predicted from the linear contrast plus its residual from the group mean. Thus the adjusted observation is the original observation after the between-group variation not explained by the contrast has been "partialed out." The correlation between the adjusted observations and the λ weights is $r_{contrast}$. It remains only to describe how to calculate the adjusted observations.

Calculating Adjusted Observations for $r_{contrast}$. To begin, we define the residual associated with each observation as the difference between that observation and the mean of its group. Each adjusted observation is each residual plus the grand mean plus the λ weight (for the group to which the observation belongs) times a regression coefficient, *b*:

$$b_{contrast} = \sqrt{\frac{MS_{contrast}}{n\Sigma\lambda_i^2}} = \frac{L}{\Sigma\lambda_i^2}. \tag{3.11}$$

We now illustrate the calculation of adjusted observations by use of the data of Table 3.3 and their associated ANOVA. Notice that in the ANOVA, we have partitioned $SS_{between}$ into a 1-degree-of-freedom portion associated with our linear contrast and a leftover, noncontrast portion with $3 - 1 = 2$ degrees of freedom. $MS_{contrast}$ can be computed from Equation 3.1:

$$\frac{5[9(-3) + 3(-1) + 27(+1) + 21(+3)]^2}{(-3)^2 + (-1)^2 + (+1)^2 + (+3)^2} = \frac{5(60)^2}{20} = 900.$$

Alternatively, $MS_{contrast}$ can be computed by the use of Equations 3.3 and 3.4 from the $r_{alerting}$ and the $SS_{between}$. The value of $r_{alerting}$, the correlation between the means (M_i) and their corresponding weights (λ_i), is $\sqrt{.50} = .707$. The value of $SS_{between}$ from

TABLE 3.3
Data for Showing Meaning of $r_{contrast}$

A. Basic Data

	Levels				
	1	2	3	4	
	12	6	30	24	
	12	6	30	24	
	9	3	27	21	
	6	0	24	18	
	6	0	24	18	Means
Sum	45	15	135	105	75
Mean	9	3	27	21	15
S_i^2	9.00	9.00	9.00	9.00	9.00
λ_i	−3	−1	+1	+3	0

B. Overall ANOVA

Source	SS	df	MS	F
Between	1,800	3	600	66.67
Contrast	900	1	900	100.00
Noncontrast	900	2	450	50.00
Within	144	16	9	
Total	1,944			

Equation 3.4 is 1,800. Consequently, $MS_{contrast}$ is $.50 \times 1800 = 900$, as before. Thus, from Equation 3.11,

$$b_{contrast} = \sqrt{\frac{MS_{contrast}}{n\Sigma\lambda_i^2}} = \sqrt{\frac{900}{5(20)}} = 3.00,$$

or

$$b_{contrast} = \frac{L}{\Sigma\lambda_i^2} = \frac{9(-3) + 3(-1) + 27(+1) + 21(+3)}{(-3)^2 + (-1)^2 + (+1)^2 + (+3)^2} = \frac{60}{20} = 3.00.$$

We are now ready to calculate the values of the adjusted observations. For each observation, the adjusted value is

Adjusted observation = Residual + $\bar{M}$ + $(\lambda_i b_{contrast})$, (3.12)

where $\bar{M}$ plus $(\lambda_i b_{contrast})$ is the predicted value for the observation from the linear contrast. In our example, $\bar{M} = 15$ (the mean of the column means). For the first

TABLE 3.4
Adjusted Data of Table 3.3

	Levels			
	1	2	3	4
	9	15	21	27
	9	15	21	27
	6	12	18	24
	3	9	15	21
	3	9	15	21
Sum	30	60	90	120
Mean	6	12	18	24
S_i^2	9.00	9.00	9.00	9.00

group, then, the predicted values are all $15 + (-3)(3.00)$. Thus, for the very first observation, the value is 12, and the residual is $12 - 9 = 3$, so the adjusted value is $3 + 15 + (-3)(3.00) = 9$. For the first observation in the second group, the value is 6, and the residual is $6 - 3 = 3$, so the adjusted value is $3 + 15 + (-1)(3.00) = 15$. All the adjusted values are shown in Table 3.4.

We can now state the meaning of $r_{contrast}$ for the data of Table 3.3. Notice first that when we employ Equation 3.2, we find, from the $F_{contrast}$ shown in Part B of Table 3.3, that

$$r_{contrast} = \sqrt{\frac{100}{100 + 16}} = .93.$$

This value of .93 is exactly the same value we obtain by directly computing the correlation between the twenty adjusted observations of Table 3.4 and their associated λs.

Distinguishing $r_{contrast}$ from $r_{effect\ size}$

In a study with only two conditions, $r_{contrast}$ is an effect size correlation, $r_{effect\ size}$. When there are more than two conditions, however, $r_{contrast}$ is generally not equivalent to $r_{effect\ size}$. Because $r_{contrast}$ is a *partial r* (i.e., the correlation between subjects' scores and the λs of the groups to which they belong *after all other between-condition effects are removed*), $r_{contrast}$ can be substantially larger than $r_{effect\ size}$ and may not correspond to our ordinary understanding of an effect size correlation.

For example, Figure 3.1 shows the results of two studies, both with $r_{contrast} = .80$. The plot of the means shows Study 1 to have a clearly linear trend in the five means: $r_{alerting} = 1.0$ (i.e., the correlation between the means and the λs for a linear trend). Study 2, however, does not show a clearly linear trend, and $r_{alerting}$ is only .45. Indeed, the five means of Study 2 show a greater quadratic than linear trend, with $r_{alerting} = .76$ using lambdas for quadratic trend of $-2, +1, +2, +1, -2$. The

44 One-Way Contrast Analyses

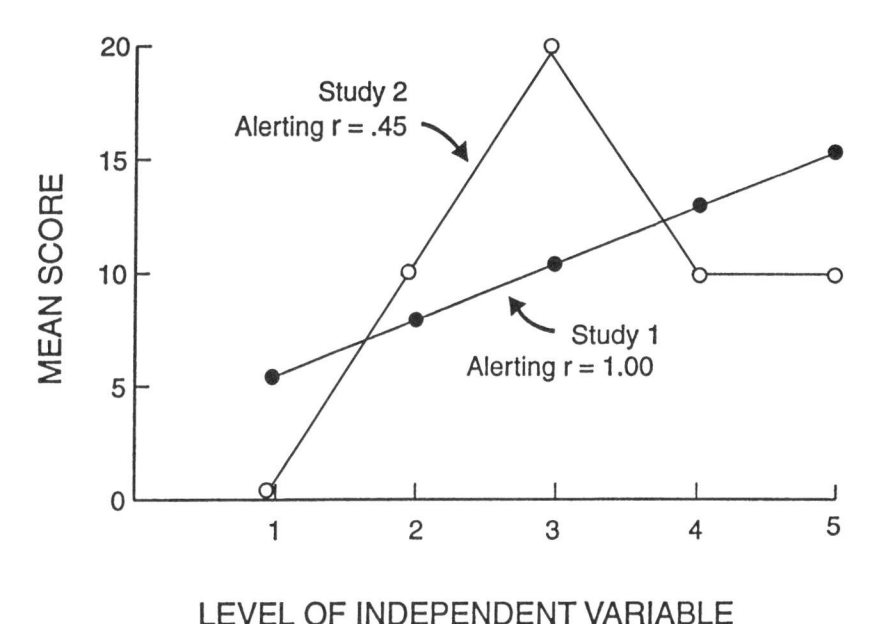

```
                20 ┌
                   │              ○
                   │   Study 2    ╱╲
                15 │   Alerting r = .45╲          ●
                   │                  ╱  ╲    ╱
        MEAN      │                 ╱    ╲ ╱
        SCORE  10 │        ○      ╱    ╱ ╲  ●
                   │       ╱      ╱  ╱     ○───────○
                   │      ╱     ●╱ ╱
                   │    ╱    ╱     Study 1
                 5 │  ●   ╱        Alerting r = 1.00
                   │  ╱
                   │╱
                 0 │○
                   └──┴──────┴──────┴──────┴──────┴──
                      1      2      3      4      5
                        LEVEL OF INDEPENDENT VARIABLE
```

FIGURE 3.1
Results of two studies with very different patterns of means and alerting rs, but, surprisingly, with identical underlying partial rs ($r_{contrast}$).

reason that both studies have the same value of $r_{contrast}$ for the linear trend despite their different patterns displayed in Figure 3.1 is that Study 2, with its smaller value of $r_{alerting}$, shows far greater noncontrast variability among the means than does Study 1. Consequently, we have a smaller proportion of a larger variability in Study 2 yielding the same size *partial* correlation, $r_{contrast}$, as in Study 1.

Were we to compute a simple correlation (putting all the noncontrast sources of between-group variation into the error term – i.e., unpartialed), we would find Study 1 still to have a simple correlation of .80, but Study 2 would have a simple correlation of only .42. These simple correlations, not controlling for other between-group sources of variability in a one-way design, are what we intuitively think of as effect size correlations because they are the correlations between the dependent variable's data and the λs. When the leftover, noncontrast between-group variability (i.e., $SS_{noncontrast}$) is small relative to the contrast variability (i.e., $SS_{contrast}$), $r_{effect\ size}$ is quite similar to $r_{contrast}$. In other words, when $r^2_{alerting}$ is nearly 1.00, $r_{effect\ size}$ and $r_{contrast}$ will be nearly equal. A specific equation will display this relationship shortly.

Consider the means and analysis of variance of Table 3.3. The between-conditions variability has been divided into a portion associated with the linear contrast ($SS = 900$) and a leftover (or residual) portion not associated with the linear contrast ($SS = 900$). The value of $r_{contrast}$, then, is .93 from Equation 3.2:

$$r_{contrast} = \sqrt{\frac{100}{100 + 16}} = .93.$$

This example is one in which $r_{contrast}$ (.93) is substantially larger than $r_{effect\ size}$ because the noncontrast between-groups variability is relatively large. To compute $r_{effect\ size}$, which is the simple correlation, we treat the noncontrast between variability as additional error variance. Then, $r_{effect\ size}$ is

$$r_{effect\ size} = \sqrt{\frac{F_{contrast}}{F_{contrast} + F_{noncontrast}(df_{noncontrast}) + df_{within}}}, \qquad (3.13)$$

where $df_{noncontrast} = k - 2$, two fewer than the number of groups. Notice that the denominator of this equation adds the noise components of (a) the denominator of $r_{contrast}$ (the df_{within} of Equation 3.2) and (b) the denominator of $r_{alerting}$ (the $F_{noncontrast}$ times $df_{noncontrast}$ of Equation 3.5).

In our example, we find

$$r_{effect\ size} = \sqrt{\frac{100}{100 + 50(2) + 16}} = .68.$$

Notice that $r_{effect\ size}$, .68, is substantially smaller than $r_{contrast}$, .93.

Another way to compute $r_{effect\ size}$ employs $r_{contrast}$ and $r_{alerting}$. Specifically,

$$r_{effect\ size} = \frac{r_{contrast}}{\sqrt{1 - r_{contrast}^2 + \frac{r_{contrast}^2}{r_{alerting}^2}}}. \qquad (3.14)$$

For the example just above with $r_{contrast} = .928$ and $r_{alerting} = .707$,

$$r_{effect\ size} = \frac{.928}{\sqrt{1 - (.928)^2 + \frac{(.928)^2}{(.707)^2}}} = .68.$$

For an example of an $r_{contrast}$ that is very similar to an $r_{effect\ size}$, we return to the example of Tables 1.1 and 3.2. Here, $r_{alerting} = .99$, $r_{contrast} = .29$, and $r_{effect\ size} = .29$. When $r_{alerting}^2 = 1.00$, then $r_{effect\ size} = r_{contrast}$, as can be seen from Equation 3.14, but otherwise $r_{effect\ size}$ is smaller than $r_{contrast}$.

For another example comparing $r_{contrast}$ and $r_{effect\ size}$, consider a simple three-condition experiment in which nine patients are randomly assigned to each of the following three treatments: (A) Psychotherapy plus Medication, (B) Psychotherapy Alone, and (C) Medication Alone. The investigator predicted that combined treatments (A) would be more effective than either treatment alone (B, C). Appropriate contrast weights for this hypothesis are $+2, -1, -1$ for treatments A, B, and C, respectively. The mean benefit scores obtained for these treatments are

	A	B	C
Means	9	6	4
λ	+2	−1	−1

The correlation between the means and their assigned λs, $r_{alerting}$, is .92. The value of $SS_{between}$ from Equation 3.4 is 114, $SS_{contrast}$ (from Equations 3.1 or 3.3) is 96, and

MS_{within} is 16. Hence, $F_{contrast}$ is 96/16, or 6.00, and from Equation 3.2, we find

$$r_{contrast} = \sqrt{\frac{F_{contrast}}{F_{contrast} + df_{within}}} = \sqrt{\frac{6}{6+24}} = .45.$$

To compute $r_{effect\ size}$, we will also need $F_{noncontrast}$ and $df_{noncontrast}$. Because $SS_{noncontrast} = SS_{between} - SS_{contrast}$, we find $114 - 96 = 18$ as our $SS_{noncontrast}$. Because $df_{noncontrast} = df_{between} - 1 = 2 - 1 = 1$ in this example, we find $MS_{noncontrast}$ to be $SS_{noncontrast}/df_{noncontrast} = 18/1 = 18$. Then $F_{noncontrast} = MS_{noncontrast}/MS_{within} = 18/16 = 1.125$. Now, from Equation 3.13, we find

$$r_{effect\ size} = \sqrt{\frac{6.00}{6.00 + 1.125(1) + 24}} = .44.$$

Thus, in this example, $r_{contrast}$ and $r_{effect\ size}$ are very similar, .45 versus .44.

Interpreting as a BESD an Effect Size for a Contrast Involving Three or More Groups

When there are three or more groups involved in a contrast, it is not immediately obvious how to display the results in a 2 × 2 binomial effect size display. The problem is that the BESD has two levels of the independent variable, but there are actually three or more levels of the independent variable in the study. For a simple example we return to the data in Table 3.2 with five age levels. Should we consider the BESD the result we would expect if we repeated our experiment but divided our available subjects into two conditions corresponding to the conditions we predicted to be furthest apart? For the data in Table 3.2, those conditions would be the 11-year-olds ($\lambda = -2$) and the 15-year-olds ($\lambda = +2$). When our total N of 50 was allocated equally ($n = 10$) to each of our five age groups, we found $t_{contrast} = 2.02$, $r_{contrast} = .29$, $r_{effect\ size} = .29$, from Equations 3.10, 2.3, and 3.13, respectively. However, if we had allocated half our N of 50 to each of our extreme conditions, we would have expected to find the same means in those groups and thus would have expected to find

$$t = \frac{25(-2) + 55(+2)}{\sqrt{1575\left[\frac{(-2)^2}{25} + \frac{(+2)^2}{25}\right]}} = \frac{60}{\sqrt{504}} = 2.67,$$

with $r_{contrast} = r_{effect\ size} = .36$ in this two-group study. This $r_{effect\ size}$ is larger than our obtained $r_{effect\ size}$ of .29 for the linear trend over all five conditions.

Suppose we had compared the two conditions close to the midmost ages (e.g., the 12- versus the 14-year-olds) in our replication. We would have expected to find the same means in those groups and thus would have expected to find, in a study with 25 in each group,

$$t = \frac{30(-1) + 50(+1)}{\sqrt{1575\left[\frac{(-1)^2}{25} + \frac{(+1)^2}{25}\right]}} = \frac{20}{\sqrt{126}} = 1.78,$$

with $r_{contrast} = r_{effect\ size} = .25$ in this two-group study. This $r_{effect\ size}$ is smaller than our obtained $r_{effect\ size}$ of .29 for the linear trend over all five conditions.

This example illustrates that even when the noncontrast sum of squares is negligible, neither the most extreme (ages 11 and 15) nor the more central (ages 12 and 14) groups and their associated ages generate a value of $r_{effect\ size}$ that we would expect to see in a replication involving only two age groups with the same total sample size. What two groups are most appropriate when we want to represent our obtained results as a BESD, and what is the value of the correlation in this BESD?

A simple exact answer to these questions is available under the assumption that the noncontrast sum of squares is truly noise, that is, under the assumption that the relationship between the outcome variable, Y, and the treatment conditions is fully captured by our contrast. Without this assumption we cannot interpolate between the levels represented in our study, and in general, such interpolation is needed to obtain a BESD.

The BESD Correlation, r_{BESD}

When we assume that the relationship between the dependent (or outcome) variable, Y, and the treatment conditions is fully captured by our contrast, we can compute r_{BESD} from

$$r_{BESD} = \sqrt{\frac{F_{contrast}}{F_{contrast} + F_{noncontrast}(df_{noncontrast} + df_{within})}}, \qquad (3.15)$$

where if $F_{noncontrast}$ is less than 1.00, it is entered into Equation 3.15 as equal to 1.00. This restriction on $F_{noncontrast}$ in this equation effectively requires the noise level underlying MS_{within} to be at least as large as the noise level underlying $MS_{noncontrast}$. The restriction arises because we are viewing the noncontrast variability as the appropriate index of the noise level. For the example under discussion, the value of $F_{noncontrast}$ is $18/16 = 1.125$ so that

$$r_{BESD} = \sqrt{\frac{6.00}{6.00 + 1.125(1 + 24)}} = .42.$$

In this example, r_{BESD} is only slightly smaller than $r_{effect\ size}$ because the value of $F_{noncontrast}$ is not large. In general, the maximum value of r_{BESD} is $r_{effect\ size}$, but r_{BESD} can be appreciably smaller than $r_{effect\ size}$ when $F_{noncontrast}$ is large.

The use of $F_{noncontrast}$ in Equation 3.15 with its restriction to be at least 1.00 formalizes the assumption that the noncontrast variation is noise and forces r_{BESD} to be less than, or at most equal to, $r_{effect\ size}$. By simultaneously (a) requiring that $F_{noncontrast}$ be at least 1.00 and (b) adding the $df_{noncontrast}$ and df_{within}, we are regarding r_{BESD} as reflecting a random rather than a fixed view of our between conditions. Although this random view of our between conditions tends to make r_{BESD} smaller than $r_{effect\ size}$, it also permits generalization not only to other subjects in the same conditions, but also to other levels of the same independent variable.

How Shall We Think of r_{BESD}?

The value of r_{BESD} is the value of $r_{effect\ size}$ we would expect to see in a two-group replication of the current study with the same total N that has the two treatment levels chosen in the following way. The lower level is set at $-1\ \sigma_\lambda$ and the higher level is set at $+1\ \sigma_\lambda$, where σ_λ is defined as

$$\sigma_\lambda = \sqrt{\frac{\Sigma \lambda^2}{k}}, \tag{3.16}$$

with, as before, $k =$ the number of groups or conditions in the contrast. The reason for this definition of the levels of the BESD is as follows. Under our assumption that the relationship between Y and our treatments is fully captured by our contrast, any study that chooses values of the treatments to have the same variance as the variance in this study will be expected to give the same correlation. More technically, if the regression of Y on the treatment conditions is linear in the contrast with constant residual variance, then the expected correlation will be the same for any study with the same variance of the treatment conditions.

For the data in Table 3.2,

$$\sigma_\lambda = \sqrt{\frac{(-2)^2 + (-1)^2 + (0)^2 + (+1)^2 + (+2)^2}{5}} = \sqrt{2} = 1.414.$$

In the example in Table 3.2, we find r_{BESD} from Equation 3.15 to be

$$r_{BESD} = \sqrt{\frac{4.06}{4.06 + 1.00(3 + 45)}} = .28,$$

where the value 1.00 replaces the obtained $F_{noncontrast}$ value of 0.021, as required by the statement following Equation 3.15. The appropriate interpretation of the BESD associated with the five λs in Table 3.2 is that it shows the comparison of the rate of above-average performance of those children whose ages fall 1 σ_λ or 1.4 λ units above the mean age with the average performance of those whose ages fall 1 σ_λ or 1.4 λ units below the mean age. In this example, children whose ages fall 1.4 λ units above the mean age are age 14.4 because the mean age is 13 and σ_λ is 1.4 years (i. e., $13 + 1.4 = 14.4$). Analogously, children whose ages fall 1.4 λ units below the mean age are age 11.6 (i.e., $13 - 1.4 = 11.6$).

Table 3.5 shows the $r_{effect\ size}$ and associated BESD for each of our three examples of defining the levels of the independent variable of the data in Table 3.2. Part A of Table 3.5 shows the $r_{effect\ size}$ and the BESD obtained when we select the most extreme levels of the independent variable. Part B shows the $r_{effect\ size}$ and the BESD obtained when we select more central levels of the independent variable. Finally, Part C shows the $r_{effect\ size}$, which is equal to r_{BESD}, and the BESD obtained with levels of the independent variable at $-1\ \sigma_\lambda$ and $+1\ \sigma_\lambda$; the BESD shown in Part C is the appropriate one for the data in Table 3.2 and its linear trend contrast.

TABLE 3.5
Effect Size rs and BESDs for Three Examples of Defining the Levels of the Independent Variable for the Data in Table 3.2

Choice of two age levels	Hypothetical $r_{effect\ size}$		BESD Above median outcome	Below median outcome	
A. Most extreme	.36[a]	High age (Mean = 15.0)	68	32	100
		Low age (Mean = 11.0)	32	68	100
			100	100	200
			Above median outcome	Below median outcome	
B. More central	.25[a]	High age (Mean = 14.0)	62.5	37.5	100
		Low age (Mean = 12.0)	37.5	62.5	100
			100	100	200
			Above median outcome	Below median outcome	
C. $\pm\sigma_\lambda$	.28[b]	High age (Mean = 14.4)	64	36	100
		Low age (Mean = 11.6)	36	64	100
			100	100	200

[a] Computed from Equation 2.3 or 2.5.
[b] Computed from Equation 3.15.

An Overview of the Four rs

In this chapter, we have distinguished four correlations useful in assessing the magnitude of experimental effects. Table 3.6 summarizes these four rs and shows that the only differences among them occur in the second (or third) term of the denominator. Thus,

1. $r_{alerting}$ ignores within-group noise, and its second denominator term incorporates information only about noncontrast between-group variation.

2. $r_{contrast}$ ignores noncontrast between-group variation, and its second denominator term incorporates information only about within-group variation.

3. $r_{effect\ size}$ incorporates information about both the noncontrast between-group variation and the within-group variation – indeed, the second and third terms of

TABLE 3.6
An Overview of the Four rs

Type of r	Computed from	Equation
$r_{alerting}$ =	$\sqrt{\dfrac{F_{contrast}}{F_{contrast} + F_{noncontrast}(df_{noncontrast})}}$	(3.17)*
$r_{contrast}$ =	$\sqrt{\dfrac{F_{contrast}}{F_{contrast} + df_{within}}}$	(3.2)
$r_{effect\ size}$ =	$\sqrt{\dfrac{F_{contrast}}{F_{contrast} + F_{noncontrast}(df_{noncontrast}) + df_{within}}}$	(3.13)
r_{BESD} =	$\sqrt{\dfrac{F_{contrast}}{F_{contrast} + F^a_{noncontrast}(df_{noncontrast} + df_{within})}}$	(3.15)

* Based on Equation 3.5, which defined $r^2_{alerting}$.
^a When $F_{noncontrast}$ is less than 1.00, it is entered here as equal to 1.00.

the denominator are simply the second denominator terms imported from $r_{alerting}$ and $r_{contrast}$.

4. r_{BESD} also incorporates information about both the noncontrast between-group variation and the within-group variation, but with the restriction that the noise level of the within-group variation must be set at least as large as the noise level of the noncontrast variation, as it is the latter that we are regarding as the appropriate index of the noise level for doing interpolation to levels of the independent variable not in this study.

It is possible for $r_{contrast}$, $r_{effect\ size}$, and r_{BESD} to show identical values in a particular case, but in general, $r_{effect\ size}$ is larger than r_{BESD}, and $r_{contrast}$ is larger than $r_{effect\ size}$, these differences sometimes being quite substantial; $r_{alerting}$ tends to be larger than the other three rs but need not be, as we saw in our discussion of Figure 3.1, in which both cases had an $r_{contrast}$ of .80, but one case was associated with an $r_{alerting}$ of 1.00, and the other case was associated with an $r_{alerting}$ of .45.

Making Old Noncontrast Noise into New Contrast Signal

When we think of $SS_{noncontrast}$ as reflecting explainable, nonerror variability, we can typically improve our understanding of the phenomena of interest by trying to form a new contrast that combines some of our original contrast with some of the original noncontrast variation. For an example, we return to Study 2 in Figure 3.1, which showed means of 0, 10, 20, 10, 10 for increasing levels of our independent variable. Our initial interest was in a linear trend contrast with λs of -2, -1, 0, $+1$, $+2$. However, the value of $SS_{contrast}$ for linear trend was only about 20% of the value of $SS_{between}$, implying $r_{alerting} = .45$, whereas the $r_{alerting}$ for a quadratic trend (with λs of −2, +1, +2, +1, −2) was .76, associated with about 58% of the $SS_{between}$. In some situations, the simple addition of the λs of the two contrasts leads to a new contrast that makes good theoretical sense. Assuming that to be the case here, we can simply add the linear and quadratic λs as follows, to create a new contrast:

	Group 1	Group 2	Group 3	Group 4	Group 5
Linear λs:	−2	−1	0	+1	+2
Quadratic λs:	−2	+1	+2	+1	−2
Total	−4	0	+2	+2	0.

In this case, the resulting contrast compares the first group ($\lambda = -4$) with the average of the third ($\lambda = +2$) and fourth ($\lambda = +2$) groups, with the second ($\lambda = 0$) and fifth ($\lambda = 0$) groups falling between and equal to each other. The result is an $r_{alerting}$ of .87, or about 75% of the $SS_{between}$.

Incidentally, it should be noted that when we added the linear and quadratic λs, just above, the quadratic λs contributed somewhat more to the total than did the linear λs, because the variance of the quadratic λs was greater (2.8) than the variance of the linear λs (2.0). If we want to weight these two contrasts equally when forming our combined contrast, we can do so by first dividing each of the linear λs by the standard deviation of those λs ($\sigma_\lambda = \sqrt{2}$) and each of the quadratic λs by the standard deviation of those λs ($\sigma_\lambda = \sqrt{2.8}$). For the present example, the standardized contrast weights (i.e., weights divided by their standard deviations) are as follows:

Linear	−1.414	−0.707	0.000	+0.707	+1.414
Quadratic	−1.195	+0.598	+1.195	+0.598	−1.195
Total	−2.609	−0.109	+1.195	+1.305	+0.219

Table 3.7 shows an analysis of variance of the data of Study 2 in Figure 3.1. The SS, df, and MS are shown for the overall between-conditions effect, the three contrasts shown just above, and the within-condition source. Also shown for each contrast are the values of SS, MS, and F for the noncontrast portion of the between-conditions effect. Table 3.8 shows for each of the three contrasts the values of $r_{alerting}$, $r_{contrast}$, $r_{effect\ size}$, and r_{BESD}. Table 3.9 shows for each contrast the BESD based on r_{BESD}. The five levels of the independent variable were 1, 2, 3, 4, and 5, and for each contrast, the high and low levels of the independent variable for the BESD are indicated in Table 3.9 by the values of the independent variable at 1 σ_λ above the mean and 1 σ_λ below the mean, respectively. In this example, just as in actual research contexts, $r_{contrast}$ is larger than $r_{effect\ size}$, which is larger than r_{BESD} for all three contrasts.

Counternull Values for r_{BESD}

Whenever we compute r_{BESD}, we should routinely display its counternull value with the associated p value. Therefore, we compute the counternull values for each r_{BESD} in Table 3.9, based on the linear, quadratic, and combined trends.

TABLE 3.7
Analysis of Variance of Data of Study 2 of Figure 3.1[a]

Source	SS	df	MS	F	p	$SS_{noncontrast}$ $(SS_{between} - SS_{contrast})$	$MS_{noncontrast}$ $(SS_{noncontrast}/df^b_{noncontrast})$	$F_{noncontrast}$ $(MS_{noncontrast}/MS_{within})$
Between	400.00	4	100	11.11	.011			
Linear	80.00	1	80.00	8.89	.031	320	106.67	11.85
Quadratic	228.57	1	228.57	25.40	.0040	171.43	57.14	6.35
Lin. + quad.[c]	289.62	1	289.62	32.18	.0024	110.38	36.79	4.09
Within	45.00	5	9.00					

[a] The analysis assumes $n = 2$ per condition.
[b] Where $df_{noncontrast} = df_{between} - 1$, which is $4 - 1 = 3$ in this case.
[c] The sum of standardized linear and standardized quadratic λs so that each has contributed equally to the sum of the λs.

TABLE 3.8
Three Contrasts of Table 3.7 with Their Associated $r_{alerting}$, $r_{contrast}$, p values, $r_{effect\ size}$, r_{BESD}, and $r_{BESD\ counternull}$

	Contrasts		
	Linear	Quadratic	Combined
$r_{alerting}$	.45[a]	.76	.85
$r_{contrast}$	.80[b]	.91	.93
p value	.031	.0040	.0024
$r_{effect\ size}$	.42	.72[c]	.81
r_{BESD}	.29	.58	.70[d]
$r_{BESD\ counternull}$	.52	.82	.89
$\sigma_\lambda = \sqrt{\dfrac{\Sigma\lambda^2}{k}}$	1.4	1.7	1.4

[a] Computed as $\sqrt{\dfrac{8.89}{8.89 + 11.85(3)}}$

[b] Computed as $\sqrt{\dfrac{8.89}{8.89 + 5}}$

[c] Computed as $\sqrt{\dfrac{25.40}{25.40 + 6.35(3) + 5}}$

[d] Computed as $\sqrt{\dfrac{32.18}{32.18 + 4.09(3 + 5)}}$

For the linear trend contrast, r_{BESD} was .29, from which we obtain $r_{BESD\ counternull}$ from Equation 2.16 as follows:

$$r_{BESD\ counternull} = \sqrt{\dfrac{4r_{BESD}^2}{1 + 3r_{BESD}^2}} = \sqrt{\dfrac{4(.29)^2}{1 + 3(.29)^2}} = .52,$$

a correlation that we display in the BESD that follows:

Counternull linear trend contrast ($p = .031$)

		Above median	Below median	Σ
$(+1\sigma_\lambda)$	Higher level	76	24	100
$(-1\sigma_\lambda)$	Lower level	24	76	100
	Σ	100	100	200

The interpretation of this display of $r_{BESD\ counternull}$ is that it is just as likely as the following BESD reflecting the null hypothesis:

		Above median	Below median	Σ
$(+1\sigma_\lambda)$	Higher level	50	50	100
$(-1\sigma_\lambda)$	Lower level	50	50	100
	Σ	100	100	200

TABLE 3.9
Three r_{BESD}s of Table 3.8 Displayed in BESDs

Independent variable[a]	Contrasts							
	Linear outcome			Quadratic outcome			Combined outcome	
		Above median	Below median		Above median	Below median		Above median	Below median
$+1\sigma_x$ high level	Mean = 4.4	64.5	35.5	Mean = 4.7	79	21	Mean = 4.4	85	15
$-1\sigma_x$ low level	Mean = 1.6	35.5	64.5	Mean = 1.3	21	79	Mean = 1.6	15	85

[a] Mean level of the independent variable was 3.0; see Study 2 in Figure 3.1.

The $r_{BESD\ counternull}$s for the quadratic and combined trends in Table 3.9 are found analogously by application of Equation 2.16 to the corresponding r_{BESD}s of .58 and .70. The $r_{BESD\ counternull}$s are .82 and .89, respectively, and are displayed in the following BESDs:

Counternull quadratic trend contrast ($p = .0040$)

		Above median	Below median	Σ
$(+1\ \sigma_\lambda)$	Higher level	91	9	100
$(-1\ \sigma_\lambda)$	Lower level	9	91	100
	Σ	100	100	200

Counternull combined trend contrast ($p = .0024$)

		Above median	Below median	Σ
$(+1\ \sigma_\lambda)$	Higher level	94.5	5.5	100
$(-1\ \sigma_\lambda)$	Lower level	5.5	94.5	100
	Σ	100	100	200

Using λs of 0 to Set Aside Conditions for Effect Size Estimation

In general, when we assign λs to the various conditions of our research studies, we are predicting a relationship between the λs and the mean score obtained for that condition. We assign larger λs to conditions predicted to yield larger means. For example, we attach a λ of 0 to a condition when our prediction is that the mean of that condition will fall halfway between the means of the conditions to which we have assigned $\lambda = +1$ and $\lambda = -1$, or $\lambda = +2$ and $\lambda = -2$, and so on. In such a case, the $\lambda = 0$ is functioning just as any other number.

Sometimes, however, we use a λ of 0 when our intent is to set aside that group. For example, suppose that for the data in Table 3.2 we want to compare the 11-year-olds to the 12-year-olds, setting aside the three older groups. We would then assign the weights of -1 and $+1$ to the two ages of interest and the weight of 0 to the remaining three groups. In this case, the λs of 0 do not represent a prediction that these three groups of older children will score between the means of the 11- and 12-year-olds. Rather, they suggest a new analysis omitting the subjects from the $\lambda = 0$ groups.

Significance levels (and F and t) are not affected by how we regard our λs of 0, as long as we assume the within-condition variances are the same across all groups. But the appropriate calculations of $r_{alerting}$, $r_{contrast}$, $r_{effect\ size}$, and r_{BESD} will all tend to give larger values when conditions with $\lambda = 0$ are set aside than when these conditions are viewed as intermediate. The typical increase in values of these correlations is due both to the decrease in $df_{noncontrast}$ and to the decrease of df_{within} when groups are set aside (see Equations 3.5, 3.2, 3.13, and 3.15 for computational equations, and see Table 3.6 for a summary). Another way to think about the effect on these correlations of setting aside one or more conditions with $\lambda = 0$ is that the variance of the nonzero λs is at least as large as the variance of all the λs because zero is always the mean λ. For example, with contrast weights of $+2, 0, -1, -1$, we find, $\sigma_\lambda = 1.22$. But when we set aside the condition with $\lambda = 0$, $\sigma_\lambda = 1.41$, an increase of about 15%.

Computing the Four rs. When conditions are set aside, four quantities required for computing the various correlations summarized in Table 3.6 change their values: $df_{between}$, $df_{noncontrast}$, df_{within}, and $F_{noncontrast}$. Both $df_{between}$ and $df_{noncontrast}$ in the original study are reduced by the number of conditions set aside, and the result is the new quantities, $df^*_{between}$ and $df^*_{noncontrast}$. The df_{within} of the original study are reduced by $n-1$ for each of the conditions set aside, and the result is a new quantity df^*_{within}. The final new quantity required, $F^*_{noncontrast}$, is obtained from

$$F^*_{noncontrast} = \frac{(SS^*_{between} - MS_{contrast})/df^*_{noncontrast}}{MS_{within}} \qquad (3.18)$$

or the equivalent

$$F^*_{noncontrast} = \frac{F^*_{between}(df^*_{between}) - F_{contrast}}{df^*_{noncontrast}}. \qquad (3.19)$$

In Equation 3.18, $SS^*_{between}$ is computed by use of Equation 3.4 on the means of the conditions remaining after the set-aside conditions have been removed. Because $MS_{contrast}$ is not affected by set-asides, we need no new computation to get that quantity, and $df^*_{noncontrast}$ is obtained as described just above. Finally, the value of MS_{within} in Equation 3.18 can be obtained in two different ways: (a) we can actually recompute MS_{within} just from the conditions remaining after removing the data from the set-aside conditions, or (b) we can employ the original MS_{within}. In general, we recommend the second option because it typically yields a more stable estimate, unless the within variances of the set-aside conditions are suspected of being atypical of the remaining conditions.

To illustrate the procedures described, Table 3.10 shows four levels of an independent variable (medication dosage level) with three observations at each level. For simplicity, the four within-condition variances are identical. Part A shows the basic data, and Part B shows the values of $SS_{between}$, $SS_{contrast}$, $SS_{noncontrast}$, and SS_{within} based on all four conditions (A, B, C, and D) corresponding to four dosage levels. We consider the contrast with λs of $-1, 0, 0, +1$. Because two of the λs are 0 (those for Conditions B and C), there are four ways we can view this contrast.

1. *No set-asides.* In this view of the contrast, both of the λs of 0 are regarded as intermediate numbers, reflecting a prediction that the means of Conditions B and C will fall halfway between the means of Conditions A and D. The analysis of variance shown in Part B of Table 3.10 is the one we would compute with this view of the contrast where there are four groups, all of whose means are of substantive interest. The first column of data of Table 3.11 shows the values of $SS_{between}$, $SS_{contrast}$, $SS_{noncontrast}$, $df_{between}$, $df_{noncontrast}$, $MS_{noncontrast}$, $F_{noncontrast}$, $F_{contrast}$, and df_{within}, all of which are obtained from Part B of Table 3.10.

2. *Condition B set aside.* In this view of the contrast, Condition B is regarded as of no relevance and is therefore set aside, whereas the $\lambda = 0$ of Condition C is regarded as an intermediate number. The ANOVA quantities of the column labeled "B" of Table 3.11 were computed as described above. Comparing the ANOVA quantities of the first and second columns of data of Table 3.11 shows, not surprisingly,

TABLE 3.10
Hypothetical Data with Analysis of Variance for Contrast with Two λs of 0

A. Basic data

	Medication dosage levels			
	0 mg	100 mg	200 mg	300 mg
	A	B	C	D
	4	5	8	8
	2	3	6	6
	0	1	4	4
Sum	6	9	18	18
M_i	2	3	6	6
S_i^2	4	4	4	4
λ_i	−1	0	0	+1

B. Analysis of variance of basic data

Source	SS	df	MS	F
Between	38.25	3	12.75	3.19
Contrast	24.00	1	24.00	6.00
Noncontrast	14.25	2	7.125	1.78
Within	32.00	8	4.00	
Total	70.25	11		

that most have changed in going from no set-asides to Condition B set aside. A few pages earlier, we noted that the appropriate calculation of $r_{alerting}$, $r_{contrast}$, $r_{effect\ size}$, and r_{BESD} will tend to give larger values when conditions with $\lambda = 0$ are set aside. In the present case, when Condition B was set aside, all four of these effect size correlations increased, on average, about 10%. Exceptions to these types of increases occur only under fairly unusual circumstances, for example, when the variance within the group set aside is substantially smaller than the pooled within-group variance, and when that variance is not included in computing MS_{within} when that group is set aside. Under some circumstances (e.g., when the sample size of the group set aside is noticeably larger than the average sample size), effect size correlations can actually decrease substantially when the variance within the group set aside was especially small and was not included in computing MS_{within}.

3. *Condition C set aside.* This view of the contrast is analogous to the one in number 2 except that Condition C instead of B is set aside. Column C of Table 3.11 shows that although the $df_{noncontrast}$ and df_{within} have not changed in going from B

TABLE 3.11
ANOVA Quantities, the Four rs, p Values, and σ_λ Obtained from the Data of Table 3.10: Weights for Conditions A, B, C, D Are $-1, 0, 0, +1$

No conditions set aside			Conditions set aside		
			B	C	B and C
$SS_{between}$	38.25	$SS^*_{between}$	32.00	26.00	24.00
$SS_{contrast}$	24.00	$SS_{contrast}$	24.00	24.00	24.00
$SS_{noncontrast}$	14.25	$SS^*_{noncontrast}$	8.00	2.00	0.00
$df_{between}$	3	$df^*_{between}$	2	2	1
$df_{noncontrast}$	2	$df^*_{noncontrast}$	1	1	0
$MS_{noncontrast}$	7.125	$MS^*_{noncontrast}$	8.00	2.00	0.00
$F_{noncontrast}$	1.78	$F^*_{noncontrast}$	2.00	0.50	0.00
$F_{contrast}$	6.00	$F_{contrast}$	6.00	6.00	6.00
df_{within}	8	df^*_{within}	6	6	4
MS_{within}	4.00	MS_{within}	4.00	4.00	4.00
$r_{alerting}$	.79	$r_{alerting}$	.87	.96	1.00
$r_{contrast}$	.65	$r_{contrast}$	.71	.71	.77
p value	.04	p value	.04	.04	.04
$r_{effect\ size}$	.58	$r_{effect\ size}$	.65	.69	.77
r_{BESD}	.50	r_{BESD}	.55	.68	.77
$r_{BESD\ counternull}$	.76	$r_{BESD\ counternull}$	.80	.88	.92
σ_λ	.71	σ_λ	.82	.82	1.00

set aside to C set aside, the other ANOVA quantities have changed, as have three of the four correlations. As we expect, compared to the situation with no set-asides, when Condition C is set aside, the effect size correlations increased – on average, about 20% in this example.

4. *Conditions B and C set aside.* In this view of the contrast, both $\lambda = 0$ conditions are set aside, and the result is changed ANOVA quantities and changed correlations. These changes are not surprising because we have set aside half our data rather than just one-quarter of the data, as in the two preceding cases. Also changed is the value of σ_λ, the standard deviation of the λs remaining after some have been set aside. When both Conditions B and C are set aside, the effect size correlations increase even more dramatically over the no set-asides – about 30% in this example, on average. Part A of Table 3.12 shows, for each of our four cases, the BESD based on the r_{BESD}; Part B shows the associated counternull value of r_{BESD}.

Counternull Values for r_{BESD} with Set-Asides

For each of the four BESDs in Table 3.12, we also display the BESD corresponding to its counternull value of r_{BESD} (i.e., the $r_{BESD\ counternull}$). For illustration, consider

TABLE 3.12
BESDs for the Four r_{BESD}s and the four $r_{BESD\ counternull}$s in Table 3.11

A. r_{BESD}s

		Conditions set aside							
		None		B		C		B and C	
		Outcome		Outcome		Outcome		Outcome	
Independent variable		Above median	Below median	Above median	Below median	Above median	Below median	Above median	Below median
High level	$.71\lambda$	75	25	77.5	22.5	84	16	88.5	11.5
Low level	$-.71\lambda$	25	75	22.5	77.5	16	84	11.5	88.5

B. $r_{BESD\ counternull}$s

		Conditions set aside							
		None		B		C		B and C	
		Outcome		Outcome		Outcome		Outcome	
Independent variable		Above median	Below median	Above median	Below median	Above median	Below median	Above median	Below median
High level	$.71\lambda$	88	12	90	10	94	6	96	4
Low level	$-.71\lambda$	12	88	10	90	6	94	4	96

Note: All *p* values are .040 and all null-counternull intervals are, therefore, 1 − .040 = .96, or 96% intervals.

the r_{BESD} of column C of Table 3.11. We compute r_{BESD} from Equation 3.15:

$$r_{BESD} = \sqrt{\frac{6.00}{6.00 + (1.00)(1+6)}} = .68,$$

a value noticeably higher than the r_{BESD} of .50 obtained when the two $\lambda = 0$ conditions are regarded as intermediate numbers rather than as set-asides.

Representing our r_{BESD} as a BESD yields the following result (where $\sigma_\lambda = 0.82$):

		Above median	Below median	Σ
(+1 σ_λ)	Higher level	84	16	100
(−1 σ_λ)	Lower level	16	84	100
	Σ	100	100	200

And from Equation 2.16 we find

$$r_{BESD\ counternull} = \sqrt{\frac{4r^2_{BESD}}{1 + 3r^2_{BESD}}} = \sqrt{\frac{4(.68)^2}{1 + 3(.68)^2}} = .88,$$

with $p = .040$, resulting in the counternull BESD shown in Table 3.12. This counternull BESD, based on the counternull value of r_{BESD} (i.e., .88), is as likely to reflect the actual state of nature as is the BESD based on the null value of the effect size. For this result, an obtained r_{BESD} of .68 and $p = .040$, the null-counternull interval (from $r = .00$ to $r = .88$) is a 96% interval (i.e., $1 - .04 = .96$).

THE FOUR rs IN THE META-ANALYTIC CONTEXT

The four correlations we have been discussing in this chapter are all easy to compute when the data are our own. However, when we are doing the meta-analytic work of summarizing other investigators' results, we typically find that all four rs ($r_{alerting}$, $r_{contrast}$, $r_{effect\ size}$, and r_{BESD}) have not been reported. However, if the researchers have reported means, standard deviations, and sample sizes for all conditions, we can readily compute any required test statistic, as well as the four rs. Here we continue to assume, as we have thus far in this chapter, that the sample sizes in each condition are the same.

$r_{alerting}$

If the means of all the conditions entering into a contrast are given, we can, of course, compute $r_{alerting}$ directly by computing the correlation between the means and their associated contrast weights. Even if the means are not reported – and sometimes they are not – we can compute $r_{alerting}$ if we can obtain the values of $F_{contrast} = t^2_{contrast}$ and $F_{noncontrast}$, because from Equation 3.17 (Table 3.6)

$$r_{alerting} = \sqrt{\frac{F_{contrast}}{F_{contrast} + F_{noncontrast}(df_{noncontrast})}}.$$

$F_{contrast}$ and $df_{noncontrast}$ are almost always available, but $F_{noncontrast}$ is often not given directly. If the mean squares are available, we can also get $r_{alerting}$ from

$$r_{alerting} = \sqrt{\frac{F_{contrast}(MS_{within})}{MS_{between}(df_{between})}}. \tag{3.20}$$

If the overall between-condition $F_{between}$ is given, we can also get $r_{alerting}$ from

$$r_{alerting} = \sqrt{\frac{F_{contrast}}{F_{between}(df_{between})}}. \tag{3.21}$$

$r_{contrast}$

If the value of $F_{contrast}$ is available, as it usually is, we can obtain $r_{contrast}$ from Equation 3.2:

$$r_{contrast} = \sqrt{\frac{F_{contrast}}{F_{contrast} + df_{within}}}$$

where df_{within} is based on the df collected from all the conditions entering into the contrast.

Some investigators do not report values of test statistics, such as F, when they are not significant, and then Equation 3.2 cannot be used. In such cases, the mean squares required to compute our own Fs are unlikely to be available either. Given means and the total sample size, however, we can use Equation 3.1 to get the mean square for our contrast, and from standard deviations, if provided, we can get MS_{within} for the denominator of our $F_{contrast}$. Alternatively, we can use Equation 3.10 to get $t_{contrast}$, which is the square root of $F_{contrast}$.

$r_{effect\ size}$

To compute $r_{effect\ size}$, we need to have both $F_{contrast}$ and $F_{noncontrast}$ to be able to use Equation 3.13:

$$r_{effect\ size} = \sqrt{\frac{F_{contrast}}{F_{contrast} + F_{noncontrast}(df_{noncontrast}) + df_{within}}}.$$

As noted in our discussion of $r_{alerting}$, however, $F_{noncontrast}$ is usually not available directly. However, if the mean squares are available, we can get $r_{effect\ size}$ from

$$r_{effect\ size} = \sqrt{\frac{F_{contrast}}{F_{between}(df_{between}) + df_{within}}}. \tag{3.22}$$

It should be recalled that we can also obtain $r_{effect\ size}$ from $r_{contrast}$ and $r_{alerting}$, as shown in Equation 3.14:

$$r_{effect\ size} = \frac{r_{contrast}}{\sqrt{1 - r_{contrast}^2 + \frac{r_{contrast}^2}{r_{alerting}^2}}}.$$

r_{BESD}

Computing r_{BESD} requires us to have the information needed to compute both $F_{contrast}$ and $F_{noncontrast}$. $F_{noncontrast}$ is only rarely provided directly in other people's data, as we have mentioned, but it can often be obtained indirectly. Thus, if both $F_{contrast}$ and $F_{between}$ are reported, we can obtain $F_{noncontrast}$ from

$$F_{noncontrast} = \frac{F_{between}(df_{between}) - F_{contrast}}{df_{between} - 1}, \tag{3.23}$$

which can then be used to get r_{BESD} from Equation 3.15:

$$r_{BESD} = \sqrt{\frac{F_{contrast}}{F_{contrast} + F_{noncontrast}(df_{noncontrast} + df_{within})}}.$$

Recall, however, that if $F_{noncontrast}$ is less than 1.00, it is entered in this expression (Equation 3.15) as equal to 1.00.

General Comment

In doing meta-analytic work it would be ideal if, for each study in our meta-analysis, we were able to compute all four correlations: $r_{alerting}$, $r_{contrast}$, $r_{effect\ size}$, and r_{BESD}. Indeed, we would be able to compute all four correlations if means, standard deviations, and sample sizes were routinely provided for each condition of the study. Often we could do almost as well if we had complete ANOVA tables. In actual practice, however, it often happens that one or more of these correlations is not calculable from the information provided. The most frequent such situation occurs when no estimates of effect magnitude are given, no test statistics are given, and we are merely told that "the effect was not significant." Unfortunately, this egregious example of poor scientific reporting occurs all too often in the literature of the social, behavioral, and educational sciences. Finally, it should be noted that if means are provided for each condition, we are able to compute contrasts involving set-asides.

EXTENSION TO UNEQUAL SAMPLE SIZES IN THREE OR MORE GROUPS

The results presented so far in this chapter are for the situation of equal sample sizes in all groups and an approximately normally distributed outcome. Here we extend these results to the case of one-way analyses with unequal-sized groups with an approximately normally distributed outcome.

Obtaining Significance Levels

The significance of a contrast based on data with unequal sample sizes across groups can be tested by the following $F_{contrast}$:

$$F_{contrast} = \frac{[\Sigma(M_i \lambda_i)]^2}{MS_{within}} \left(\frac{1}{\Sigma \frac{\lambda_i^2}{n_i}} \right), \tag{3.24}$$

where each λ_i^2 is divided by its associated sample size, n_i.

Also, we can write

$$F_{contrast} = \bar{F}_{contrast}\left(\frac{n_h^\lambda}{\bar{n}}\right), \qquad (3.25)$$

where $\bar{F}_{contrast}$ is obtained from the standard equal-n equation for F, but with the quantity n replaced by $\bar{n}$, the average of all the k sample sizes, $\bar{n} = (1/k)\Sigma n_i$;

$$\bar{F}_{contrast} = \frac{[\Sigma(M_i \lambda_i)]^2}{MS_{within}}\left[\frac{1}{(\Sigma \lambda_i^2)/\bar{n}}\right], \qquad (3.26)$$

and

$$n_h^\lambda = \frac{\Sigma \lambda_i^2}{\Sigma(\lambda_i^2/n_i)} \qquad (3.27)$$

is the λ^2-weighted harmonic mean of the sample sizes. The expression $n_h^\lambda/\bar{n}$ in Equation 3.25 is called the power-loss index for that contrast. When (n_h^λ) equals $\bar{n}$, the power-loss index, of course, is 1.00. The smaller the λ^2-weighted harmonic mean (n_h^λ) relative to the arithmetic mean $(\bar{n})$, the greater the cost in power due to the inequality of the sample sizes. It is when the smallest sample sizes $(n_i s)$ are associated with the largest $\lambda_i^2 s$ that the costs of inequality of sample size are greatest. When the largest sample sizes $(n_i s)$ are associated with the largest $\lambda_i^2 s$, the inequality of sample size can serve to increase power, and the power-loss index for that contrast can be greater than 1.00. For a contrast in which all the λs are $+1$s and -1s, the quantity n_h^λ equals n_h, the simple harmonic mean, defined for two samples in Equation 2.21 and for k samples as

$$n_h = \frac{k}{\Sigma\dfrac{1}{n_i}}. \qquad (3.28)$$

The significance of a contrast with unequal sample sizes can also be tested by

$$t_{contrast} = \frac{\Sigma(M_i \lambda_i)}{\sqrt{MS_{within}\left[\Sigma\dfrac{\lambda_i^2}{n_i}\right]}}, \qquad (3.29)$$

which is simply the square root of Equation 3.24. The degrees of freedom for t, and for the denominator of its square, $F_{contrast}$, are the degrees of freedom in MS_{within}.

Effect Size Estimation

The effect sizes we want to estimate in most behavioral research are those we would expect to find in a replication study that uses equal sample sizes across all groups. In such a replication, we would expect to see essentially the same means and variances as those found in our study with unequal sample sizes.

To compute our four correlations, therefore, we need only to calculate the equal-n quantities $F_{contrast}$ and $F_{noncontrast}$ of the equations in Table 3.6, using the observed means and variances, but with n (the common sample size) replaced by $\bar{n}$, the *average* sample size.

Thus, where

$$F_{contrast} = \frac{MS_{contrast}}{MS_{within}}$$

and

$$MS_{contrast} = \frac{nL^2}{\Sigma\lambda_i^2}$$

as shown in Equation 3.1, we need only replace n of the numerator of Equation 3.1 by $\bar{n}$, the average n of the k conditions of our study, to obtain $\bar{F}_{contrast}$ of Equation 3.26:

$$\bar{F}_{contrast} = \frac{\bar{n}L^2/\Sigma\lambda_i^2}{MS_{within}}.$$

With unequal sample sizes, n_i, we can also obtain $\bar{F}_{contrast}$ directly from $F_{contrast}$, the F computed using unequal sample sizes (for obtaining significance levels), from the following

$$\bar{F}_{contrast} = F_{contrast}\left[\frac{\bar{n}}{n_h^\lambda}\right]. \tag{3.30}$$

Examples of Unequal Sample Sizes

Table 3.13 shows the hypothetical results of a four-condition study with unequal sample sizes. The means (M_i), weights (λ_i), variances (S_i^2), and total sample

TABLE 3.13
Results of a Four-Condition Study with Two Different Allocations of Unequal Sample Sizes and Power-Loss Indices of .29 and 1.10 for a Specific Contrast

		Condition				
		A	B	C	D	Σ
	1. Means	6	8	12	16	42
	2. λ_i	−3	−1	+1	+3	0
Original	3. $M_i\lambda_i$	−18	−8	+12	+48	34
allocation of n_i	4. n_i	1	9	8	2	20
	5. $\bar{n}$	5	5	5	5	20
	6. $\lambda_i^2/\bar{n}$	9/5	1/5	1/5	9/5	4
	7. λ_i^2/n_i	9/1	1/9	1/8	9/2	13.74
Alternative	8. n_i	9	1	2	8	20
Allocation of n_i	9. λ_i^2/n_i	9/9	1/1	1/2	9/8	3.625

TABLE 3.14
Analysis of Variance and Contrast Quantities for the Two Allocations of Sample Sizes from Table 3.13

	Sample size allocations to conditions A, B, C, D							
	A	B	C	D	A	B	C	D
	1	9	8	2	9	1	2	8
1. $SS_{between}(\bar{n})$	295				295			
2. $SS_{contrast}(\bar{n})$	289				289			
3. $SS_{noncontrast}(\bar{n})$	6				6			
4. $df_{between}$	3				3			
5. $df_{noncontrast}$	2				2			
6. $MS_{noncontrast}(\bar{n})$	3				3			
7. MS_{within}	10				10			
8. df_{within}	16				16			
9. $\bar{F}_{contrast}$	28.90				28.90			
10. $\bar{F}_{noncontrast}$	0.30				0.30			
*11. n_h^λ	1.46				5.52			
*12. Power loss ($n_h^\lambda/\bar{n}$)	.29				1.10			
*13. $F_{contrast}$	8.42				31.89			
*14. $t_{contrast}$	2.90				5.65			
*15. p	.0052				.000018			

* These quantities differ according to the differences in allocation of sample sizes.

size (N) are those of Table 3.1, but in Table 3.13, the sample sizes (n_i) are allocated in two different ways to the four conditions: 1, 9, 8, and 2 for one allocation and 9, 1, 2, and 8 for the other allocation. Quantities used in the computation of $\bar{F}_{contrast}$, $\bar{F}_{noncontrast}$, and $F_{contrast}$ and $t_{contrast}$ are provided for both allocations in Table 3.14.

For computing $\bar{F}_{contrast}$, for example, we divided $\overline{SS}_{contrast}$ (i.e., the $SS_{contrast}$ computed assuming all sample sizes to be $\bar{n}$) by MS_{within}. For computing $\bar{F}_{noncontrast}$, we divide $\overline{MS}_{noncontrast}$ (the $MS_{noncontrast}$ computed assuming all sample sizes to be $\bar{n}$) by MS_{within}. $F_{contrast}$ is computed from Equation 3.24 or 3.25, and $t_{contrast}$ (the square root of $F_{contrast}$) is computed directly from Equation 3.29, all ingredients of which are given in Tables 3.13 and 3.14.

Tables 3.13 and 3.14 also show the results of a hypothetical study where the means are unchanged, but where the sample sizes, n_i, have been allocated so that the larger sample sizes are associated with the larger weights. Although most of the quantities shown in Tables 3.13 and 3.14 do not differ (because they were computed assuming equal sample sizes for all conditions), there are great differences in the quantities $\Sigma(\lambda^2/n_i)$, n_h^λ, $n_h^\lambda/\bar{n}$, $F_{contrast}$, and $t_{contrast}$. These are the quantities required for obtaining significance levels, and they show that the $F_{contrast}$ of the alternative allocation of n_i (i.e., 31.89) is 3.79 times greater than the $F_{contrast}$ of the original allocation (i.e., 8.42). The reason is that the alternative allocation has its heavy concentration of sample size on the larger λs, so that $F_{contrast}$ must be larger for any given $\Sigma M_i \lambda_i$, as we can see by examining Equation 3.24.

Although the levels of significance differ dramatically for the data of the two allocations of sample size, the four rs are identical for the two allocations because $\bar{F}_{contrast}$ and $\bar{F}_{noncontrast}$ are identical for the two allocations. For both allocations, our four rs are, from the equations in Table 3.6,

$$r_{alerting} = \sqrt{\frac{\bar{F}_{contrast}}{\bar{F}_{contrast} + \bar{F}_{noncontrast}(df_{noncontrast})}}$$

$$= \sqrt{\frac{28.90}{28.90 + 0.30(2)}} = .99,$$

$$r_{contrast} = \sqrt{\frac{\bar{F}_{contrast}}{\bar{F}_{contrast} + df_{within}}}$$

$$= \sqrt{\frac{28.90}{28.90 + 16}} = .80,$$

$$r_{effect\ size} = \sqrt{\frac{\bar{F}_{contrast}}{\bar{F}_{contrast} + \bar{F}_{noncontrast}(df_{noncontrast}) + df_{within}}}$$

$$= \sqrt{\frac{28.90}{28.90 + 0.30(2) + 16}} = .80,$$

and

$$r_{BESD} = \sqrt{\frac{\bar{F}_{contrast}}{\bar{F}_{contrast} + \bar{F}_{noncontrast}(df_{noncontrast} + df_{within})}}$$

$$= \sqrt{\frac{28.90}{28.90 + 0.30(2 + 16)}}$$

$$= \sqrt{\frac{28.90}{28.90 + 1.00(2 + 16)}} = .78.$$

Note that in the computation of r_{BESD}, when $\bar{F}_{noncontrast}$ is less than 1.00, it is entered as equal to 1.00.

Dealing with Conditions Set Aside

In our earlier discussion of λs of 0, we noted that setting aside one or more groups does not affect tests of significance of the contrasts of which the λs of 0 are a part. That is still the situation when the sample sizes are unequal.

Similarly, unequal sample sizes do not change the computation of the four rs. We treat each condition as having the same sample size $\bar{n}$, the average of the k sample sizes, and we proceed exactly as we did when our sample sizes were equal. That is, for every condition set aside, we reduce both $df_{noncontrast}$ and $df_{between}$ by 1, and we reduce df_{within} by $\bar{n} - 1$. Thus, just as was the case with equal sample sizes discussed earlier in this chapter, setting one or more conditions aside will tend to increase the values of the four correlations. These four correlations are calculated in the usual way, summarized in Table 3.6, but, as just shown, with $F_{contrast}$ and $F_{noncontrast}$ replaced by $\bar{F}_{contrast}$ and $\bar{F}_{noncontrast}$, respectively.

When we compute r_{BESD} for contrasts of unequal sample sizes, whether or not we have set aside any conditions with $\lambda_i = 0$, we view it as the replication we would expect to obtain given equal sample sizes with the high and low levels of the independent variable set at $+1\,\sigma_\lambda$ and $-1\,\sigma_\lambda$ respectively. The hypothetical sample size at each level of the independent variable in this two-group replication is $N/2$.

Counternull values for r_{BESD}

Whenever we compute r_{BESD} and display it in a BESD, it is generally instructive also to compute the counternull value of r_{BESD} and display it in a BESD. Fortunately, no special complications arise in computing $r_{BESD\ counternull}$ when sample sizes are unequal. Whether or not we have one or more conditions as set-asides, we can employ Equation 2.16 (or its restatement in 2.18) so long as we (a) have used $\bar{F}_{contrast}$ and $\bar{F}_{noncontrast}$ to obtain r_{BESD} from Equation 3.15 and (b) remember to decrease $df_{noncontrast}$ by the number of conditions set aside and to decrease df_{within} by $\bar{n} - 1$ for each condition we set aside.

REVIEW QUESTIONS

1. In a study with $k = 4$ randomized groups with equal ns ($n = 5$ per group), the group means on the dependent variable are reported as 3, 4, 5, 8, and the overall ANOVA was as follows:

Source	SS	DF	MS	F	p
Between conditions	70	3	23.333	9.33	.00084
Within (error)	40	16	2.5		

Using lambdas of $-3, -1, +1, +3$, compute a linear contrast t by each of the three methods described in this chapter, and compute the associated "four rs."

Answer: (a) One method computes t indirectly by taking the square root of F obtained by dividing Equation 3.1 by the MS within. This method gives us linear contrast $F(1, 16) = [5(16)^2/20]/2.5 = 64/2.5 = 25.60$, $t(16) = 5.06$. The "four rs" are $r_{alerting} = .96$, $r_{contrast} = .78$, $r_{effect\ size} = .76$, and $r_{BESD} = .74$. (b) The second method described in this chapter also computes t indirectly from F, but by dividing Equation 3.3 by the MS_{within}. To solve for the $r^2_{alerting}$ needed in this approach, we can compute the product-moment r directly on the group means and group lambdas, which gives $r = .9562$. Because we have already done the work, we can also take the square root of the $SS_{contrast}$ computed above, divided by the $SS_{between}$ above (see Equation 3.5), which, of course, also yields an $r_{alerting}$ of .9562 because

$$\sqrt{\frac{5(16)^2/20}{70}} = .9562,$$

and (for Equation 3.3) $r^2_{alerting} = .9143$. Our linear contrast $F\ (1, 16)$ is now computed as $(.9143 \times 70)/2.5 = 25.60$, which again gives $t(16) = 5.06$. (c) The third method described in this chapter computes the contrast t directly by means of Equation 3.10; in this case, the result is

$$t = \frac{\Sigma(M\lambda)}{\sqrt{S^2 \Sigma\left(\frac{\lambda^2}{n}\right)}} = \frac{(3)(-3) + (4)(-1) + (5)(+1) + (8)(+3)}{\sqrt{2.5\left[\frac{(-3)^2}{5} + \frac{(-1)^2}{5} + \frac{(+1)^2}{5} + \frac{(+3)^2}{5}\right]}}$$

$$= \frac{16}{\sqrt{10}} = 5.06.$$

2. Given $k = 4$, but with the following unequal ns, compute the linear contrast t directly (using the same lambda weights as above):

	A	B	C	D
	1	4	5	8
	4	5	7	
	3	3	3	
	2			
	5			
M_i	3	4	5	8
n_i	5	3	3	1
λ_i	-3	-1	$+1$	$+3$
S_i^2	2.5	1.0	4.0	0.0

Answer: Substituting in Equation 3.10 gives

$$t = \frac{(3)(-3) + (4)(-1) + (5)(+1) + (8)(+3)}{\sqrt{2.5\left[\frac{(-3)^2}{5} + \frac{(-1)^2}{3} + \frac{(+1)^2}{3} + \frac{(+3)^2}{1}\right]}}$$

$$= \frac{16}{\sqrt{2.5(11.4667)}} = 2.99,$$

with $df = 8$, one-tailed $p = .0087$.

3. From the analysis of variance in Table 1.1 based on five age levels, 11, 12, 13, 14, 15 (Figure 1.1 and Table 3.2), compute the F or t associated with the contrast comparing the age 11 with the age 12 children (λs of $-1, +1, 0, 0, 0$). Then compute the four rs twice, once assuming the zero weights for ages 13, 14, and 15 to be numbers and once assuming them to be set-asides.

Answer: The new table of variance showing contrast and noncontrast sources of variance is as follows:

Source	SS	df	MS	F
Between conditions	6,500	4	1,625	1.03
contrast				
$(-1, +1, 0, 0, 0)$	125	1	125	0.08
noncontrast	6,375	3	2,125	1.35
Within (error)	70,875	45	1,575	

From this table, we find the two sets of "four rs" to be:

	Zero λ as number	Zero λ as set-aside
$r_{alerting}$	.139	1.000
$r_{contrast}$	.042	.066
$r_{effect\ size}$	.040	.066
r_{BESD}	.035	.066

Note that the reduced table of variance based on $\lambda = 0$ as set-asides is as follows:

Source	SS	df	MS
Between (contrast)	125	1	125
Within (error)	28,350	18	1,575
Total	28,475	19	

where the SS_{within} is obtained from the full table MS_{within} of 1,575 multiplied by the 18 df associated with just the two groups being compared.

CHAPTER 4

Contrasts in Factorial Designs

In this chapter, we discuss planned and ad hoc contrasts in two-way and higher-order factorial designs. Our emphasis, as in the previous discussion, will be on effect size estimation, although obtaining significance levels will also be discussed. We will see that with factorial designs in which all factors are *substantive*, a term we define, the calculations are exactly the same as in Chapter 3. When there are nonsubstantive factors, these calculations are adjusted for the nonsubstantive factors.

PROLOGUE

This chapter is more complex than the previous chapters. At first reading, it may appear to repeat some of the earlier material because it is a detailed exposition of the application of the concepts outlined in Chapter 3 to special and complex cases that arise with factorial designs. In fact, some of these concepts really come to life in these more complex cases.

$r_{alerting}$: A PRELIMINARY LOOK AT THE DATA

As in Chapter 3, we can think of $r_{alerting}$ as based on a one-way layout of conditions in which the condition or cell means are correlated with their associated contrast weights (i.e., their associated λs). Table 4.1 shows the means and analysis of variance of a 3×4 factorial design in which the column factor "number of weekly treatments" has four levels (0, 1, 2, 3) and the row factor "severity of illness" has three levels (mild, moderate, severe). The dependent variable is effectiveness of functioning.

Suppose our primary research question is whether there is a linear increase in functioning with an increased number of weekly treatments. Our contrast weights would then be the following:

	0	1	2	3
Mild	−3	−1	+1	+3
Moderate	−3	−1	+1	+3
Severe	−3	−1	+1	+3

TABLE 4.1
Means and Analysis of Variance of a 3 × 4 Factorial Design

A. Table of means ($n = 10$ per condition)

		Number of treatments weekly				
		0	1	2	3	Mean
Severity of illness	Mild	3	10	9	12	8.5
	Moderate	1	4	8	9	5.5
	Severe	1	4	6	5	4.0
	Mean	1.67	6.00	7.67	8.67	6.0

B. Analysis of variance of table of means

Source	SS	df	MS	F	p
Between	1,420	11	129.09	5.16	.000002
Treatments	860	3	286.67	11.47	.000002
Severity	420	2	210.00	8.40	.0004
Treat. × severity	140	6	23.33	0.93	.47
Within	2,700	108	25.00		
Total	4,120	119			

To compute $r_{alerting}$, we simply correlate these twelve weights with their corresponding means in Table 4.1 and find $r_{alerting} = .7367$. Multiplying $r^2_{alerting}$, .5427 in this example, by the $SS_{between}$ (i.e., the $SS_{treatment} + SS_{severity} + SS_{treatment \times severity}$), or 1,420 in this example of Table 4.1, yields the $MS_{contrast}$ value of 770.67.

The only new aspect of $r_{alerting}$ that emerges when we go to factorial designs is that another $r_{alerting}$ can sometimes be computed from the means of one of the factors. This circumstance occurs when the same contrast weights are used at each level of some factor. For our example, the same λ weights do appear at each of the three levels of severity. In this case, therefore, we could also have computed the value of $r_{alerting}$ between the means of the treatment factor and the weights of $-3, -1, +1, +3$, representing a linear trend. Had we done so in this example, we would have found a very different value of $r_{alerting}$ (.9468 instead of .7367) and of $r^2_{alerting}$ (.8964 instead of .5427).

When using $r^2_{alerting}$ to compute $MS_{contrast}$, it is important to "align" the $r^2_{alerting}$ with the appropriate SS. Thus, when using $r^2_{alerting}$ based on all the conditions of the design, we multiply $r^2_{alerting}$ by the $SS_{between}$ based on all factors of the design to obtain $MS_{contrast}$; in this case, $SS_{between} = SS_{treatment} + SS_{severity} + SS_{treat \times severity}$. When using $r^2_{alerting}$ based not on all conditions, but on the means of the dependent variable across the levels of one of the factors, we multiply $r^2_{alerting}$ by the SS associated specifically with that factor. Thus, in the present example, we can compute $MS_{contrast}$ quite appropriately in two different ways:

Based on	$r^2_{alerting}$	×	SS	=	$MS_{contrast}$
12 conditions	.5427	×	1,420	=	770.67
4 treatments	.8964	×	860	=	770.67

The smaller $r^2_{alerting}$ of .5427 was multiplied by a larger SS of 1,420 (the $SS_{between}$), and the larger $r^2_{alerting}$ of .8964 was multiplied by a smaller SS of 860 (the $SS_{treatment}$), but both products yielded identical values of 770.67.

The situation where the same λ weights occur at each level of a factor is also important in the computation of $r_{effect\ size}$ and r_{BESD}, as we shall see shortly.

OBTAINING SIGNIFICANCE LEVELS

The F statistic for our contrast (i.e., $F_{contrast}$) is $MS_{contrast}/MS_{within}$, which in our example yields $770.67/25.00 = 30.83$, an F that, with 1 and 108 degrees of freedom, has $p = .0000002$.

We could also have computed $MS_{contrast}$ from $nL^2/\Sigma\lambda_i^2$ (Equation 3.1) as

$$MS_{contrast} = \frac{10[(3)(-3) + (10)(-1) + (9)(+1) + (12)(+3) + (1)(-3) + (4)(-1) + (8)(+1) + (9)(+3) + (1)(-3) + (4)(-1) + (6)(+1) + (5)(+3)]^2}{(-3)^2 + (-1)^2 + (+1)^2 + (+3)^2 + (-3)^2 + (-1)^2 + (+1)^2(+3)^2 + (-3)^2 + (-1)^2 + (+1)^2 + (+3)^2}$$

$$= \frac{10[68]^2}{60} = 770.67,$$

a value already calculated using $r^2_{alerting}$.

Finally, we can also obtain the significance level by computing $t_{contrast}$ from Equation 3.10, using

$$t_{contrast} = \frac{\Sigma(M_i\lambda_i)}{\sqrt{MS_{within}\left[\Sigma\frac{\lambda_i^2}{n}\right]}} = \frac{L}{\sqrt{MS_{within}\left[\Sigma\frac{\lambda_i^2}{n}\right]}},$$

which thereby yields

$$t_{contrast} = \frac{68}{\sqrt{25\left(\frac{60}{10}\right)}} = 5.55,$$

which is identical to the value of $\sqrt{F_{contrast}}$, $\sqrt{30.83}$.

$r_{contrast}$: THE MAXIMALLY PARTIALED CORRELATION

In factorial designs, we compute $r_{contrast}$ just as in one-way designs (i.e., from Equation 3.2). For the present example, therefore, we find

$$r_{contrast} = \sqrt{\frac{F_{contrast}}{F_{contrast} + df_{within}}} = \sqrt{\frac{30.83}{30.83 + 108}} = .471.$$

As discussed in Chapter 3, $r_{contrast}$ is a partial correlation. In the case of a factorial design, $r_{contrast}$ can be viewed as "maximally partialed" because we have partialed out all of the noncontrast effects of the factors, just as we did in Chapter 3 for a one-factor design.

To interpret $r_{contrast}$ in a design with more than one factor, we calculate adjusted observations, just as in Chapter 3, and correlate them with the corresponding λ weights. Specifically, we use Equation 3.12 to find:

$$\text{Adjusted observation} = \text{Residual} + \bar{M} + (\lambda b_{contrast}),$$

where residual is the observation minus its cell mean, and $\bar{M} + \lambda b_{contrast}$ is the value for the observation predicted from the linear contrast, with $\bar{M}$ the grand mean of the observations, λ the observation's contrast weight, and, from Equation 3.11,

$$b_{contrast} = \sqrt{\frac{MS_{contrast}}{n\Sigma\lambda_i^2}} = \frac{L}{\Sigma\lambda_i^2}.$$

The correlation between the adjusted observations and the λ weights is $r_{contrast}$, the partial correlation between the observations and the corresponding λ weights after all between-cell sources of variation have been eliminated, other than the variation for the contrast in question.

We illustrate this calculation for the data in Table 4.2 and its associated analysis of variance. Notice that $SS_{between}$ has been partitioned into treatment, sex, and treatment × sex sources of variation. In addition, $SS_{contrast}$ is shown as part of the between source of variation. The ten λ weights are shown in Table 4.2, each beneath the cell mean with which λ_i is associated.

We find $b_{contrast}$ from Equation 3.11,

$$b_{contrast} = \sqrt{\frac{MS_{contrast}}{n\Sigma\lambda_i^2}} = \sqrt{\frac{44.10}{2(20)}} = 1.05,$$

or

$$b_{contrast} = \frac{L}{\Sigma\lambda_i^2} = \frac{3(-2)........6(+2)}{(-2)^2.....(+2)^2} = 1.05.$$

For the data in Table 4.2, the value of $\bar{M} = 4.5$. For the two observations of the upper left cell, then, the predicted values are both $4.5 + (-2)(1.05) = 2.4$. Thus, for the very first observation, the value is 4, the residual is $4 - 3 = 1$, so, when

TABLE 4.2
Data for Showing Meaning of $r_{contrast}$ in a Factorial Design

A. Basic data

	Levels					
	1	2	3	4	5	Means
Females	4	6	8	9	13	
	2	2	4	5	7	
Cell mean	3	4	6	7	10	6.0
λ	−2	−1	0	+1	+2	
Males	6	4	2	3	8	
	2	0	0	1	4	
Cell mean	4	2	1	2	6	3.0
λ	−2	−1	0	+1	+2	
Column mean	3.5	3.0	3.5	4.5	8.0	4.5
Column λ	−2	−1	0	+1	+2	

B. Overall ANOVA

Source	SS	df	MS	F
Between	137.0	9	15.22	2.11
(Contrast)	(44.1)	(1)	(44.10)	(6.125)
Treatment	66.0	4	16.50	2.29
Sex	45.0	1	45.00	6.25
Treat. × sex	26.0	4	6.50	0.90
Within	72.0	10	7.20	
Total	209.0	19		

Equation 3.12 is used, the adjusted value is $1 + 4.5 + (-2)(1.05) = 3.4$. For the first observation of the lower right cell, the value is 8, and the residual is $8 - 6 = 2$, so, when Equation 3.12 is used, the adjusted value is $2 + 4.5 + (+2)(1.05) = 8.6$. All the adjusted values are shown in Table 4.3.

We can now state the meaning of $r_{contrast}$ for the data in Table 4.2. Notice first that when we use Equation 3.2, we find, from the value of $F_{contrast}$ ($F = 6.125$, $p = .033$) shown in Table 4.2B, that

$$r_{contrast} = \sqrt{\frac{6.125}{6.125 + 10}} = .62.$$

TABLE 4.3
Adjustment of Data in Table 4.2

	Levels									
	1	(λ)	2	(λ)	3	(λ)	4	(λ)	5	(λ)
	3.4	(−2)	5.45	(−1)	6.5	(0)	7.55	(+1)	9.6	(+2)
	1.4	(−2)	1.45	(−1)	2.5	(0)	3.55	(+1)	3.6	(+2)
Cell mean	2.4		3.45		4.5		5.55		6.6	
	4.4	(−2)	5.45	(−1)	5.5	(0)	6.55	(+1)	8.6	(+2)
	0.4	(−2)	1.45	(−1)	3.5	(0)	4.55	(+1)	4.6	(+2)
Cell mean	2.4		3.45		4.5		5.55		6.6	

This value of .62 is identical to the value we obtain by directly computing the correlation between the twenty adjusted observations in Table 4.3 and their associated λs.

Should we want to compute $r_{alerting}$ for the data in Table 4.2, we would simply correlate the ten cell means in that table with their associated ten λ weights. The value of $r_{alerting}$, based on these ten pairs of scores, is .5674. In this example of Table 4.2, where the same λ weights occur at each level of the sex of subject, we can also compute $r_{alerting}$ for just the five column means of the treatment conditions. The value of $r_{alerting}$ between the five column means and their associated five λs is .8174. We can use either of these values of the $r_{alerting}$ to compute $MS_{contrast}$. We first square the $r_{alerting}$ to obtain $r^2_{alerting}$, which gives $r^2_{alerting}$ values of .3219 and .6681, respectively. We then find $MS_{contrast}$ from these $r^2_{alerting}$ values as follows:

Based on	$r^2_{alerting}$	×	SS	=	$MS_{contrast}$
10 conditions	.3219	×	137	=	44.1
5 conditions	.6681	×	66	=	44.1

It should be noted that analogous calculations can be performed no matter how many between factors are involved. All conditions or cells of the design are simply listed as a one-way layout for both obtaining significance levels and calculating $r_{contrast}$ and $r_{alerting}$.

ANOTHER EXAMPLE OF THE CALCULATION OF $r_{alerting}$, SIGNIFICANCE LEVELS, AND $r_{contrast}$

Table 4.4 shows the means and analysis of variance of a 3 × 4 factorial design in which the factors are treated as additive, a term defined shortly. The column factor is the same as that in Table 4.1, number of weekly treatments (0, 1, 2, 3),

TABLE 4.4
Means and Analysis of Variance of a Factorial Design with Factors Treated as Additive

A. Table of means ($n = 10$ per condition)

		Number of treatments weekly				
		0	1	2	3	Mean
Medication	100 mg	3	10	9	12	8.5
Dosage	50 mg	1	4	8	9	5.5
Levels	0 mg	1	4	6	5	4.0
	Mean	1.67	6.00	7.67	8.67	6.0

B. Analysis of variance of table of means

Source	SS	df	MS	F	p
Between	1,420	11	129.09	5.16	.000002
Treatments	860	3	286.67	11.47	.000002
Medication	420	2	210.00	8.40	.0004
Treat. × medication	140	6	23.33	0.93	.47
Within	2,700	108	25.00		
Total	4,120	119			

and the row factor has levels of medication dosage (0, 50, 100 mg). The dependent variable again is effectiveness of functioning.

Suppose our general theory is that both increases in the number of weekly treatments and increases in the level of medication dosage will improve effectiveness of functioning. We can create our contrast weights in a reasonable way to examine this question by awarding one point more for the increase of one level of the number-of-treatments factor and one point more for the increase of one level of the medication dosage. Applying this simple rule yields the allocation of points for each of the twelve conditions shown in Part A of Table 4.5. Each entry is simply the sum of the points contributed by the row factor and the column factor. This prediction is, by definition, for an *additive* effect of the row factor and the column factor.

These predicted points of Part A of Table 4.5 are not contrast weights because they do not sum to zero, but we can make them into contrast weights simply by subtracting the mean of the twelve predicted values (2.5) from each prediction, with the results shown in Table 4.5, Part B. For convenience, we can multiply these contrast weights by 2 to make integers of our weights, as shown in Part C of Table 4.5. The row and column means of Part C show that our additive prediction (i.e., contrast) is reflected in a linear trend in both the rows and the columns.

Another Example of the Calculation of $r_{alerting}$, Significance Levels, and $r_{contrast}$

TABLE 4.5
Allocation of Points to Twelve Treatment Conditions (A), Converting These Points to Contrast Weights (B), and Doubling These Weights to Make Integer Values (C)

A. Point allocations

		Points per level				
Points		0	1	2	3	Mean
2	100 mg	2	3	4	5	3.5
1	50 mg	1	2	3	4	2.5
0	0 mg	0	1	2	3	1.5
	Mean	1.0	2.0	3.0	4.0	2.5

B. Points converted to contrast weights

	0	1	2	3	Mean
100 mg	−0.5	+0.5	+1.5	+2.5	+1.0
50 mg	−1.5	−0.5	+0.5	+1.5	0.0
0 mg	−2.5	−1.5	−0.5	+0.5	−1.0
Mean	−1.5	−0.5	+0.5	+1.5	0.0

C. Contrast weights of B converted to integer values

	0	1	2	3	Mean
100 mg	−1	+1	+3	+5	+2
50 mg	−3	−1	+1	+3	0
0 mg	−5	−3	−1	+1	−2
Mean	−3	−1	+1	+3	0

From Equation 3.1 we compute $MS_{contrast}$ from $nL^2/\Sigma \lambda_i^2$ as

$$MS_{contrast} = \frac{10[(3)(-1) + (10)(+1) + (9)(+3) + (12)(+5) + (1)(-3) + (4)(-1) + (8)(+1) + (+9)(+3) + (1)(-5) + (4)(-3) + (6)(-1) + (5)(+1)]^2}{(-1)^2 + (+1)^2 + (+3)^2 + (+5)^2 + (-3)^2 + (-1)^2 + (+1)^2 + (+3)^2 + (-5)^2 + (-3)^2 + (-1)^2 + (+1)^2}$$

$$= \frac{10[104]^2}{92} = 1175.65.$$

We obtain $F_{contrast}$ from $MS_{contrast}/MS_{within}$, which yields $1175.65/25.00 = 47.03$, an F with 1 and 108 degrees of freedom that has $p < 5/10^{10}$.

We can also compute $F_{contrast}$ from Equation 3.3, where $MS_{contrast} = r^2_{alerting} \times SS_{between}$, which in this example gives $.8279 \times 1420 = 1175.65$, a value identical to the value of $MS_{contrast}$ obtained from Equation 3.1.

Finally, we note that we can also obtain our significance level from $t_{contrast}$ computed from Equation 3.10,

$$t_{contrast} = \frac{\Sigma(M\lambda)}{\sqrt{MS_{within}\left(\Sigma \frac{\lambda^2}{n}\right)}} = \frac{104}{\sqrt{25\left(\frac{92}{10}\right)}} = 6.86,$$

which is identical to $\sqrt{F_{contrast}}$ or $\sqrt{47.03}$, as indeed it must be.

The value of $r_{alerting}$ is the correlation between the $r \times c$ contrast weights and their associated $r \times c$ means. In the present example, this correlation, $r_{alerting}$, is .9099.

The value of $r_{contrast}$ is computed from Equation 3.2 just as in the case of one-way designs. For the present example, then, we find

$$r_{contrast} = \sqrt{\frac{F_{contrast}}{F_{contrast} + df_{within}}} = \sqrt{\frac{47.03}{47.03 + 108}} = .55.$$

$r_{alerting}$, SIGNIFICANCE LEVELS, AND $r_{contrast}$ IN MULTIFACTOR DESIGNS WITH UNEQUAL SAMPLE SIZES

The calculation of $r_{alerting}$, significance levels, and $r_{contrast}$ never becomes more complicated than what we have now seen. No matter how many factors there are in a between-subjects design, we can always view it as a one-way layout and compute $r_{alerting}$, significance levels, and $r_{contrast}$, by means of the procedures in Chapter 3. Even when the sample sizes are unequal for the cells or conditions of our factorial design, we need only array them as a one-way layout and apply the procedures for unequal sample sizes in Chapter 3. Moreover, for the calculation of $r_{alerting}$, significance levels, and $r_{contrast}$ when certain cells are to be set aside, we can view the remaining cells as a one-way layout and use the procedures in Chapter 3.

$r_{effect\ size}$

$r_{effect\ size}$ in General

In factorial designs, $r_{effect\ size}$ can be calculated just as in Chapter 3, by means of Equation 3.13,

$$r_{effect\ size} = \sqrt{\frac{F_{contrast}}{F_{contrast} + F_{noncontrast}(df_{noncontrast}) + df_{within}}},$$

where $F_{noncontrast}$ is the noncontrast F for all sources of variation other than the contrast, and $df_{noncontrast}$ is the noncontrast degrees of freedom associated with it.

In the example in Table 4.4, therefore, we find $F_{noncontrast}$ from Equation 3.6,

$$F_{noncontrast} = \frac{(SS_{between} - MS_{contrast})/df_{noncontrast}}{MS_{within}},$$

or from Equation 3.7,

$$F_{noncontrast} = \frac{F_{between}(df_{between}) - F_{contrast}}{df_{noncontrast}}.$$

We provide here both Equations 3.6 and 3.7 because Equation 3.6 is more convenient when we have access to all the sums of squares, whereas Equation 3.7 is appropriate when we have access only to various F statistics, a situation frequently encountered when we reanalyze other investigators' results (e.g., in meta-analytic applications). For the present data, we find

$$F_{noncontrast} = \frac{(1420 - 1175.65)/10}{25.00} = .98$$

from Equation 3.6 and

$$F_{noncontrast} = \frac{5.164(11) - 47.03}{10} = .98$$

from Equation 3.7.

The degrees of freedom for noncontrast sources of variation are obtained from

$$df_{noncontrast} = df_{between} - 1, \tag{4.1}$$

which for the present example yields $11 - 1 = 10$. Therefore, for the present example,

$$r_{effect\ size} = \sqrt{\frac{47.03}{47.03 + 0.98(10) + 108}} = .5342,$$

a correlation not much smaller than the $r_{contrast}$ value of .55 in this example. However, $r_{effect\ size}$ can be substantially smaller than $r_{contrast}$. The reason for large differences when they do occur is that in the case of $r_{effect\ size}$, none of the noncontrast sources of the between-conditions variation are partialed out (i.e., all the noncontrast between-conditions variation is regarded as noise, whereas all of it is partialed out in the case of $r_{contrast}$). The meaning of the correlation $r_{effect\ size}$ is, as in Chapter 3, the simple correlation between the outcome variable and the contrast (λ) weights across all subjects.

Effect Size Correlation with Nonsubstantive Factors: $r_{effect\ size|NS}$

The value of $r_{effect\ size}$ calculated from Equation 3.13 treats all designs as one-way layouts with all noncontrast variation as uncontrollable subject-to-subject variation. With some contrasts in some factorial designs, however, some noncontrast variation can be considered *nonsubstantive* (or not essential to the question of interest), and a different and larger effect size correlation can be calculated.

For example, consider the data in Table 4.1 and the linear contrast used in the discussion of those data. At each level of the factor "severity," the contrast weights are the same (−3, −1, +1, +3), reflecting a linear trend in the treatment factor. Thus we can think of the overall contrast as a contrast pooled across the three levels of the severity factor after allowing for separate mean responses at each level of severity. For this contrast, one factor, "severity," can therefore be called *nonsubstantive* (i.e., not essential) because the contrast weights imply the same trend at each level of severity. More generally, several factors can be nonsubstantive in this sense. For example, in a treatment × severity × sex factorial design, when the same contrast weights are used at each level of severity and for both sexes, both the factors of severity and of sex and the interaction of severity × sex are nonsubstantive (i.e., not essential).

Graphically, in our example of the data in Table 4.1, within each level of severity we can plot y observations against their λ weights; we can then subtract the mean y for each of the three groups and combine (or pool) the plots, thereby controlling for the main effect of severity. The correlation between these "de-meaned" scores and their associated λ weights is $r_{effect\ size|NS}$, an effect size correlation controlling for the nonsubstantive factor of severity. (For $r_{effect\ size|NS}$ read "$r_{effect\ size}$ given NS," i.e., adjusted for nonsubstantive factors.)

A faster way of calculating this effect size correlation, which does not require actually de-meaning the data and calculating directly the correlation between the λ weights and the de-meaned data, uses a modification of Equation 3.13. In this modification, the noncontrast variation represented in Equation 3.13 by $F_{noncontrast}(df_{noncontrast})$ is replaced by $F_{NC|NS}(df_{NC|NS})$, where $F_{NC|NS}$ is the F statistic for noncontrast variation adjusting for nonsubstantive factors, and $df_{NC|NS}$ is its associated numerator degrees of freedom:

$$F_{NC|NS} = \frac{(SS_{between} - MS_{contrast} - SS_{NS})/df_{NC|NS}}{MS_{within}}, \quad (4.2)$$

where SS_{NS} is the sum of squares due to nonsubstantive factors and df_{NS} is their associated degrees of freedom, and

$$df_{NC|NS} = df_{between} - 1 - df_{NS} \quad (4.3)$$
$$= df_{noncontrast} - df_{NS}. \quad (4.4)$$

The modification of Equation 3.13 is then

$$r_{effect\ size|NS} = \sqrt{\frac{F_{contrast}}{F_{contrast} + F_{NC|NS}(df_{NC|NS}) + df_{within}}}. \quad (4.5)$$

For the data in Table 4.1, we can use Equation 4.5 to find

$$r_{effect\ size|NS} = \sqrt{\frac{30.83}{30.83 + 1.15(8) + 108}} = .4564,$$

where we use Equation 4.2 to find $F_{NC|NS}$:

$$F_{NC|NS} = \frac{(1420 - 770.67 - 420)/8}{25} = 1.15$$

and use Equation 4.3 to find $df_{NC|NS}$:

$$df_{NC|NS} = df_{between} - 1 - df_{NS} = 11 - 1 - 2 = 8.$$

A MORE DETAILED EXAMPLE OF THE CALCULATION OF $r_{effect\ size}$ AND $r_{effect\ size|NS}$

Table 4.6 shows the basic data in Table 4.2 in two ways. Part A shows the original scores with their associated λ weights; Part B shows the data in Part A after

TABLE 4.6
Data in Table 4.2 Showing Each Observation with Its Associated λ Weight (A), and De-meaning Each Score of the Mean of Its Nonsubstantive Factor (Sex of Subject) (B)

A. Original scores with associated λ weights

		Levels				
		1	2	3	4	5
Females (Mean = 6.0)	Score	4	6	8	9	13
	(λ)	(−2)	(−1)	(0)	(+1)	(+2)
	Score	2	2	4	5	7
	(λ)	(−2)	(−1)	(0)	(+1)	(+2)
Males (Mean = 3.0)	Score	6	4	2	3	8
	(λ)	(−2)	(−1)	(0)	(+1)	(+2)
	Score	2	0	0	1	4
	(λ)	(−2)	(−1)	(0)	(+1)	(+2)

B. De-meaned scores with associated λ weights

		Levels				
		1	2	3	4	5
Females (Mean = 0.0)	Score	−2	0	2	3	7
	(λ)	(−2)	(−1)	(0)	(+1)	(+2)
	Score	−4	−4	−2	−1	1
	(λ)	(−2)	(−1)	(0)	(+1)	(+2)
Males (Mean = 0.0)	Score	3	1	−1	0	5
	(λ)	(−2)	(−1)	(0)	(+1)	(+2)
	Score	−1	−3	−3	−2	1
	(λ)	(−2)	(−1)	(0)	(+1)	(+2)

the mean scores of 6.0 for female subjects and 3.0 for male subjects have been subtracted from each corresponding score of Part A.

When we calculate the correlation between the original scores of Part A and their associated λ weights, we find $r_{effect\ size} = .46$. When we calculate the correlation between the de-meaned scores of Part B and their associated λ weights we find $r_{effect\ size|NS} = .52$. As an alternative, usually faster, way of calculating $r_{effect\ size}$ and $r_{effect\ size|NS}$, we can use Equations 3.13 and 4.5, respectively. The quantities required for these equations include $F_{contrast}$, $F_{noncontrast}$, $df_{noncontrast}$, df_{within}, $F_{NC|NS}$, and $df_{NC|NS}$. All of these quantities either are given directly in Part B of Table 4.2 or are readily computed from the information in Part B of Table 4.2. Thus we find $F_{noncontrast}$ from Equation 3.6 as

$$F_{noncontrast} = \frac{(SS_{between} - MS_{contrast})/df_{noncontrast}}{MS_{within}}$$

$$= \frac{(137 - 44.1)/8}{7.2} = 1.61.$$

We obtained $df_{noncontrast}$ from Equation 4.1:

$$df_{noncontrast} = df_{between} - 1 = 9 - 1 = 8.$$

Now we can use Equation 3.13 to get

$$r_{effect\ size} = \sqrt{\frac{6.125}{6.125 + 1.61(8) + 10}} = .46,$$

exactly the same value that we obtained by correlating the scores of Table 4.6, Part A, with their associated contrast weights.

We use Equation 4.5 to get

$$r_{effect\ size|NS} = \sqrt{\frac{6.125}{6.125 + .95(7) + 10}} = .52,$$

exactly the same value that we obtained by correlating the de-meaned scores of Table 4.6, Part B, with their associated contrast weights.

Earlier, we reported the significance level of the contrast examined in Table 4.2 (with weights of −2, −1, 0, +1, +2) as $p = .033$, associated with our $F_{contrast}$ of 6.125. In addition, from Equation 3.2 we reported

$$r_{contrast} = \sqrt{\frac{6.125}{6.125 + 10}} = .62.$$

As we would expect, of the three correlations ($r_{effect\ size}$, $r_{effect\ size|NS}$, and $r_{contrast}$), $r_{effect\ size}$ is smallest (.46) because it controls for, or partials out, nothing. The value of $r_{effect\ size|NS}$ is larger (.52) because it controls for, or partials out, the nonsubstantive (i.e., not essential) factor of sex of subject. The value of $r_{contrast}$ is largest

TABLE 4.7
Data in Table 4.2 Showing Cell Means Adjusted for Sex-of-Subject Factor and Their Associated λ Weights

		Levels				
		1	2	3	4	5
Females	Mean	−3	−2	0	1	4
(Mean = 0.0)	(λ)	(−2)	(−1)	(0)	(+1)	(+2)
Males	Mean	1	−1	−2	−1	3
(Mean = 0.0)	(λ)	(−2)	(−1)	(0)	(+1)	(+2)

(.62) because it controls for, or partials out, all sources of variation other than the contrast itself.

To complete our discussion of correlations adjusted for, or partialing out, the effects of nonsubstantive factors, we note that $r_{alerting}$ for the data in Table 4.2 was calculated between the ten cell means and their associated ten contrast weights and was reported earlier to be .57. It is also possible to compute $r_{alerting|NS}$ that adjusts for, or partials out, the effects of the nonsubstantive factor. Table 4.7 shows the cell means of Table 4.2 after the mean of the cell means of 6.0 for female subjects or 3.0 for male subjects have been subtracted from each cell mean in Table 4.2.

The value of $r_{alerting|NS}$ is simply the correlation between the ten adjusted cell means in Table 4.7 and their associated λ weights; $r_{alerting|NS} = .69$ in this example is larger than the $r_{alerting}$ of .57, as we would expect.

A THREE-FACTOR EXAMPLE

Table 4.8 gives the results of a 2 × 2 × 5 factorial experiment in which the two sexes (female, male) are crossed by two levels of age (young, old), and both of these factors are crossed by five levels of a treatment variable (with contrast weights of −2, −1, 0, +1, +2). Table 4.8 shows that the contrast weights are identical for each level of sex of subject and age of subject, so that sex, age, and the sex × age interaction are all regarded as nonsubstantive.

Table 4.9 shows the analysis of variance of the data in Table 4.8. The F statistic for our contrast (i.e., $F_{contrast}$), is $MS_{contrast}/MS_{within}$, which for Table 4.9 yields $88.20/7.20 = 12.25$, an F that with 1 and 20 degrees of freedom has $p = .0023$. We could have computed $MS_{contrast}$ from Equation 3.1 or 3.3. Had we used Equation 3.3, we would have computed $r_{alerting}$, the correlation between the twenty means of Table 4.8 and their associated λs, and found it to be .4508. Then

$$MS_{contrast} = r^2_{alerting} \times SS_{between}$$
$$= (.4508)^2 \times 434 = 88.20.$$

TABLE 4.8
Basic Data of a 2 × 2 × 5 Factorial Design

Sex	Age	Levels					Mean
		1	2	3	4	5	
Females	Young	6	8	10	11	15	
		4	4	6	7	9	
	Cell mean	5	6	8	9	12	8.0
	λ	−2	−1	0	+1	+2	
	Old	2	4	6	7	11	
		0	0	2	3	5	
	Cell mean	1	2	4	5	8	4.0
	λ	−2	−1	0	+1	+2	
Males	Young	8	6	4	5	10	
		4	2	2	3	6	
	Cell mean	6	4	3	4	8	5.0
	λ	−2	−1	0	+1	+2	
	Old	4	2	0	1	6	
		0	−2	−2	−1	2	
	Cell mean	2	0	−1	0	4	1.0
	λ	−2	−1	0	+1	+2	

TABLE 4.9
Analysis of Variance of the Data in Table 4.8

Source	SS	df	MS	F	p
Between	434	19	22.8	3.17	.0068
(Contrast)	(88.2)	(1)	(88.20)	(12.25)	(.0023)
Treatment	132	4	33.00	4.58	.0086
Sex	90	1	90.00	12.50	.0021
Age	160	1	160.00	22.22	.00013
Treat. × sex	52	4	13.00	1.81	.17
Treat. × age	00	4	0.00	—	—
Sex × age	00	1	0.00	—	—
Tr. × sex × age	00	4	0.00	—	—
Within	144	20	7.20		
Total	578	39			

From Equation 3.2, we find

$$r_{contrast} = \sqrt{\frac{F_{contrast}}{F_{contrast} + df_{within}}} = \sqrt{\frac{12.25}{12.25 + 20}} = .62,$$

and from Equation 3.13, we find

$$r_{effect\ size} = \sqrt{\frac{F_{contrast}}{F_{contrast} + F_{noncontrast}(df_{noncontrast}) + df_{within}}}$$

$$= \sqrt{\frac{12.25}{12.25 + 2.67(18) + 20}} = .39,$$

where $F_{noncontrast}$ was found from Equation 3.6,

$$F_{noncontrast} = \frac{(SS_{between} - MS_{contrast})/df_{noncontrast}}{MS_{within}}$$

$$= \frac{(434 - 88.2)/18}{7.20} = 2.67,$$

and $df_{noncontrast}$ was found from Equation 4.1,

$$df_{noncontrast} = df_{between} - 1 = 19 - 1 = 18.$$

Table 4.10 shows the data in Table 4.8 after the twenty cell means have been adjusted for the sex, age, and sex × age interaction effects summarized in

TABLE 4.10
Data in Table 4.8 Showing Cell Means Adjusted for Sex and Age with Associated λ Weights

		Levels					
		1	2	3	4	5	Means
Female Young	Mean (λ)	−3 (−2)	−2 (−1)	0 (0)	1 (+1)	4 (+2)	0.0
Female Old	Mean (λ)	−3 (−2)	−2 (−1)	0 (0)	1 (+1)	4 (+2)	0.0
Male Young	Mean (λ)	1 (−2)	−1 (−1)	−2 (0)	−1 (+1)	3 (+2)	0.0
Male Old	Mean (λ)	1 (−2)	−1 (−1)	−2 (0)	−1 (+1)	3 (+2)	0.0

Table 4.9. For each of the four rows of Table 4.8, the mean of that row was subtracted from each of the five cell means in that row. From this table of de-meaned data, we can directly compute $r_{alerting|NS}$. The correlation between the twenty adjusted cell means of Table 4.10 and their associated twenty contrast weights yields an $r_{alerting|NS}$ of .69, a value substantially larger than the $r_{alerting}$ of .45, as we would expect.

From Equation 4.5, we find

$$r_{effect\ size|NS} = \sqrt{\frac{F_{contrast}}{F_{contrast} + F_{NC|NS}(df_{NC|NS}) + df_{within}}}$$

$$= \sqrt{\frac{12.25}{12.25 + 0.89(15) + 20}} = .52,$$

a value noticeably larger than the value of $r_{effect\ size}$ of .39, as we would expect. The only difference between $r_{effect\ size}$ (Equation 3.13) and $r_{effect\ size|NS}$ (Equation 4.5) is that the latter adjusts the noncontrast variation in the denominator for the variation due to nonsubstantive factors. For the present example, $F_{NC|NS}$ and $df_{NC|NS}$ are obtained from Equations 4.2 and 4.3, where

$$SS_{NS} = SS_{sex} + SS_{age} + SS_{sex \times age}$$
$$= 90 + 160 + 0 = 250,$$

$$df_{NS} = df_{sex} + df_{age} + df_{sex \times age}$$
$$= 1 + 1 + 1 = 3,$$

$$df_{NC|NS} = df_{between} - 1 - df_{NS}$$
$$= 19 - 1 - 3 = 15,$$

and

$$F_{NC|NS} = \frac{(434 - 88.2 - 250)/15}{7.20} = 0.89.$$

In our discussion of this three-factor design, in which two of the factors (sex and age) are nonsubstantive, we have implicitly treated these two factors and their interaction as just a single factor. We now make this treatment quite explicit. Whenever two or more factors and their interactions with each other are nonsubstantive, we simply "uncross" these factors and array all their cells along a single dimension as the varying levels of just a single nonsubstantive factor. By *nonsubstantive*, we mean simply, as before, that the contrast weights of the substantive factor (or factors) do not change across the varying levels of the nonsubstantive factor and thus are not essential to the question of interest.

Table 4.11 shows the analysis of variance of Table 4.9 simplified so that the two nonsubstantive factors of age and sex, and their interaction, have been expressed as a single nonsubstantive factor called *demographics*. The sum of squares for this

TABLE 4.11
Three-Way Analysis of Variance of Table 4.9 Simplified into a Two-Way Analysis

Source	SS	df	MS	F	p
Between	434	19	22.84	3.17	.0068
(Contrast)	(88.2)	(1)	(88.20)	(12.25)	(.0023)
Treatment	132	4	33.00	4.58	.0086
Demographics	250	3	83.33	11.57	.00013
Treat. × demog.	52	12	4.33	0.60	.82
Within	144	20	7.20		
Total	578	39			

new factor is simply the sum of the sums of squares of the sex, age, and sex × age sources of variation. The sum of squares for the interaction of treatment × demographics is simply the sum of the sums of squares of the treatment × sex, treatment × age, and treatment × sex × age sources of variation. Analogously, the degrees of freedom of the demographics factor are the sum of the degrees of freedom of its constituent sources of variation (i.e., $1+1+1=3$), and the degrees of freedom of the treatment × demographics interaction are the sum of the degrees of freedom of its constituent sources of variation (i.e., $4+4+4=12$).

A FOUR-FACTOR EXAMPLE

Table 4.12 shows the results of a 2 × 2 × 2 × 2 factorial experiment in which female and male patients with either high or low levels of education and either good or poor levels of general health are assigned either to a treatment or control condition. The outcome variable is level of health achieved.

Table 4.12 also shows that the contrast weights at each level of education and general health are identical, indicating that the education and general health factors, and their interaction, are all nonsubstantive sources of variation. The contrast weights for treatment effects are different for female and male patients, however, indicating that sex of patient is a substantive factor, as is the treatment factor.

Table 4.13 shows the analysis of variance of the data in Table 4.12, including the $F_{contrast}$ of $MS_{contrast}/MS_{within} = 56.89/2.00 = 28.44$. For the data in Table 4.12, the correlation between the sixteen condition or cell means and their associated contrast weights (λs) (i.e., the $r_{alerting}$) is .6242. From Equation 3.2, we find

$$r_{contrast} = \sqrt{\frac{F_{contrast}}{F_{contrast} + df_{within}}} = \sqrt{\frac{28.44}{28.44 + 16}} = .80,$$

TABLE 4.12
Means and Contrast Weights of a 2 × 2 × 2 × 2 Factorial Design

Level of education	General health		Sex of patient				Mean
			Female		Male		
			Control	Treatment	Control	Treatment	
High	Poor	Mean	3	6	3	3	3.75
		λ	−1	+5	−3	−1	
	Good	Mean	5	9	5	5	6.00
		λ	−1	+5	−3	−1	
Low	Poor	Mean	2	3	1	2	2.00
		λ	−1	+5	−3	−1	
	Good	Mean	4	8	3	6	5.25
		λ	−1	+5	−3	−1	

TABLE 4.13
Analysis of Variance of the Data in Table 4.12

Source	SS	df	MS	F	p
Between	146.0	15	9.73	4.87	.0016
(Contrast)	(56.89)	(1)	(56.89)	(28.44)	(.000067)
Treatment	32.0	1	32.0	16.00	.0010
Sex	18.0	1	18.0	9.00	.0085
Health	60.5	1	60.5	30.25	.000048
Education	12.5	1	12.5	6.25	.024
Treatment × sex	8.0	1	8.0	4.00	.063
Treatment × health	4.5	1	4.5	2.25	.15
Treatment × education	0.5	1	0.5	0.25	.62
Sex × health	0.5	1	0.5	0.25	.62
Sex × education	0.5	1	0.5	0.25	.62
Health × education	2.0	1	2.0	1.00	.33
Treat. × sex × health	0.5	1	0.5	0.25	.62
Treat. × sex × educ.	4.5	1	4.5	2.25	.15
Treat. × health × educ.	2.0	1	2.0	1.00	.33
Sex × health × educ.	0.0	1	0.0	0.00	1.00
Tr. × sex × hlth. × educ.	0.0	1	0.0	0.00	1.00
Within	32.0	16	2.0		
Total	178.0	31			

and from Equation 3.13, we find

$$r_{effect\ size} = \sqrt{\frac{F_{contrast}}{F_{contrast} + F_{noncontrast}(df_{noncontrast}) + df_{within}}}$$

$$= \sqrt{\frac{28.44}{28.44 + 3.18(14) + 16}} = .57,$$

where $F_{noncontrast}$ is found from Equation 3.6,

$$F_{noncontrast} = \frac{(SS_{between} - MS_{contrast})/df_{noncontrast}}{MS_{within}}$$

$$= \frac{(146 - 56.89)/14}{2.00} = 3.18,$$

or from Equation 3.7,

$$F_{noncontrast} = \frac{F_{between}(df_{between}) - F_{contrast}}{df_{noncontrast}}$$

$$= \frac{4.867(15) - 28.44}{14} = 3.18,$$

and $df_{noncontrast}$ is found from Equation 4.1,

$$df_{noncontrast} = df_{between} - 1 = 15 - 1 = 14.$$

Table 4.14 shows the data in Table 4.12 after the sixteen cell means have been adjusted for the education, health, and education × health interaction effects shown in Table 4.13. For each of the four rows in Table 4.12, the mean of that row was subtracted from each of the four cell means in that row. From this table of de-meaned data, we can directly compute $r_{alerting|NS}$. The correlation between the sixteen adjusted cell means in Table 4.14 and their associated sixteen contrast weights yields $r_{alerting|NS} = .90$, a value substantially larger than the value of $r_{alerting} = .62$, as we would expect.

From Equation 4.5, we find

$$r_{effect\ size|NS} = \sqrt{\frac{F_{contrast}}{F_{contrast} + F_{NC|NS}(df_{NC|NS}) + df_{within}}}$$

$$= \sqrt{\frac{28.44}{28.44 + 0.64(11) + 16}} = .74,$$

a value noticeably larger than the value of $r_{effect\ size}$ of .57, as we would expect. The difference between $r_{effect\ size}$ and $r_{effect\ size|NS}$ (Equations 3.13 and 4.5, respectively)

TABLE 4.14
Data from Table 4.12 Showing Cell Means Adjusted for Health and Education with Associated λ Weights

		Substantive factor				
		Female		Male		
		Control	Treatment	Control	Treatment	Mean
High education Poor health	Mean λ	−0.75 −1	2.25 +5	−0.75 −3	−0.75 −1	0.0
High education Good health	Mean λ	−1.00 −1	3.00 +5	−1.00 −3	−1.00 −1	0.0
Low education Poor health	Mean λ	0.00 −1	1.00 +5	−1.00 −3	0.00 −1	0.0
Low education Good health	Mean λ	−1.25 −1	2.75 +5	−2.25 −3	0.75 −1	0.0

is that the latter adjusts the noncontrast variation in the denominator for the nonsubstantive factors. In the present example, $F_{NC|NS}$ and $df_{NC|NS}$ are obtained from Equations 4.2 and 4.3, with

$$SS_{NS} = SS_{educ} + SS_{health} + SS_{educ \times health}$$
$$= 12.5 + 60.5 + 2.0 = 75,$$

and

$$df_{NS} = df_{educ} + df_{health} + df_{educ \times health} = 1 + 1 + 1 = 3.$$

In the present 2 × 2 × 2 × 2 factorial design, two factors are substantive (sex and treatment) and two factors are nonsubstantive (education and health). Once we have seen from the pattern of contrast weights which factors are nonsubstantive (i.e., the contrast weights do not change as we move from level to level of the nonsubstantive factor), there is no compelling reason to continue to regard the design as a four-factor design. It is more convenient to think of this design and *any* factorial design involving one or more nonsubstantive and one or more substantive factors as a basic two-factor design. The two resulting factors are always the substantive factor (e.g., the column effect) and the nonsubstantive factor (e.g., the row effect).

Table 4.15 shows the analysis of variance of Table 4.13 simplified so that the two substantive factors and the two nonsubstantive factors have been condensed into a single substantive and a single nonsubstantive factor. The quantity $SS_{substantive}$ is

TABLE 4.15
Four-Way Analysis of Variance of Table 4.13 Data Simplified into a Two-Way Analysis

Source	SS	df	MS	F	p
Between	146.0	15	9.73	4.87	.0016
(Contrast)	(56.89)	(1)	(56.89)	(28.44)	(.000067)
Substantive	58.0	3	19.33	9.67	.00070
Nonsubstantive	75.0	3	25.00	12.50	.00018
Subst. × nonsubst.	13.0	9	1.44	0.72	.55
Within	32.0	16	2.00		
Total	178.0				

the sum of the sums of squares of the three sources of variation comprising the "composite" substantive factor:

$$SS_{treatment} + SS_{sex} + SS_{treatment \times sex} = 32 + 18 + 8 = 58.$$

The quantity $SS_{nonsubstantive}$ is the sum of the sums of squares of the three sources of variation comprising the "composite" nonsubstantive factor:

$$SS_{education} + SS_{health} + SS_{educ \times health} = 12.5 + 60.5 + 2.0 = 75.$$

Note that

$$SS_{between} = SS_{substantive} + SS_{NS} + SS_{subs \times NS}.$$

The degrees of freedom of the substantive and nonsubstantive factors are simply the sums of the degrees of freedom of the constituent sources of variation; for the substantive factor,

$$df_{subs} = df_{treat} + df_{sex} + df_{treat \times sex} = 1 + 1 + 1 = 3,$$

and for the nonsubstantive factor,

$$df_{NS} = df_{educ} + df_{health} + df_{educ \times health} = 1 + 1 + 1 = 3.$$

r_{BESD}

The use of r_{BESD} to represent effect sizes was straightforward in Chapter 2, where there was only one factor and it had only two levels. In Chapter 3, where the one factor under consideration had more than two levels, using r_{BESD} was complicated by the need to use the results of our completed study to predict the results of a future two-group study whose levels were not necessarily represented in our completed study. Two issues arose in Chapter 3, and they also arise here, where there are two or more factors. First, what is the appropriate noise level for the new study? Second, what are the levels associated with the two new groups?

The Appropriate Noise Level for r_{BESD}

Because of the needed extrapolation to two levels that were not necessarily represented in our completed study, the appropriate noise level must include all noncontrast variation that cannot be controlled (i.e., not controlled in the sense of not being attributable to nonsubstantive factors). Although we could also consider nonsubstantive factors to be uncontrolled in a two-level replication of the current study, we feel that typically it makes more sense to consider a replication with the same nonsubstantive factors controlled as in the current study. Thus, in the context of factorial designs, r_{BESD}, which could also be designated as $r_{BESD|NS}$, is defined as always controlling for any nonsubstantive factor(s).

Recall that by the definition of a nonsubstantive factor, within each level defined by nonsubstantive factors the contrast weights reflect the same trend. The uncontrolled between-cell noise level is the noncontrast variation with the nonsubstantive variation removed; the associated F statistic is $F_{NC|NS}$, given in Equation 4.2, with $df_{NC|NS}$ degrees of freedom given in Equation 4.3.

To illustrate for the data of Tables 4.12 and 4.13, we find

$$SS_{NS} = 60.5 + 12.5 + 2.0 = 75,$$

$$F_{NC|NS} = \frac{(146 - 56.89 - 75)/11}{2} = .64,$$

where

$$df_{NC|NS} = 15 - 1 - 3 = 11$$

is the numerator degrees of freedom associated with $F_{NC|NS}$.

The Value of r_{BESD} and $r_{BESD\ counternull}$

As in Chapter 3, if by chance the level of noise reflected by $F_{NC|NS}$ is less than the within-cell level of noise (i.e., if $F_{NC|NS}$ is less than 1), we should use the within noise level. Thus, the appropriate expression for r_{BESD} is

$$r_{BESD} = \sqrt{\frac{F_{contrast}}{F_{contrast} + F_{NC|NS}(df_{NC|NS} + df_{within})}}, \qquad (4.6)$$

where $F_{NC|NS}$ is entered as 1 if it is less than 1. The counternull value of r_{BESD} is calculated just as in Chapter 3.

For the data in Tables 4.12 and 4.13, we find

$$r_{BESD} = \sqrt{\frac{28.44}{28.44 + 1.00(11 + 16)}} = .72,$$

and from Equation 2.16, we find

$$r_{BESD\ counternull} = \sqrt{\frac{4r_{BESD}^2}{1+3r_{BESD}^2}} = \sqrt{\frac{4(.72)^2}{1+3(.72)^2}} = .90.$$

Interpretation of r_{BESD} with One Substantive Factor

The interpretation of r_{BESD} for a design with one substantive factor is that the value of r_{BESD} is the value of $r_{effect\ size}$ that we would expect to see in a hypothetical replication of the current study, with the same total N, in which the substantive factor had only two levels, and in which these two levels were compared at a randomly chosen level of the nonsubstantive factor.

In the two-group replication, the two levels of the substantive factor would be set at $-1\sigma_\lambda$ and $+1\sigma_\lambda$, where σ_λ is defined in Equation 3.16 as the standard deviation of the λ weights for the contrast:

$$\sigma_\lambda = \sqrt{\frac{\Sigma \lambda_i^2}{k}},$$

and where k is the number of conditions or levels of the substantive factor and the summation is over the k λs that are associated with the k levels of treatment. For the data in Table 4.1, for example, with one substantive and one nonsubstantive factor,

$$\sigma_\lambda = \sqrt{\frac{(-3)^2 + (-1)^2 + (+1)^2 + (+3)^2}{4}} = \sqrt{5} = 2.236.$$

The appropriate interpretation of the BESD associated with the four levels of the substantive factor (number of treatments weekly) is that it compares the rate of above-average functioning of patients whose frequency of treatment falls $1\sigma_\lambda$ or 2.2 λ units above the mean frequency of treatment with those whose frequency of treatment falls $1\sigma_\lambda$ or 2.2 λ units below the mean frequency of treatment. This two-group replication is considered conducted within one randomly chosen level of the nonsubstantive factor, in this example, using patients either at the mild, or the moderate, or the severe level of illness.

In the present example, the variance of the λ weights is larger than the variance of the original values of the four levels of treatment 0, 1, 2, 3. To set the $+1\sigma$ and -1σ levels in the original metric, we find the $+1\sigma$ level (where the standard deviation [σ] of the four levels of treatment 0, 1, 2, 3, equals 1.1) from

mean treatment level $+1\sigma$ treatment level
$= (0+1+2+3)/4 + 1.1 = 2.6,$

and the -1σ level from

mean treatment level -1σ treatment level
$= (0+1+2+3)/4 - 1.1 = 0.4.$

For the present example, therefore, the BESD compares, for groups of patients with the same severity of illness, those receiving about two and a half treatments per week with those receiving about a one-half treatment per week.

Calculating r_{BESD}: A More Detailed Example

The primary quantities required to compute r_{BESD} are the $SS_{between}$, $MS_{contrast}$, MS_{within}, SS_{NS}, $df_{between}$, $df_{noncontrast}$, df_{NS}, $df_{NC|NS}$, and df_{within}. For the data in Table 4.1 these values are as follows:

$$
\begin{aligned}
SS_{between} &= 1{,}420.00 \\
MS_{contrast} &= 770.67 \\
MS_{within} &= 25.00 \\
SS_{NS} &= 420.00 \\
df_{between} &= 11 \\
df_{noncontrast} &= 10 \\
df_{NS} &= 2 \\
df_{NC|NS} &= 8 \\
df_{within} &= 108.
\end{aligned}
$$

From these primary quantities, we can obtain the necessary secondary quantities $F_{contrast}$ and $F_{NC|NS}$. For the present data, the values of these quantities and how they were obtained are as follows:

$$F_{contrast} = MS_{contrast}/MS_{within} = 770.67/25.00 = 30.83,$$

$$F_{NC|NS} = \frac{(SS_{between} - MS_{contrast} - SS_{NS})/df_{NC|NS}}{MS_{within}}$$

$$= \frac{(1{,}420 - 770.67 - 420)/8}{25} = 1.15.$$

We can now use Equation 4.6 to calculate r_{BESD} as

$$r_{BESD} = \sqrt{\frac{F_{contrast}}{F_{contrast} + F_{NC|NS}(df_{NC|NS} + df_{within})}}$$

$$= \sqrt{\frac{30.83}{30.83 + 1.15(8 + 108)}} = .43.$$

Note that if the value of $F_{NC|NS}$ had been less than 1.00, it would have been entered as 1.00. We display our obtained value of r_{BESD} of .43 as a BESD just as we did in Chapter 3:

		Above median	Below median	Σ
$(+1\sigma_\lambda)$	Higher level	71.5	28.5	100
$(-1\sigma_\lambda)$	Lower level	28.5	71.5	100
	Σ	100	100	200

Counternull Values for r_{BESD}

Whenever we compute r_{BESD}, it is wise routinely to compute its counternull value. For the present example with $F_{contrast} = 30.83$ and $p = .0000002$, it is virtually certain that the true value of r_{BESD} is between the null and counternull values. Using Equation 2.16 to find the counternull value, we have

$$r_{BESD\ counternull} = \sqrt{\frac{4r_{BESD}^2}{1 + 3r_{BESD}^2}} = \sqrt{\frac{4(.43)^2}{1 + 3(.43)^2}} = .69.$$

We display our obtained counternull value of r_{BESD} as a BESD just as we did in Chapter 3:

		Above median	Below median	Σ
$(+1\sigma_\lambda)$	Higher level	84.5	15.5	100
$(-1\sigma_\lambda)$	Lower level	15.5	84.5	100
	Σ	100	100	200

Interpretation of r_{BESD} with Two Additive and No Nonsubstantive Factors

For an example in which there are two additive factors and no nonsubstantive factors, we return to the data in Tables 4.4 and 4.5. For those data, we found $F_{contrast} = 47.03$, $F_{noncontrast} = 0.98$, $df_{noncontrast} = 10$, and $df_{within} = 108$. Because there are no nonsubstantive factors, Equation 4.6, which is

$$r_{BESD} = \sqrt{\frac{F_{contrast}}{F_{contrast} + F_{NC|NS}(df_{NC|NS} + df_{within})}},$$

simplifies to Equation 3.15, which we use to compute r_{BESD}:

$$r_{BESD} = \sqrt{\frac{F_{contrast}}{F_{contrast} + F_{noncontrast}(df_{noncontrast} + df_{within})}},$$

with $F_{noncontrast}$ and $df_{noncontrast}$ defined as above with the restriction that if $F_{noncontrast}$ is less than 1.00 (as it is in the present example), it is replaced by 1.00 in Equation 3.15. For the present example, therefore, we find

$$r_{BESD} = \sqrt{\frac{47.03}{47.03 + 1.00(10 + 108)}} = .5338,$$

a value not noticeably lower than the $r_{contrast}$ of .55 reported earlier or the $r_{effect\ size}$ of .53. In other cases, however, r_{BESD} can be appreciably smaller than both $r_{contrast}$ and $r_{effect\ size}$. In those cases, r_{BESD} is lower because the noise level of the noncontrast variation is quite substantial. It is this variation that serves as the appropriate index of the noise level for doing interpolation to levels of the substantive factors not included in this study, and it is these interpolations (i.e., to $+1\sigma_\lambda$ and $-1\sigma_\lambda$) that are needed to define the BESD.

The interpretation of r_{BESD} for the present design with two substantive factors is somewhat more complex than it is for the earlier design with one substantive and one nonsubstantive factor. In that earlier case, we had only to reduce the multiple levels of our single substantive factor to a two-group representation, while remembering that our r_{BESD} was valid only for the situation in which we were replicating our study within a randomly chosen level of the nonsubstantive factor.

In the present case of two substantive factors, to interpret the BESD we must reduce the multiple levels of two factors to two levels of a single dimension that can reflect the levels of the two factors simultaneously. We illustrate this reduction for the additive contrast of the present example in which patients were predicted to have better outcomes as number of weekly treatments and medication dosages were increased. Favorableness of outcome was predicted in points as shown in Part A of Table 4.5, for which the contrast weights were given as shown in Part C of Table 4.5. The standard deviation of the contrast weights (σ_λ) is 2.8 and the standard deviation of the raw points predicted (σ_{points}) is 1.4. There are six levels of prediction given either in raw points or in contrast weights. For each one, we list the one, two, or three conditions that fall at that level. The first number given to describe or identify each condition is the number of weekly treatments; the second number is the dosage level in milligrams. The final row gives the mean treatment condition for each contrast weight. These mean treatment conditions reflect an assumption of an underlying linear dimension:

		$-1\sigma \downarrow$			$\downarrow +1\sigma$	
Raw points	0	1	2	3	4	5
Contrast weights	−5	−3	−1	+1	+3	+5
	0/0	0/50	0/100	1/100	2/100	3/100
		1/0	1/50	2/50	3/50	
			2/0	3/0		
Mean	0/0	.5/25	1/50	2/50	2.5/75	3/100

Two arrows have been drawn to indicate the location of -1σ and $+1\sigma$. These values are 1.1 and 3.9 for the raw point metric and -2.8 and $+2.8$ for the contrast weight metric.

What is the appropriate interpretation of the BESD associated with the four levels of the number-of-treatments factor and the three levels of the dosage factor combined additively? The BESD compares the rate of above-average functioning of patients whose additive factors fall 1σ unit above the mean (i.e., a bit less than either [a] two treatments weekly with 100 mg of medication or [b] three treatments with 50 mg) with those whose additive factors fall 1σ unit below the mean (i.e., a bit more than either [c] no treatments with 50 mg or [d] 1 treatment with 0 mg).

A more quantitative statement can be based on linear interpolation between the means of treatment conditions immediately below and above $-1\,\sigma$ and immediately below and above $+1\sigma$. To illustrate for the table just above, the raw point value of 1.1 and the contrast weight value of -2.8 correspond to the location of -1σ. But the value 1.1 is 1/10th of the distance between raw point values of 1 and 2, and the value -2.8 is 1/10th of the distance between contrast weight values of -3 and -1. Therefore, we want to go 1/10th of the distance between the mean treatment conditions associated with raw point values of 1 and 2 and contrast weight values of -3 and -1 to find the interpolated mean treatment condition between .5/25 and 1/50. Going 1/10 of the distance between .5 and 1 treatment per week (the first value reported for each mean treatment condition) yields .55 treatments per week, whereas going 1/10 of the distance between the 25- and 50-mg dosage level (the second value reported for each mean treatment condition) yields 27.5 mg.

We follow the same process of linear interpolation between the mean treatment conditions of 2/50 and 2.5/75 found immediately below and above $+1\sigma$. Because the raw point value of 3.9 and the contrast weight value of $+2.8$ correspond to the location of $+1\sigma$, we want to go 9/10 of the distance between 2/50 and 2.5/75, which gives 2.45 treatments per week and 72.5 mg.

The interpretation of the BESD associated with these interpolated values of the mean treatment condition is that it compares the rate of above-average functioning of patients given (a) 2.45 treatments per week and a 72.5-mg dosage with patients given (b) .55 treatments per week and a 27.5-mg dosage. Because these values were found by linear interpolation, an assumption of underlying linear relationships is needed for this interpretation.

Counternull Values for r_{BESD}. As usual, when computing r_{BESD} we want also to examine $r_{BESD\ counternull}$, a value we compute from Equation 2.16. In the present example,

$$r_{BESD\ counternull} = \sqrt{\frac{4r_{BESD}^2}{1 + 3r_{BESD}^2}} = \sqrt{\frac{4(.53)^2}{1 + 3(.53)^2}} = .78.$$

We can display r_{BESD}, $r_{BESD\ counternull}$, and the null hypothesis ($r = .00$ in this example and in most situations) in BESDs as illustrated earlier in this chapter and in preceding chapters. Because $p < 5/10^{10}$ in the present example, it is virtually certain that the true value of r_{BESD} is between the null and counternull values.

In the example we have been discussing, the two substantive factors of number of weekly treatments and medication dosage could be reconceptualized as a single underlying dimension of "treatment intensity," where increases in the number of weekly treatments or increases in the medication dosage could be seen as increasing the overall intensity of treatment. The use of the BESD is always reasonable when our two or more substantive factors can be thought of as reflecting a single underlying dimension.

TABLE 4.16
Means and Analysis of Variance of a Factorial Design with Two Substantive Factors

A. Table of means ($n = 15$ per condition)

Patient sex	Number of treatments weekly				Mean
	0	1	2	3	
Female	2.67	7.00	9.67	8.33	6.92
Male	0.67	5.00	5.67	9.00	5.08
Mean	1.67	6.00	7.67	8.67	6.00

B. Analysis of variance of table of means

Source	SS	df	MS	F	p
Between	1,043.33	7	149.05	5.96	.000007
Treatments	860.00	3	286.67	11.47	.000002
Sex of patient	100.83	1	100.83	4.03	.05
Treat. × sex	82.50	3	27.50	1.10	.35
Within	2,800.00	112	25.00		
Total	3,843.33	119			

Sometimes, however, it is not at all clear how we would form a single underlying dimension for our two or more substantive factors. For example, consider the data in Table 4.16, in which the two substantive factors are number of weekly treatments and sex of patient.

Our predictions were additive, with female patients predicted to score higher than males and with increases in number of treatments predicted to lead to higher scores. Table 4.17 shows these predictions in raw points predicted per condition (Part A) and in contrast weight form (Part B) computed from Part A simply by subtracting the mean predicted points (2.0) from every condition's predicted points.

The contrast we compute based on these weights is perfectly sensible and yields clearly interpretable values for $MS_{contrast}$ (865.93), $F_{contrast}$ (34.64), $r_{alerting}$ (.91), $r_{contrast}$ (.49), and $r_{effect\ size}$ (.47). However, the interpretation of r_{BESD} would be obscure because we would have to combine sex and number of treatments in a single quantitative factor. This would have so little meaning that we advise treating each of the sexes separately when computing r_{BESD}, thereby displaying the results in two clearly interpretable BESDs.

Treating Each Sex Separately. Having decided to treat each of the sexes separately, we have only a single factor in our design (number of weekly treatments), and so we will need only the procedures of Chapter 3. The primary quantities required to compute r_{BESD} from Equation 3.15 are given separately for female and

TABLE 4.17
Allocation of Points to Eight Treatment Conditions and Their Corresponding Contrast Weights

A. Point allocations

Points		Points per level				Mean
		0	1	2	3	
1	Female	1	2	3	4	2.5
0	Male	0	1	2	3	1.5
	Mean	0.5	1.5	2.5	3.5	2.0

B. Points converted to contrast weights

	0	1	2	3	Mean
Female	−1	0	+1	+2	+0.5
Male	−2	−1	0	+1	−0.5
Mean	−1.5	−0.5	+0.5	+1.5	0.0

male patients:

	Females	Males
$SS_{between}$	414.29	527.53
$MS_{contrast}$	289.59	493.83
MS_{within}	25.00	25.00
$df_{between}$	3	3
$df_{noncontrast}$	2	2
df_{within}	56	56

Note that the degrees of freedom are 56 within each sex; however, for purposes of computing significance levels, the degrees of freedom could be 112 for each sex because we could use a pooled error term based on all the data in computing the significance level for each sex.

From the primary quantities given just above, we obtain the required secondary quantities of $F_{contrast}$ and $F_{noncontrast}$ separately for female and male patients:

	Females	Males
$F_{contrast}$	11.58	19.75
$F_{noncontrast}$	2.49	0.67

Then, from Equation 3.15, we find r_{BESD} to be .27 for females and .50 for males. We find the values of $r_{BESD\ counternull}$ to be .49 for females and .76 for males. Should we want to do so, we could, of course, also compute $r_{alerting}$, $r_{contrast}$, and $r_{effect\ size}$ separately for the two sexes. For the data in Tables 4.16 and 4.17, these values are

Correlation	Equations	Females	Males
$r_{alerting}$	3.17	.84	.97
$r_{contrast}$	3.2	.41	.51
$r_{effect\ size}$	3.13	.40	.51
r_{BESD}	3.15	.27	.50
$r_{BESD\ counternull}$	2.16	.49	.76

Using these estimates, we find the predicted linear trend in number of weekly treatments in both sexes but with noticeably larger effects, especially for r_{BESD} and $r_{BESD\ counternull}$, for male than for female patients. It may have struck the reader that the drop in going from $r_{effect\ size}$ to r_{BESD} is more substantial for female patients (.40 to .27) than it is for male patients (.51 to .50). This difference is due to the presence of a larger $F_{noncontrast}$ for the females than for the males in the context of a much larger value of df_{within} relative to $df_{noncontrast}$.

Treating Each Level of Nonsubstantive Factors Separately

In the last section, we saw that in the case of two substantive (or essential) factors, it can make r_{BESD} more interpretable to treat each level of one of the factors separately, in particular when a single underlying quantitative dimension cannot readily be conceptualized. Similarly, it can often be useful to treat separately the different levels of one or more nonsubstantive factors. Once we have effectively removed the nonsubstantive factors from the design, by computing r_{BESD} separately at each level, we can compute r_{BESD} directly from Equation 3.15.

For an example, we return to the data in Table 4.1, in which severity of illness was our nonsubstantive factor. The primary quantities required to compute r_{BESD} from Equation 3.15 are given separately for each level of severity, mild, moderate, and severe:

	Mild	Moderate	Severe
$SS_{between}$	450	410	140
$MS_{contrast}$	338	392	98
MS_{within}	25	25	25
$df_{between}$	3	3	3
$df_{noncontrast}$	2	2	2
df_{within}	36	36	36

Note that the degrees of freedom are 36 within each level of the severity factor; however, for purposes of computing significance levels, the degrees of freedom would be 108 for each level of severity if we used a pooled error term based on all the data when computing the significance level for each degree of severity.

From the primary quantities given just above, we obtain the required secondary quantities of $F_{contrast}$ and $F_{noncontrast}$ separately for each level of severity:

	Mild	Moderate	Severe
$F_{contrast}$	13.52	15.68	3.92
$F_{noncontrast}$	2.24	0.36	0.84

Then, from Equation 3.15, we find the following r_{BESD} values, and from Equation 2.16, we find the corresponding $r_{BESD\ counternull}$ values:

	Mild	Moderate	Severe
r_{BESD}	.37	.54	.31
p value	.00037	.00013	.050
$r_{BESD\ counternull}$	.62	.79	.54

Note that in Equation 3.15, the $F_{noncontrast}$ values of 0.36 and 0.84 were replaced by the value 1.00 for the moderate and severe levels, respectively. In the present example, there is a substantial linear trend revealed by r_{BESD} and $r_{BESD\ counternull}$ in all three levels of severity. We might, on the one hand, regard these values as fairly homogeneous; however, we might also regard the difference between the r_{BESD} of .54 for the moderate level and the r_{BESD} of .31 for the severe level as a meaningful difference leading us to watch for this difference in future studies. When, a little earlier in this chapter, we computed r_{BESD} for all the data in Table 4.1 considered together (i.e., not separately for each level), we used Equation 4.5 and found $r_{BESD} = .46$, a value not very different from the values of r_{BESD} obtained when each level of our nonsubstantive factor was considered separately.

Should we want to do so, we could also compute $r_{alerting}$, $r_{contrast}$, and $r_{effect\ size}$ separately for the three levels of severity. For the data of Table 4.1, these values are

Correlation	Equation	Mild	Moderate	Severe
$r_{alerting}$	3.17	.87	.98	.84
$r_{contrast}$	3.2	.52	.55	.31
$r_{effect\ size}$	3.13	.50	.55	.31

The differences between the correlations obtained for the moderate and severe levels may appear to us to be substantial for both $r_{contrast}$ and $r_{effect\ size}$, and we would want to watch for such differences in future studies. When, much earlier in this chapter, we computed $r_{contrast}$ and $r_{effect\ size}$ for all the data in Table 4.1 considered together (i.e., not separately for each level of severity), we found $r_{contrast} = .47$ (from Equation 3.2), and $r_{effect\ size} = .46$ (from Equation 4.5), values not dramatically different from those obtained when each level of our nonsubstantive factor was considered separately.

EFFECT SIZE ESTIMATION WHEN CONTRAST WEIGHTS OF 0 ARE SET ASIDE

In Chapter 3, we saw that contrast weights of 0 can be used in two quite different ways. First, contrast weights of 0 may be intended to function just as any other number. Second, contrast weights of 0 may be intended to set aside the group or groups that have been given weights of 0. Significance levels (and F and t) are not affected by how we regard contrast weights of 0, as long as we assume the within-condition variances are the same across all groups.

When all of our factors are substantive, we deal with contrast weights of 0 that are to be set aside exactly as described in Chapter 3. We simply think of all the conditions of the design as constituting a one-way design. Thus the appropriate calculation of $r_{alerting}$, $r_{contrast}$, $r_{effect\ size}$, and r_{BESD} will all tend to give larger values when conditions with $\lambda = 0$ are set aside than when these conditions are viewed as ordinary intermediate numbers. The typical increase in values of these correlations is due both to the decrease in $df_{noncontrast}$ and to the decrease of df_{within} when groups are set aside (see Equations 3.17, 3.2, 3.13, and 3.15 for computational equations, and see Table 3.6 for a summary).

When one or more factors of a factorial design are nonsubstantive, our general strategy is to recalculate the analysis of variance of the overall design, omitting any levels of any factor that were given λs of 0 with the intent to set them aside, but assuming that the mean square within is the same as in the original design (i.e., MS_{within}).

We will illustrate our procedures for three situations:

1. Set-aside conditions that are defined by substantive factors.
2. Set-aside conditions that are defined by nonsubstantive factors.
3. Set-aside conditions that are defined by both substantive and nonsubstantive factors.

Set-Asides in Substantive Factors

Table 4.18 shows the same means as those in Table 4.12, but with the contrast weights changed from those of Table 4.12. In the present analysis, we wish to examine the treatment effect only for female patients; the male patients have been set aside with contrast weights of 0 for all conditions. The most convenient way to obtain the ingredient quantities we need to compute our various effect

TABLE 4.18
Means and Contrast Weights: Set-Asides Only in Substantive Factors

Level of education	General health		Sex of patient			
			Female		Male	
			Control	Treatment	Control	Treatment
High	Poor	Mean	3	6	3	3
		λ	−1	+1	0	0
	Good	Mean	5	9	5	5
		λ	−1	+1	0	0
Low	Poor	Mean	2	3	1	2
		λ	−1	+1	0	0
	Good	Mean	4	8	3	6
		λ	−1	+1	0	0

TABLE 4.19
Analysis of Variance of the Data of Table 4.18 after λs of 0 Are Set Aside

Source	SS	df	MS	F	p
Between	88	7	12.57	6.29	.0012
Treatment (contrast)	36	1	36.00	18.00	.00062
Nonsubstantive	46	3	15.33	7.67	.0021
Treat. × nonsubst.	6	3	2.00	1.00	.42
Within	16	8[a]	2.00		
Total	104	15			

[a] Represents the degrees of freedom found in the conditions involving only female patients. For computing significance levels, however, we use the degrees of freedom of the original design, 16, associated with the MS_{within} of the original design.

size correlations is to compute a separate analysis of variance for all conditions remaining after we have set aside the conditions with $\lambda = 0$. Table 4.19 shows this analysis of variance.

It should be noted that Table 4.19 shows a nonsubstantive factor with 3 degrees of freedom representing the four rows of Table 4.18. In Table 4.18, the labeling of these four rows shows that we could equally well have regarded them as representing a 2 × 2 factorial arrangement of two levels of education crossed by two levels of general health. The 3 degrees of freedom of our nonsubstantive factor would then be defined as 1 degree of freedom each for the education factor, the health factor, and the education × health interaction. In the present application, however, nothing is gained by casting the factor "nonsubstantive" into a 2 × 2 factorial, and so we use the single-factor format.

Significance Levels. Table 4.19 shows the F for treatment, our contrast with weights of -1 and $+1$ computed for female patients only, to be 18.00, for which p would be .0028 for 1 and 8 degrees of freedom. However, for purposes of computing significance levels, we assume that the within mean square of the design with set-asides is the same as that of the original design, with the original degrees of freedom. Table 4.13 shows the original within mean square is 2.00 with associated degrees of freedom of 16. The p value for an F of 18.00 based on 1 and 16 degrees of freedom is .00062, as shown in Table 4.19.

Effect Size Estimation: Primary and Secondary Quantities. The primary quantities required to compute our various effect size correlations for the data in Tables 4.18 and 4.19 are as follows:

$SS_{between}$ = 88.00
$MS_{contrast}$ = 36.00
MS_{within} = 2.00

$$SS_{NS} = 46.00$$
$$df_{between} = 7$$
$$df_{noncontrast} = 6$$
$$df_{NS} = 3$$
$$df_{NC|NS} = 3$$
$$df_{within} = 8$$

Note that for purposes of effect size estimation, the appropriate degrees of freedom for the mean square within are based only on the conditions remaining after we have set aside the conditions of the original design with $\lambda = 0$.

From the primary quantities just given, we can obtain the necessary secondary quantities: $F_{contrast}$, $F_{noncontrast}$, and $F_{NC|NS}$. For the data in Tables 4.18 and 4.19, the values of these quantities and how they were obtained are as follows:

$$F_{contrast} = MS_{contrast}/MS_{within} = 36.00/2.00 = 18.00,$$

$$F_{noncontrast} = \frac{(SS_{between} - MS_{contrast})/df_{noncontrast}}{MS_{within}},$$

$$= \frac{(88.00 - 36.00)/6}{2.00} = 4.33,$$

$$F_{NC|NS} = \frac{(SS_{between} - MS_{contrast} - SS_{NS})/df_{NC|NS}}{MS_{within}}$$

$$= \frac{(88.00 - 36.00 - 46.0)/3}{2.00} = 1.00.$$

$r_{contrast}$. From Equation 3.2, we find

$$r_{contrast} = \sqrt{\frac{F_{contrast}}{F_{contrast} + df_{within}}}$$

$$= \sqrt{\frac{18.00}{18.00 + 8}} = .83.$$

$r_{effect\ size}$. **The general case.** From Equation 3.13, we find

$$r_{effect\ size} = \sqrt{\frac{F_{contrast}}{F_{contrast} + F_{noncontrast}(df_{noncontrast}) + df_{within}}}$$

$$= \sqrt{\frac{18.00}{18.00 + 4.33(6) + 8}} = .59.$$

This is the value of $r_{effect\ size}$ in general (that is, not taking into account the presence of a nonsubstantive factor). In the following paragraph, we do take the nonsubstantive factor into account.

$r_{effect\ size|NS}$. From Equation 4.5, we find

$$r_{effect\ size|NS} = \sqrt{\frac{F_{contrast}}{F_{contrast} + F_{NC|NS}(df_{NC|NS}) + df_{within}}}$$

$$= \sqrt{\frac{18.00}{18.00 + 1.00(3) + 8}} = .79,$$

a value considerably larger than the value of $r_{effect\ size}$ not taking the nonsubstantive factor into account.

r_{BESD}. From Equation 4.6, we find

$$r_{BESD} = \sqrt{\frac{F_{contrast}}{F_{contrast} + F_{NC|NS}(df_{NC|NS} + df_{within})}}$$

$$= \sqrt{\frac{18.00}{18.00 + 1.00(3 + 8)}} = .79,$$

a value identical to that of $r_{effect\ size|NS}$ in this example because the noncontrast variation, adjusted for the nonsubstantive factor, is no larger than the noise level within conditions (i.e., the value of MS_{within}).

$r_{BESD\ counternull}$. From Equation 2.16, we find

$$r_{BESD\ counternull} = \sqrt{\frac{4r_{BESD}^2}{1 + 3r_{BESD}^2}}$$

$$= \sqrt{\frac{4(.79)^2}{1 + 3(.79)^2}} = .93.$$

$r_{alerting}$. **The General Case.** We can compute $r_{alerting}$ either by direct calculation or from Equation 3.12. By direct calculation of the correlation between the means of the eight conditions involving only female patients in Table 4.18 and their corresponding contrast weights, we find $r_{alerting} = .64$. From Equation 3.4 or 3.12, we find, equivalently, that

$$r_{alerting} = \sqrt{\frac{F_{contrast}}{F_{contrast} + F_{noncontrast}(df_{noncontrast})}}$$

$$= \sqrt{\frac{18.00}{18.00 + 4.33(6)}} = .64.$$

$r_{alerting|NS}$. To find $r_{alerting}$ adjusted for the nonsubstantive factors, $r_{alerting|NS}$, we can employ the following equation:

$$r_{alerting|NS} = \sqrt{\frac{F_{contrast}}{F_{contrast} + F_{NC|NS}(df_{NC|NS})}} \qquad (4.7)$$

TABLE 4.20
Means and Contrast Weights: Set-Asides Only in Nonsubstantive Factors

Level of education	General health		Sex of patient			
			Female		Male	
			Control	Treatment	Control	Treatment
High	Poor	Mean	3	6	3	3
		λ	0	0	0	0
	Good	Mean	5	9	5	5
		λ	−1	+5	−3	−1
Low	Poor	Mean	2	3	1	2
		λ	−1	+5	−3	−1
	Good	Mean	4	8	3	6
		λ	0	0	0	0

to find

$$= \sqrt{\frac{18.00}{18.00 + 1.00(3)}} = .93.$$

We could also have computed $r_{alerting|NS}$ directly by finding the correlation between the contrast weights for female patients in Table 4.18 and their associated means after the row means (i.e., the means of the levels of the nonsubstantive factor) are subtracted from each of the original condition means. For the data in Table 4.18, the adjusted means and their associated λs are

| Means | −1.5 | +1.5 | −2 | +2 | −.5 | +.5 | −2 | +2 |
| λs | −1 | +1 | −1 | +1 | −1 | +1 | −1 | +1 |

and the correlation between these means and their λs is $r_{alerting|NS} = .93$.

Set-Asides in Nonsubstantive Factors

Table 4.20 shows the same means as those in Table 4.18, but with different contrast weights. In the present analysis, we wish to examine our contrast (with weights of −1, +5, −3, −1) at only two of the four levels of the nonsubstantive factor, with the other levels set aside by means of contrast weights of 0. Table 4.21 shows the analysis of variance of the data in Table 4.20 setting aside the two levels of the nonsubstantive factor with weights of 0.

It should be noted that Table 4.21 shows a substantive factor with 3 degrees of freedom representing the four columns of Table 4.20. The labeling of these

TABLE 4.21
Analysis of Variance of the Data of Table 4.20 after λs of 0 Are Set Aside

Source	SS	df	MS	F	p
Between	92	7	13.14	6.57	.00091
Substantive	22	3	7.33	3.67	.035
(Contrast)	(21.78)	(1)	(21.78)	(10.89)	(.0045)
Nonsubstantive	64	1	64.00	32.00	.000036
Subst. × nonsubst.	6	3	2.00	1.00	.42
Within	16	8[a]	2.00		
Total	108	15			

[a] Represents the degrees of freedom found in the conditions remaining after the set-asides associated with $\lambda = 0$. For computing significance levels, however, we use the degrees of freedom of the original design, 16, associated with the MS_{within} of the original design.

four columns in Table 4.20 shows that we could equally well have regarded them as representing a 2 × 2 factorial arrangement of two levels of treatment crossed by two levels of sex of patient. Nothing would be gained by this arrangement, however, because our contrast weights show that our prediction is not specifically about a main effect of treatment, a main effect of sex, and a treatment × sex interaction. Accordingly, we regard the four columns of our substantive factor as a single factor.

Significance Levels. We compute the value of $MS_{contrast}$ from Equation 3.1 and find

$$MS_{contrast} = \frac{nL^2}{\Sigma\lambda^2} = \frac{2(28)^2}{72} = 21.78.$$

Table 4.21 shows MS_{within} to be 2.00, so $F_{contrast} = 21.78/2.00 = 10.89$, for which p would be .011 for 1 and 8 degrees of freedom. However, for purposes of computing significance levels, we could assume that the within mean square for the design with the set-asides is the same as that of the original design with the original degrees of freedom. Table 4.13 shows the original within mean square is 2.00 with associated degrees of freedom of 16. The p value for an F of 10.89 with 1 and 16 degrees of freedom is .0045, as shown in Table 4.21.

Effect Size Estimation: Primary and Secondary Quantities. The primary quantities required to compute our various effect size correlations for the data in Tables 4.20 and 4.21 are as follows:

$SS_{between}$ = 92.00
$MS_{contrast}$ = 21.78
MS_{within} = 2.00

$$SS_{NS} = 64.00$$
$$df_{between} = 7$$
$$df_{noncontrast} = 6$$
$$df_{NS} = 1$$
$$df_{NC|NS} = 5$$
$$df_{within} = 8$$

Note that, for purposes of effect size estimation, the appropriate degrees of freedom for the within mean square are based only on the conditions remaining after we have set aside some of the conditions of the original design.

From the primary quantities just given, we can obtain the necessary secondary quantities: $F_{contrast}$, $F_{noncontrast}$, and $F_{NC|NS}$. For the data in Table 4.20 and 4.21, the values of these quantities and how they were obtained are as follows:

$$F_{contrast} = MS_{contrast}/MS_{within} = 21.78/2.00 = 10.89,$$

$$F_{noncontrast} = \frac{(SS_{between} - MS_{contrast})/df_{noncontrast}}{MS_{within}},$$

$$= \frac{(92.00 - 21.78)/6}{2.00} = 5.85,$$

$$F_{NC|NS} = \frac{(SS_{between} - MS_{contrast} - SS_{NS})/df_{NC|NS}}{MS_{within}}$$

$$= \frac{(92.00 - 21.78 - 64.00)/5}{2.00} = 0.62.$$

Effect Size Correlations. In our discussion of set-asides in substantive factors a bit earlier, we gave all the details required to calculate the various effect size correlations. In this section, therefore, we simply report the computations for each of these correlations for the data in Tables 4.20 and 4.21:

$$r_{contrast} = \sqrt{\frac{10.89}{10.89 + 8}} = .76,$$

$$r_{effect\ size} = \sqrt{\frac{10.89}{10.89 + 5.85(6) + 8}} = .45,$$

$$r_{effect\ size|NS} = \sqrt{\frac{10.89}{10.89 + 0.62(5) + 8}} = .70,$$

$$r_{BESD} = \sqrt{\frac{10.89}{10.89 + 1.00(5 + 8)}} = .68.$$

(Note that since the value of $F_{NC|NS}$ is less than 1.00, we have replaced the value of $F_{NC|NS} = 0.62$ by the value 1.00, as required in the computation of r_{BESD}.)

$$r_{BESD\ counternull} = \sqrt{\frac{4(.68)^2}{1 + 3(.68)^2}} = .88,$$

$$r_{alerting} = \sqrt{\frac{10.89}{10.89 + 5.85(6)}} = .49,$$

$$r_{alerting|NS} = \sqrt{\frac{10.89}{10.89 + 0.62(5)}} = .88.$$

Set-Asides in Both Substantive and Nonsubstantive Factors

Table 4.22 shows the same means as those in Table 4.20, but with different contrast weights. In the present analysis, our substantive contrast has weights of −1, +2, 0, −1 with the weight of 0 intended to serve as a set-aside. Suppose, for example, that it were already well known that the untreated male patients did very poorly, and that we wanted primarily to learn whether the treated females fared better than either the untreated females or the treated males. This situation would suggest the contrast weights shown in the first, third, and fourth rows of Table 4.22. Suppose further, however, that highly educated patients in good general health were unlikely to require treatment and that we wanted, therefore, to set their data aside in the present contrast. The row of zero λ weights in Table 4.22 reflects this decision. For Table 4.22, then, all the λs of 0 are intended as set-asides. Table 4.23

TABLE 4.22
Means and Contrast Weights: Set-Asides in Both Substantive and Nonsubstantive Factors

| Level of education | General health | | Sex of patient | | | |
| | | | Female | | Male | |
			Control	Treatment	Control	Treatment
High	Poor	Mean	3	6	3	3
		λ	−1	+2	0	−1
	Good	Mean	5	9	5	5
		λ	0	0	0	0
Low	Poor	Mean	2	3	1	2
		λ	−1	+2	0	−1
	Good	Mean	4	8	3	6
		λ	−1	+2	0	−1

TABLE 4.23
Analysis of Variance of the Data of Table 4.22 after λs of 0 Are Set Aside

Source	SS	df	MS	F	p
Between	69.78	8	8.72	4.36	.0059
Substantive	23.111	2	11.56	5.78	.013
(Contrast)	(21.777)	(1)	(21.78)	(10.89)	(.0045)
Nonsubstantive	40.444	2	20.22	10.11	.0015
Subst. × nonsubst.	6.222	4	1.56	0.78	.55
Within	18.00	9[a]	2.00		
Total	87.78	17			

[a] Represents the degrees of freedom found in the conditions remaining after the set-asides associated with $\lambda = 0$. For computing significance levels, however, we use the degrees of freedom of the original design, 16, associated with the MS_{within} of the original design.

shows the analysis of variance of the data in Table 4.22, setting aside one level of a substantive factor and one level of a nonsubstantive factor.

Significance Levels. We compute $MS_{contrast}$ as before and find

$$MS_{contrast} = \frac{nL^2}{\Sigma \lambda_i^2} = \frac{2(14)^2}{18} = 21.78.$$

Table 4.23 shows this value of $MS_{contrast}$, the associated value of $F_{contrast}$, and the associated p of .0045 for 1 and 16 degrees of freedom. As before, recall that for purposes of computing significance levels, we assume that the within mean square for the design with the set-asides is the same as that of the original design with the original degrees of freedom. Table 4.13 shows the original within mean square is 2.00 with associated degrees of freedom of 16. The p value for an F of 10.89 with 1 and 16 degrees of freedom is .0045, as shown in Table 4.23.

Effect Size Estimation: Primary and Secondary Quantities. The primary quantities required to compute our various effect size correlations for the data in Tables 4.22 and 4.23 are as follows:

$SS_{between} = 69.78$
$MS_{contrast} = 21.78$
$MS_{within} = 2.00$
$SS_{NS} = 40.44$
$df_{between} = 8$
$df_{noncontrast} = 7$
$df_{NS} = 2$
$df_{NC|NS} = 5$

Note that, as before, for purposes of effect size estimation, the appropriate degrees of freedom for the within mean square are based only on the conditions remaining after we have set aside some of the conditions of the original design.

From the primary quantities just given, we can obtain the necessary secondary quantities of $F_{contrast}$, $F_{noncontrast}$, and $F_{NC|NS}$. Using the equations given a few pages ago in our discussion of set-asides in nonsubstantive factors, we find the following values:

$$F_{contrast} = \frac{21.78}{2.00} = 10.89,$$

$$F_{noncontrast} = \frac{(69.78 - 21.78)/7}{2} = 3.43,$$

$$F_{NC|NS} = \frac{(69.78 - 21.78 - 40.44)/5}{2.00} = 0.76.$$

Effect Size Correlations. In our discussion of set-asides in substantive factors, we gave all the details required to calculate the various effect size correlations. In this section, as in the last section, therefore, we simply report the computations for each of these correlations for the data in Tables 4.22 and 4.23:

$$r_{contrast} = \sqrt{\frac{10.89}{10.89 + 9}} = .74,$$

$$r_{effect\ size} = \sqrt{\frac{10.89}{10.89 + 3.43(7) + 9}} = .50,$$

$$r_{effect\ size|NS} = \sqrt{\frac{10.89}{10.89 + 0.76(5) + 9}} = .68,$$

$$r_{BESD} = \sqrt{\frac{10.89}{10.89 + 1.00(5 + 9)}} = .66.$$

(Note that since the value of $F_{NC|NS}$ is less than 1.00, we have replaced the value of $F_{NC|NS} = 0.76$ by the value 1.00, as required in the computation of r_{BESD}.)

$$r_{BESD\ counternull} = \sqrt{\frac{4(.66)^2}{1 + 3(.66)^2}} = .87,$$

$$r_{alerting} = \sqrt{\frac{10.89}{10.89 + 3.43(7)}} = .56,$$

$$r_{alerting|NS} = \sqrt{\frac{10.89}{10.89 + 0.76(5)}} = .86.$$

EXTENSION TO UNEQUAL SAMPLE SIZES IN FACTORIAL DESIGNS

The results presented so far in this chapter are for the situation of equal sample sizes in all conditions or groups of a factorial design and an approximately normally distributed outcome. In this section, we extend these results to factorial designs with unequal-size conditions or groups with an approximately normally distributed outcome.

As was the case in our discussion of unequal sample sizes in one-way contrast analyses, we assume that had investigators had a choice, they would have chosen equal rather than unequal sample sizes. This assumption has no effect on the computation of significance levels. However, when computing estimates of effect sizes, we will obtain different results depending on whether we assume that equal sample sizes would have been preferred had they been possible, because different relative sample sizes represent different target populations.

Obtaining Significance Levels

The procedures for obtaining significance levels for contrasts with unequal sample sizes in the conditions of factorial designs are the same as those employed for contrasts in one-way contrast analyses. For example, consider the data in Table 4.4, for which Table 4.5 gives the predicted outcomes in raw points and in contrast weights. The total size of the study was $N = 120$ with equal numbers ($n = 10$) in each of the twelve conditions. Suppose instead that the sample sizes (n_i) had been as follows for each of the twelve conditions

	0	1	2	3
100 mg	1	5	2	1
50 mg	2	1	9	3
0 mg	3	53	38	2

We use Equation 3.24 to find

$$F_{contrast} = \frac{[\Sigma(M_i \lambda_i)]^2}{MS_{within}} \left[\frac{1}{\Sigma \frac{\lambda_i^2}{n_i}} \right].$$

We compute first

$$\Sigma M_i \lambda_i = (3)(-1) + (10)(+1) + (9)(+3) + (12)(+5) + (1)(-3) + (4)(-1)$$
$$+ (8)(+1) + (9)(+3) + (1)(-5) + (4)(-3) + (6)(-1) + (5)(+1)$$
$$= 104$$

and then

$$\Sigma \frac{\lambda_i^2}{n_i} = \frac{(-1)^2}{1} + \frac{(+1)^2}{5} + \frac{(+3)^2}{2} + \frac{(+5)^2}{1} + \frac{(-3)^2}{2} + \frac{(-1)^2}{1} + \frac{(+1)^2}{9} + \frac{(+3)^2}{3}$$
$$+ \frac{(-5)^2}{3} + \frac{(-3)^2}{53} + \frac{(-1)^2}{38} + \frac{(+1)^2}{2} = 48.34.$$

Then we find

$$F_{contrast} = \frac{(104)^2}{25}\left[\frac{1}{48.34}\right] = 8.95,$$

with 1 and 108 degrees of freedom, so $p = .0034$.

An alternative computational procedure is based on Equation 3.25,

$$F_{contrast} = \bar{F}_{contrast}\frac{n_h^\lambda}{\bar{n}},$$

where $\bar{F}_{contrast}$ is computed from the standard equal-n equation for F, but with the quantity n replaced by $\bar{n}$, the average of all the k sample sizes ($\bar{n} = (1/k)\sum n_i$; Equation 3.26 gives

$$\bar{F}_{contrast} = \frac{[\sum(M_i\lambda_i)]^2}{MS_{within}}\left[\frac{1}{(\sum\lambda_i^2)/\bar{n}}\right],$$

and where, from Equation 3.27,

$$n_h^\lambda = \frac{\sum\lambda_i^2}{\sum\left(\frac{\lambda_i^2}{n_i}\right)},$$

is the λ^2-weighted harmonic mean of the sample sizes; $n_h^\lambda/\bar{n}$ is the "power-loss" index for this contrast, which can be either less than or greater than 1.00. In the present example, based on Table 4.4 with the very unequal sample sizes given above, we find

$$\bar{F}_{contrast} = \frac{(104)^2}{25}\left[\frac{1}{\frac{92}{10}}\right] = 47.03,$$

$$\bar{n} = (1/k)\sum n_i = (1/12)(1+5+2+1+2+1+9+3+3+53+38+2)$$
$$= (1/12)120 = 10,$$

and

$$n_h^\lambda = \frac{\sum\lambda_i^2}{\sum\left(\frac{\lambda_i^2}{n_i}\right)} = \frac{92}{48.34} = 1.903.$$

Then, from Equation 3.25, we find

$$F_{contrast} = \bar{F}_{contrast}\frac{n_h^\lambda}{\bar{n}} = 47.03\left(\frac{1.903}{10}\right) = 8.95,$$

the same value obtained from Equation 3.24.

We could also have obtained the significance level of our contrast based on unequal sample sizes from Equation 3.29:

$$t_{contrast} = \frac{\Sigma(M_i \lambda_i)}{\sqrt{MS_{within} \Sigma \frac{\lambda_i^2}{n_i}}},$$

which is simply the square root of Equation 3.24. The degrees of freedom for t, and for the denominator of its square, $F_{contrast}$, are the degrees of freedom in MS_{within}. For the present example,

$$t_{contrast} = \frac{104}{\sqrt{25(48.34)}} = 2.99,$$

with degrees of freedom = 108 and $p = .0017$, one-tailed.

Effect Size Estimation with No Nonsubstantive Factors

As stated earlier, the effect sizes we want to estimate in most behavioral research are those we would expect to find in a replication study that used equal sample sizes across all groups. In such a replication, we would expect to see essentially the same means and variances as those found in our study with unequal sample sizes.

To compute our four correlations, therefore, we need only to calculate the equal-n quantities $F_{contrast}$ and $F_{noncontrast}$ of the equations in Table 3.6, using the observed means and variances, but with n (the common sample size) replaced by $\bar{n}$ (the average sample size).

Thus, where

$$F_{contrast} = \frac{MS_{contrast}}{MS_{within}}$$

and

$$MS_{contrast} = \frac{nL^2}{\Sigma \lambda_i^2},$$

as shown in Equation 3.1, we need only replace the quantity n of the numerator of Equation 3.1 by $\bar{n}$ (the average sample size of the k conditions of our study) to obtain $\bar{F}_{contrast}$ of Equation 3.26:

$$\bar{F}_{contrast} = \frac{\bar{n} L^2 / \Sigma \lambda_i^2}{MS_{within}}. \tag{4.8}$$

With unequal sample sizes, n_i, we can also obtain $\bar{F}_{contrast}$ directly from $F_{contrast}$, the F computed from unequal sample sizes (for significance testing) by the following rearrangement of Equation 3.25, given by Equation 3.30:

$$\bar{F}_{contrast} = F_{contrast} \frac{\bar{n}}{n_h^\lambda}.$$

For our present example we found that $\bar{F}_{contrast} = 47.03$, the same value we found for $F_{contrast}$ in our earlier analysis of these data of Table 4.4 when sample sizes were equal. Analogously, we find $\bar{F}_{noncontrast}$ to be the value we obtained earlier from Equation 3.6 when our sample sizes were equal (i.e., $\bar{F}_{noncontrast} = 0.98$). The degrees of freedom for noncontrast are obtained from Equation 4.1 (i.e., $df_{noncontrast} = df_{between} - 1 = 11 - 1 = 10$) for the present example. We now have all the ingredients required to compute our basic effect size correlations. From the equations in Table 3.6, with $\bar{F}$ replacing F, we find

$$r_{alerting} = \sqrt{\frac{\bar{F}_{contrast}}{\bar{F}_{contrast} + \bar{F}_{noncontrast}(df_{noncontrast})}}$$

$$= \sqrt{\frac{47.03}{47.03 + 0.98(10)}} = .91;$$

$$r_{contrast} = \sqrt{\frac{\bar{F}_{contrast}}{\bar{F}_{contrast} + df_{within}}}$$

$$= \sqrt{\frac{47.03}{47.03 + 108}} = .55;$$

$$r_{effect\ size} = \sqrt{\frac{\bar{F}_{contrast}}{\bar{F}_{contrast} + \bar{F}_{noncontrast}(df_{noncontrast}) + df_{within}}}$$

$$= \sqrt{\frac{47.03}{47.03 + 0.98(10) + 108}} = .53;$$

and

$$r_{BESD} = \sqrt{\frac{\bar{F}_{contrast}}{\bar{F}_{contrast} + \bar{F}_{noncontrast}(df_{noncontrast} + df_{within})}}$$

$$= \sqrt{\frac{47.03}{47.03 + 1.00(10 + 108)}} = .53.$$

Note that because $\bar{F}_{noncontrast}$ is less than 1.00, we enter the value 1.00 in the computation of r_{BESD}. As is usual when we compute r_{BESD}, we also report $r_{BESD\ counternull}$ from Equation 2.16:

$$r_{BESD\ counternull} = \sqrt{\frac{4r_{BESD}^2}{1 + 3r_{BESD}^2}}$$

$$= \sqrt{\frac{4(.53)^2}{1 + 3(.53)^2}} = .78,$$

with its associated p value of .0034.

Effect Size Estimation in the Presence of Nonsubstantive Factors

For our example, we return to the data in Table 4.4 (with the same means as Table 4.1), but this time we regard medication dosage levels as a nonsubstantive factor. Our contrast weights reflect the nonsubstantive nature of the dosage-levels factor in that our contrast weights are identical from level to level of that factor; these are the weights we used in our analysis of the data of Table 4.1:

	0	1	2	3
100 mg	−3	−1	+1	+3
50 mg	−3	−1	+1	+3
0 mg	−3	−1	+1	+3

The sample sizes corresponding to each of these conditions are

	0	1	2	3
100 mg	1	5	2	1
50 mg	2	1	9	3
0 mg	3	53	38	2

Obtaining Significance Levels. We obtain significance levels just as we would in one-way contrast analyses. We use Equation 3.24 to find

$$F_{contrast} = \frac{[\Sigma(M_i \lambda_i)]^2}{MS_{within}} \left[\frac{1}{\Sigma \frac{\lambda_i^2}{n_i}} \right].$$

We compute first

$$\Sigma M_i \lambda_i = (3)(-3) + (10)(-1) + (9)(+1) + (12)(+3) + (1)(-3) + 4(-1)$$
$$+ (8)(+1) + (9)(+3) + (1)(-3) + (4)(-1) + (6)(+1) + (5)(+3)$$
$$= 68,$$

and then

$$\Sigma \frac{\lambda_i^2}{n_i} = \frac{(-3)^2}{1} + \frac{(-1)^2}{5} + \frac{(+1)^2}{2} + \frac{(+3)^2}{1} + \frac{(-3)^2}{2} + \frac{(-1)^2}{1} + \frac{(+1)^2}{9} + \frac{(+3)^2}{3}$$
$$+ \frac{(-3)^2}{3} + \frac{(-1)^2}{53} + \frac{(+1)^2}{38} + \frac{(+3)^2}{2} = 34.86.$$

Then we find

$$F_{contrast} = \frac{(68)^2}{25} \left[\frac{1}{34.86} \right] = 5.31,$$

with 1 and 108 degrees of freedom, so $p = .023$.

An alternative computational procedure is based on Equation 3.25,

$$F_{contrast} = \bar{F}_{contrast} \frac{n_h^\lambda}{\bar{n}},$$

where $\bar{F}_{contrast}$ is computed from the standard equal-n equation for F, but with the quantity n replaced by $\bar{n}$, the average of all the k sample sizes ($\bar{n} = (1/k)\Sigma n_i$). Equation 3.26 gives

$$\bar{F}_{contrast} = \frac{[\Sigma(M_i\lambda_i)]^2}{MS_{within}} \left[\frac{1}{(\Sigma\lambda_i^2)/\bar{n}} \right],$$

and Equation 3.27 gives

$$n_h^\lambda = \frac{\Sigma\lambda_i^2}{\Sigma\left(\frac{\lambda_i^2}{n_i}\right)},$$

which is the λ^2-weighted harmonic mean of the sample sizes. In the present example, based on Table 4.4 with the very unequal sample sizes given above, we find

$$\bar{F}_{contrast} = \frac{(68)^2}{25} \left[\frac{1}{\frac{60}{10}} \right] = 30.83,$$

$$\bar{n} = (1/k)\Sigma n_i = (1/12)(1 + 5 + 2 + 1 + 2 + 1 + 9 + 3 + 3 + 53 + 38 + 2)$$

$$= (1/12)120 = 10,$$

and

$$n_h^\lambda = \frac{\Sigma\lambda_i^2}{\Sigma\left(\frac{\lambda_i^2}{n_i}\right)} = \frac{60}{34.86} = 1.721.$$

Then, from Equation 3.25, we find

$$F_{contrast} = \bar{F}_{contrast} \frac{n_h^\lambda}{\bar{n}} = 30.83 \left(\frac{1.721}{10} \right) = 5.31,$$

the same value obtained from Equation 3.24. In this example, the power-loss index, $n_h^\lambda/\bar{n} = 1.721/10 = .17$, which is a substantial loss of power for this contrast due to the nonconstant sample sizes.

We could also have obtained the significance level of our contrast based on unequal sample sizes from Equation 3.29:

$$t_{contrast} = \frac{\Sigma(M_i\lambda_i)}{\sqrt{MS_{within}\Sigma\frac{\lambda_i^2}{n_i}}},$$

which is simply the square root of Equation 3.24. The degrees of freedom for t, and for the denominator of its square, $F_{contrast}$, are the degrees of freedom in MS_{within}. For the present example,

$$t_{contrast} = \frac{68}{\sqrt{25(34.86)}} = 2.30,$$

with degrees of freedom = 108 and $p = .012$, one-tailed.

Effect Size Estimation. Just as was the case earlier, the effect sizes we want to estimate are those we would expect to find in a replication study that uses equal sample sizes across all groups. In such a replication, we would expect to see essentially the same means and variances as those found in our study with unequal sample sizes.

To compute our effect size correlations, therefore, we need only to calculate the equal-n quantities $F_{contrast}$ and $F_{noncontrast}$ of the equations in Table 3.6 and Equations 4.5, 4.6, and 4.7 using the observed means and variances, but with n (the common sample size) replaced by $\bar{n}$ (the *average* sample size).

Therefore, since

$$F_{contrast} = \frac{MS_{contrast}}{MS_{within}}$$

and

$$MS_{contrast} = \frac{nL^2}{\Sigma \lambda_i^2}$$

(from Equation 3.1), we simply replace the quantity n of the numerator of Equation 3.1 by $\bar{n}$ (the average sample size of the k conditions of our study), to obtain $\bar{F}_{contrast}$ of Equation 4.8:

$$\bar{F}_{contrast} = \frac{\bar{n}L^2 / \Sigma \lambda_i^2}{MS_{within}}.$$

As we saw earlier, with unequal sample sizes, n_i, we can obtain $\bar{F}_{contrast}$ directly from $F_{contrast}$ (the F computed using unequal sample sizes for obtaining significance levels) from Equation 3.30:

$$\bar{F}_{contrast} = F_{contrast} \frac{\bar{n}}{n_h^\lambda}.$$

For our present example, we found that $\bar{F}_{contrast} = 30.83$, the same value we found for $F_{contrast}$ in an earlier analysis of these same data shown in Table 4.1 when sample sizes were equal. Analogously, we find $\bar{F}_{noncontrast}$ from Equation 3.6,

$$\bar{F}_{noncontrast} = \frac{(SS_{between} - MS_{contrast})/df_{noncontrast}}{MS_{within}}$$

$$= \frac{(1420 - 770.67)/10}{25.00} = 2.60,$$

or from Equation 3.7,

$$\bar{F}_{noncontrast} = \frac{F_{between}(df_{between}) - F_{contrast}}{df_{noncontrast}}$$

$$= \frac{5.164(11) - 30.83}{10} = 2.60.$$

We select Equation 3.6 or 3.7, depending on which required quantities are more readily at hand. The degrees of freedom for noncontrast are obtained from Equation 4.1 (i.e., $df_{noncontrast} = df_{between} - 1 = 11 - 1 = 10$) for the present example. We now have most of the ingredients required to compute our basic effect size correlations. Still needed is the quantity $\bar{F}_{NC|NS}$, a quantity specific to designs and analyses employing nonsubstantive factors. We compute $\bar{F}_{NC|NS}$ from Equation 4.2, assuming all sample sizes have been set at $\bar{n}$:

$$F_{NC|NS} = \frac{(SS_{between} - MS_{contrast} - SS_{NS})/df_{NC|NS}}{MS_{within}},$$

where SS_{NS} is the sum of squares due to nonsubstantive factors, df_{NS} is their associated degrees of freedom, and

$$df_{NC|NS} = df_{between} - 1 - df_{NS} \tag{4.3}$$

$$= df_{noncontrast} - df_{NS}. \tag{4.4}$$

For the present data, we find $df_{NS} = 2$, $df_{NC|NS} = df_{between} - 1 - df_{NS} = 11 - 1 - 2 = 8$, and

$$\bar{F}_{NC|NS} = \frac{(1{,}420 - 770.67 - 420)/8}{25} = 1.15.$$

Effect Size Correlations: No Adjustment for Nonsubstantive Factors. In this section, we present the effect size correlations for the contrast we have been considering *without* adjusting for nonsubstantive factors. From Equations 3.17, 3.12, and 3.13, respectively, replacing F by $\bar{F}$, we have

$$r_{alerting} = \sqrt{\frac{\bar{F}_{contrast}}{\bar{F}_{contrast} + \bar{F}_{noncontrast}(df_{noncontrast})}}$$

$$= \sqrt{\frac{30.83}{30.83 + 2.60(10)}} = .74;$$

$$r_{contrast} = \sqrt{\frac{\bar{F}_{contrast}}{\bar{F}_{contrast} + df_{within}}}$$

$$= \sqrt{\frac{30.83}{30.83 + 108}} = .47;$$

and

$$r_{effect\ size} = \sqrt{\frac{\bar{F}_{contrast}}{\bar{F}_{contrast} + \bar{F}_{noncontrast}(df_{noncontrast}) + df_{within}}}$$

$$= \sqrt{\frac{30.83}{30.83 + 2.60(10) + 108}} = .43.$$

Effect Size Correlations with Adjustments for Nonsubstantive Factors. In this section, we present the effect size correlations for the contrast we have been considering, with the appropriate adjustments for the nonsubstantive factor of our design. There are three such effect size correlations: $r_{effect\ size|NS}$ (Equation 4.5), r_{BESD} (Equation 4.6), and $r_{alerting|NS}$ (Equation 4.7). Recall that r_{BESD} is defined as always adjusting for the nonsubstantive factor. For the present contrast, the three effect size correlations are as follows:

$$r_{effect\ size|NS} = \sqrt{\frac{\bar{F}_{contrast}}{\bar{F}_{contrast} + \bar{F}_{NC|NS}(df_{NC|NS}) + df_{within}}}$$

$$= \sqrt{\frac{30.83}{30.83 + 1.15(8) + 108}} = .46;$$

$$r_{BESD} = \sqrt{\frac{\bar{F}_{contrast}}{\bar{F}_{contrast} + \bar{F}_{NC|NS}(df_{NC|NS} + df_{within})}}$$

$$= \sqrt{\frac{30.83}{30.83 + 1.15(8 + 108)}} = .43;$$

$$r_{alerting|NS} = \sqrt{\frac{\bar{F}_{contrast}}{\bar{F}_{contrast} + \bar{F}_{NC|NS}(df_{NC|NS})}}$$

$$= \sqrt{\frac{30.83}{30.83 + 1.15(8)}} = .88.$$

The adjusted effect size correlations, $r_{effect\ size|NS}$ and $r_{alerting|NS}$, are almost always larger than their unadjusted counterparts, but the differences are larger when the sum of squares associated with the nonsubstantive factor represents a larger proportion of the overall between sum of squares.

PREVIEW

This chapter described contrasts in factorial designs. In these designs, all factors are between-subjects factors (i.e., each subject contributed only a single score to the study). In the next chapter, however, each subject contributes two or more scores to the study.

REVIEW QUESTIONS

1. In a test of a new incentive program for improving morale in a company, samples of day shift and night shift workers are assigned to one of four levels of incentive, designated as 0, 1, 2, 3, with ten workers randomly assigned to each cell of this 2×4 between-subjects design ($N = 80$). The mean scores on morale (representing a composite score of self-ratings) appear in the table.

   | | Level of incentive | | | | |
Work group	0	1	2	3	Mean
Day shift	1	3	5	6	3.750
Night shift	1	2	4	5	3.000
Mean	1.0	2.5	4.5	5.5	3.375

   Suppose the hypothesis of interest was that there is a positive linear trend in level of incentive, which can be represented by weights of $-3, -1, +1, +3$. How can we compute the $MS_{contrast}$ using the sums of squares of the rows, columns, and interaction and then examine our hypothesis by means of F?

   Answer: One possibility is to correlate the linear weights with all eight cell means, which will give us an alerting r. That is, we correlate -3 with 1 (row 1, column 1) and 1 (row 2, column 1), -1 with 3 (row 1, column 2) and 2 (row 2, column 2), and so on, which gives us $r_{alerting} = .9636$. We then square this value and multiply the result ($r^2_{alerting} = .9285$) by the $SS_{between}$ based on $SS_{rows} + SS_{columns} + SS_{interaction}$ to obtain $MS_{contrast}$. Alternatively, we can correlate the four linear weights with the four column means, that is, -3 with 1.0, -1 with 2.5, $+1$ with 4.5, and $+3$ with 5.5. Now we have $r_{alerting} = .9928$, and because this value was carved out of the column means, we will multiply $r^2_{alerting} = .9856$ by $SS_{columns}$ to obtain our $MS_{contrast}$. Either way, the result is the same, but we must remember to align our $r^2_{alerting}$ with its appropriate sum of squares. To examine our hypothesis using F, we then divide the $MS_{contrast}$ by the pooled S^2 (i.e., MS_{within}).

2. In this chapter the $r_{contrast}$ is referred to as a "maximally partialed correlation." What does this mean in the case of a factorial design?

   Answer: The $r_{contrast}$ denotes the correlation between the outcome scores or scores on the dependent variable (i.e., the individual scores, which we can symbolize as Y scores) and the contrast coefficients (λ) associated with each score or condition, with the proviso that the noncontrast variation (NC) is removed. Another way of symbolizing $r_{contrast}$ would be as $r_{Y\lambda \cdot NC}$ (Rosnow & Rosenthal, 1997), and in this chapter, we showed how to adjust the values of Y for the removed noncontrast variation. Correlating these adjusted values with their associated contrast weights was another way of computing $r_{contrast}$ (i.e., $r_{Y\lambda \cdot NC}$).

3. Returning to the table of means in Question 1, suppose we had predicted not only that the level of morale will improve with higher levels of incentives, but also that working the day shift (as opposed to the night shift) will be associated with a higher level of morale. How can we now create contrast weights to test this prediction?

Answer: Now the assumption is that the row factor and the column factor are additive. To create our contrast weights, we award one point more for the day shift and one point more for each increase in the level of incentive. Applying this rule gives us the following allocation of points:

	Level of incentive				
Work group	0	1	2	3	Mean
Day shift	2	3	4	5	3.5
Night shift	1	2	3	4	2.5
Mean	1.5	2.5	3.5	4.5	3.0

To make these scores into contrast weights so that $\Sigma\lambda = 0$, we simply subtract the grand mean of 3.0 from each score; the result is the following table of lambda (λ) weights:

	Level of incentive			
Work group	0	1	2	3
Day shift	−1	0	+1	+2
Night shift	−2	−1	0	+1

4. Let's change the hypothesis once again and suppose that the shift the subjects work is of no interest. All that interests us is that the predicted increase in morale occurred as a result of the increase in incentive level. How should we think of the $r_{\text{effect size}}$ in this case?

Answer: Because the row factor is "nonsubstantive" (i.e., of no interest), the $r_{\text{effect size}}$ in which we are interested will focus only on the column factor, and the nonsubstantive row factor is eliminated from the equation for $r_{\text{effect size}|NS}$ (i.e., effect size correlation adjusted for removal of nonsubstantive factor), this value is calculated from Equation 4.5:

$$r_{\text{effect size}|NS} = \sqrt{\frac{F_{\text{contrast}}}{F_{\text{contrast}} + F_{NC|NS}(df_{NC|NS}) + df_{\text{within}}}},$$

and from Equation 4.2, we find

$$F_{NC|NS} = \frac{(SS_{\text{between}} - MS_{\text{contrast}} - SS_{NS})/df_{NC|NS}}{MS_{\text{within}}},$$

where $df_{NC|NS}$ is defined in either Equation 4.3 or 4.4.

5. Suppose we had a factorial design with four between-subjects factors, unequal cell means, and an overall prediction involving all the cell means. How can we test this prediction?

Answer: No matter how many factors are operating, and regardless of whether there are equal or unequal ns in the cells, we can think of the design as a one-way layout and then apply the procedure that is most appropriate, as described in the previous chapters.

6. How should we interpret the meaning of an $r_{BESD} = .30$ if the factor of interest has more than two levels and other factors are of no interest whatsoever? How can we find the counternull value of this r_{BESD}, and what does it tell us?

Answer: We view the factors that are of no interest as "nonsubstantive," and the r_{BESD} is therefore defined in Equation 4.6 as

$$r_{BESD} = \sqrt{\frac{F_{contrast}}{F_{contrast} + F_{NC|NS}(df_{NC|NS} + df_{within})}},$$

which refers to the difference in the rate of responding between $-1\sigma_\lambda$ and $+1\sigma_\lambda$ that we would expect in a replication with one substantive factor, where

$$\sigma_\lambda = \sqrt{\frac{\Sigma \lambda_i^2}{k}},$$

and k = number of conditions or levels of the substantive factor. So in this example, with $r_{BESD} = .30$, our binomial effect size display would be as follows:

	Rate of responding	
Substantive factor	**Above median**	**Below median**
Higher level ($+1\sigma_\lambda$)	65	35
Lower level ($-1\sigma_\lambda$)	35	65

To find the counternull value of $r_{BESD} = .30$, we substiute in Equation 2.16, which gives us:

$$r_{BESD\ counternull} = \sqrt{\frac{4r_{BESD}^2}{1 + 3r_{BESD}^2}} = \sqrt{\frac{4(.30)^2}{1 + 3(.30)^2}} = .53,$$

a value of r_{BESD} that is exactly as likely as an r_{BESD} value of .00

CHAPTER 5

Contrasts in Repeated Measures

The contrasts discussed in earlier chapters were from studies in which each subject contributed only a single score. In the present chapter, contrasts are from studies in which each subject contributes two or more scores. Such studies are often referred to as repeated measures studies because each subject is measured repeatedly. Two broad types of repeated measures studies can be distinguished: those that must be conducted as repeated measures studies and those that are conducted as repeated measures studies for reasons of design efficiency.

INTRINSICALLY REPEATED MEASURES STUDIES

In intrinsically repeated measures studies, the repeated measures are required in order to construct an outcome measure (or score) for each subject. For example, suppose we wanted to know whether individual females or individual males were more variable in the scores they earned on verbal, quantitative, and analytic subtests of the Graduate Record Examination. It would then be necessary to create an outcome measure that indexes the variability, for each subject, of the three scores earned on the three subtests. We might define variability for each subject by computing the range or the standard deviation of the three scores. This study would be a repeated measures study in the intrinsic sense because we could not have defined a sensible outcome measure indexing variability without obtaining repeated measures from each subject.

However, once we have created our new outcome measure of variability in this study of male-female differences, we address our basic question of sex differences in score variability by using the procedures in Chapter 2. If we wanted instead to learn whether there was a linear trend across several age groups in score variability, we would use the procedures in Chapter 3 on our newly created scores of variability. If we wanted to consider a contrast of our variability scores with several factors present, we would use the procedures in Chapter 4. In short, in studies that are intrinsically repeated measures designs, the repeated measures are used to create scores that are then analyzed by the between-subjects analyses in Chapters 2, 3, or 4. We now present examples of each such case.

TABLE 5.1
Three Repeated Measures with Associated Composite Scores for Four Female and Four Male Research Participants

	Measurements			Composite scores per subject		
	1	2	3	Sum	Standard deviation	Linear trend $(L)^a$
Females						
Person 1	3	5	6	14	1.53	+3
Person 2	2	4	5	11	1.53	+3
Person 3	1	3	6	10	2.52	+5
Person 4	4	5	6	15	1.00	+2
Sum	10	17	23	50	6.58	13
Mean	2.5	4.25	5.75	12.5	1.645	3.25
Males						
Person 5	1	6	7	14	3.21	+6
Person 6	3	8	6	17	2.52	+3
Person 7	2	8	5	15	3.00	+3
Person 8	3	9	6	18	3.00	+3
Sum	9	31	24	64	11.73	15
Mean	2.25	7.75	6.00	16.0	2.932	3.75

[a] Computed as $L = \Sigma(Y_i \lambda_i) = Y_1(-1) + Y_2(0) + Y_3(+1)$.

An Example with One Between-Subjects Factor with Two Levels

Table 5.1 shows three repeated measures for each of four female and four male research participants along with three *composite scores:* the sum of the three measurements, the standard deviation of the three measurements, and the linear trend "L score" using contrast weights of $-1, 0, +1$. (The construction of L scores will be discussed a little later.)

Suppose we have hypothesized that males' variability among their three measurements would be greater than females' variability among their three measurements. We can then obtain the level of significance and various effect size estimates associated with the difference between female and male participants by using the procedures described in Chapter 2, simply treating the second composite value in Table 5.1, the standard deviation, as the outcome measurement Y.

Obtaining Significance Levels. Equation 2.1 shows how we compute t comparing two groups with equal sample size:

$$t = \left(\frac{M_1 - M_2}{S_{within}}\right)\left(\frac{\sqrt{N}}{2}\right),$$

where M_1 and M_2 are the group means, N is the total number of sampling units with $n = N/2$ in each of the two groups, and S_{within} is the square root of the pooled estimate of the population variance computed from Equation 2.2 as

$$S^2_{within} = \frac{(n-1)S_1^2 + (n-1)S_2^2}{df_{within}},$$

where $df_{within} = N - 2$, S_1^2 is the usual unbiased estimate of within-group 1 variance (i.e., with denominator $n - 1$), and analogously for S_2^2. For the present data in Table 5.1, we find $S_1^2 = 0.4027$, $S_2^2 = 0.0854$, and

$$S^2_{within} = \frac{(4-1)0.4027 + (4-1)0.0854}{8 - 2} = 0.24405.$$

Then

$$t = \left(\frac{2.932 - 1.645}{\sqrt{0.24405}}\right)\left(\frac{\sqrt{8}}{2}\right) = 3.684,$$

which, with $N - 2 = 8 - 2 = 6$ degrees of freedom, has $p = .0051$. Note that the within-group variances (S_1^2 and S_2^2) of 0.4027 and 0.0854 appear to be rather different. This difference might be worrisome in certain situations but is of less concern in the present example for two reasons: (a) The two sample sizes are equal, and (b) the sample sizes are so small that the variance ratio might in fact be 1. Indeed, if we were to test the difference between these variances, we would find p to be substantially greater than .10 (i.e., .24).

Effect Size Correlation, $r_{contrast}$. The effect size correlation associated with the difference between two groups can be computed from Equation 2.3 in Chapter 2, which for the present example yields

$$r_{contrast} = \sqrt{\frac{t^2}{t^2 + df_{within}}} = \sqrt{\frac{(3.684)^2}{(3.684)^2 + 6}} = .833.$$

This effect size correlation is interpreted exactly as described in Chapter 2 and illustrated in Table 2.2, Y being the composite score. Note that in the two-group situation, there is no distinction between $r_{contrast}$, $r_{effect\ size}$, and r_{BESD}, and that we do not compute $r_{alerting}$ because it can take on only values of $+1.00$, 0.00, or -1.00.

Computing $r_{counternull}$. From Equation 2.16, we find the $r_{counternull}$ associated with our effect size correlation as follows:

$$r_{counternull} = \sqrt{\frac{4r^2}{1 + 3r^2}} = \sqrt{\frac{4(.833)^2}{1 + 3(.833)^2}} = .949.$$

Just as was the case in Chapter 2, we interpret the value of $r_{counternull}$ as indicating that the true value of the effect size correlation is just as likely to be .949 as .00. To aid in the interpretation of the practical importance of both the effect size correlation and its counternull value, we can display each one as a BESD. Table 5.2 shows the BESD based on the obtained result, the null result, and the counternull result, as well as the null-counternull interval.

TABLE 5.2
BESD Based on the Obtained Result, the Null Result, and the Counternull Result for Composite Scores in Table 5.1 (i.e., the Within-Subject Standard Deviation)

Null result	Obtained result	Counternull result
($r = .00$)	($r = .833$, $p = .010$, two-tailed)	($r = .949$)

	High	Lo			High	Low	Σ			High	Lo
Hi	50	50		Predicted high	92	8	100		Hi	97	3
Lo	50	50		Predicted low	8	92	100		Lo	3	97
				Σ	100	100	200				

99% Null-counternull interval

$r = .00$ $r = .949$

Note: The values shown in the BESD are rounded to avoid decimal values.

An Example with More Than Two Between-Subjects Groups

So far in our discussion of intrinsically repeated measures designs, we have restricted our discussion to the simple situation in which we want to compare the composite scores of just two groups, males and females in the previous example. It often happens, however, that there are three or more groups to be compared. Whenever there are three or more groups in a one-way layout, we can directly use the procedures described in Chapter 3, applying these procedures to the composite scores we have constructed for each subject, just as if the values of the composite score were directly observed values of the dependent variable. We compute contrasts among the three or more conditions of our one-way layout, obtain significance levels, and compute the various effect size correlations exactly as described in Chapter 3.

Table 5.3 shows four repeated measures for three children at each of three age levels, 8, 10, and 12, along with four composite scores: the sum of the four measurements; the standard deviation of the four scores; the linear trend L score employing contrast weights of $-3, -1, +1, +3$; and the correlation between the four scores and these contrast weights.

We have already seen an example using the standard deviation of a person's repeated measures as a composite score when we compared the variability of females' and males' scores on three subtests of the Graduate Record Examination.

Another composite score, a contrast score or "L score," is very commonly used in computing contrasts in repeated measures. Contrast (or L) scores for individuals

TABLE 5.3
Four Repeated Measures with Associated Composite Scores for Three Age Groups

	Measurements				Composite scores			
	1	2	3	4	Sum	σ	L	r
Age 8								
Child 1	3	2	3	3	11	.43	1	.26
Child 2	1	2	1	2	6	.50	2	.45
Child 3	4	5	5	5	19	.43	3	.77
Sum	8	9	9	10	36	1.36	6	1.48
Mean	2.67	3	3	3.33	12	.45	2	.49
S^2							1.00	.066
Age 10								
Child 4	4	5	4	6	19	.83	5	.67
Child 5	5	6	5	6	22	.50	2	.45
Child 6	5	7	6	7	25	.83	5	.67
Sum	14	18	15	19	66	2.16	12	1.79
Mean	4.67	6	5	6.33	22	.72	4	.60
S^2							3.00	.016
Age 12								
Child 7	6	6	7	8	27	.83	7	.94
Child 8	5	6	6	8	25	1.09	9	.92
Child 9	7	8	8	9	32	.71	6	.95
Sum	18	20	21	25	84	2.63	22	2.81
Mean	6	6.67	7	8.33	28	.88	7.33	.94
S^2							2.33	.0002
Grand sum	40	47	45	54	186	6.15	40	6.08
Grand mean	4.44	5.22	5	6	20.67	.68	4.44	.68
Mean S^2							2.11	.027

are computed from:

$$L = \Sigma (Y_i \lambda_i) = Y_1 \lambda_1 + Y_2 \lambda_2 + \cdots + Y_k \lambda_k. \tag{5.1}$$

The L scores given for each child in Table 5.3 are linear trend L scores because one research hypothesis held that children's performance would show linear improvement with practice in going from the first to the fourth measurement, with contrast weights of $-3, -1, +1, +3$. Accordingly, the linear trend L score for the 10-year-old Child 4 is

$$L = \Sigma(Y_i \lambda_i) = (4)(-3) + (5)(-1) + (4)(+1) + (6)(+3) = 5.$$

TABLE 5.4
A Comparison of L Scores and r Scores for Two Children

	Measurement				Composite	
	1	2	3	4	L	r
(λ)	(−3)	−1	+1	+3)		
Child A	1	8	2	9	18	.57
Child B	1	2	3	4	10	1.00

Especially when the number of repeated measures per person is large, it is often useful to compute the correlation (r score) between a person's scores (Y_i) and the contrast weights (λ_i) associated with each score. In Table 5.3 this correlation between scores and λ weights for Child 4 is .67.

L scores are more sensitive to the absolute value of the scores used, whereas r scores are more sensitive to the agreement in the patterning of scores and their associated λ weights. To illustrate this difference between L scores and r scores, consider two children (A and B) measured four times with the hypothesis that there will be a linear increase in performance. Table 5.4 shows that Child A shows better agreement (18) with the hypothesis than does Child B (10) when agreement is defined by the L score. However, when agreement is defined by the r score, Child B (1.00) shows better agreement than does Child A (.57). Which result is more meaningful will depend on the research question or hypothesis of interest. In the computational examples that follow, we use both the L scores and the r scores given in Table 5.3.

Obtaining Significance Levels. In the study shown in Table 5.3, the specific hypothesis was that the linear improvement with practice, expected for the study overall, would be more marked with increasing age. Thus the contrast weights associated with the three ages (8, 10, 12) are −1, 0, +1. First we compute $MS_{contrast}$ for the L scores using Equation 3.1:

$$MS_{contrast} = \frac{nL^2}{\Sigma \lambda_i^2} = \frac{3[(2)(-1) + (4)(0) + (7.33)(+1)]^2}{(-1)^2 + (0)^2 + (+1)^2}$$

$$= \frac{3(5.33)^2}{2} = 42.61.$$

Table 5.3 shows the MS_{within} (i.e., S^2) for the L scores to be 2.11, so that

$$F_{contrast} = \frac{MS_{contrast}}{MS_{within}} = \frac{42.61}{2.11} = 20.19.$$

This value of $F_{contrast}$, with degrees of freedom equal to 1 and 6, has $p = .0041$.

The analogous analysis for the r scores yields

$$MS_{contrast} = \frac{nL^2}{\Sigma\lambda_i^2} = \frac{3[(.49)(-1) + (.60)(0) + (.94)(+1)]^2}{(-1)^2 + (0)^2 + (+1)^2}$$

$$= \frac{3(.45)^2}{2} = .304.$$

Table 5.3 shows the MS_{within} (or S^2) for the r scores to be .027, so that

$$F_{contrast} = \frac{MS_{contrast}}{MS_{within}} = \frac{.304}{.027} = 11.26.$$

This value of $F_{contrast}$, with degrees of freedom equal to 1 and 6, has $p = .015$. Thus the analyses of both L scores and r scores support the prediction of increasing linearity of practice effects with increasing age. However, in this example, the value of F for L scores is substantially larger than the F for r scores.

Effect Size Correlation, $r_{contrast}$. We obtain the value of $r_{contrast}$ from Equation 3.2. For the $F_{contrast}$ for the L scores, we find

$$r_{contrast} = \sqrt{\frac{F_{contrast}}{F_{contrast} + df_{within}}} = \sqrt{\frac{20.19}{20.19 + 6}} = .878.$$

Analogously, for the r scores, we find

$$r_{contrast} = \sqrt{\frac{11.26}{11.26 + 6}} = .808,$$

a value lower than the $r_{contrast}$ for L scores but still of very substantial magnitude.

Effect Size Correlation, $r_{alerting}$. When there are three or more conditions, it is often useful to compute $r_{alerting}$, the correlation between the group means and their corresponding λ weights. For the data in Table 5.3, the values of $r_{alerting}$ are .990 and .959, respectively, for the L scores and the r scores. These high correlations indicate that the three mean L scores and the three mean r scores follow a fairly linear trend with age. However, we should not make too much of this very close fit when there are only three group means to be correlated with their corresponding λ weights. As the number of groups increases, so does the stability and interpretability of $r_{alerting}$.

Effect Size Correlation, $r_{effect\ size}$. We use Equation 3.13 to compute $r_{effect\ size}$ for the L score and r score data:

$$r_{effect\ size} = \sqrt{\frac{F_{contrast}}{F_{contrast} + F_{noncontrast}(df_{noncontrast}) + df_{within}}}$$

$$= \sqrt{\frac{20.19}{20.19 + 0.44(1) + 6}} = .871$$

for the L-score data and

$$r_{\text{effect size}} = \sqrt{\frac{11.26}{11.26 + 0.44(1) + 6}} = .798$$

for the r-score data.

Effect Size Correlation, r_{BESD}. We use Equation 3.15 to compute r_{BESD} for the L-score and r-score data:

$$r_{BESD} = \sqrt{\frac{F_{contrast}}{F_{contrast} + F_{noncontrast}(df_{noncontrast} + df_{within})}}$$

$$= \sqrt{\frac{20.19}{20.19 + 1.00(1 + 6)}} = .862$$

for the L-score data and

$$r_{BESD} = \sqrt{\frac{11.26}{11.26 + 1.00(1 + 6)}} = .785$$

for the r-score data. Note that in Equation 3.15, if $F_{noncontrast}$ has a value less than 1.00, we replace that value with 1.00.

Effect Size Correlation, $r_{BESD\ counternull}$. We use Equation 2.16 to compute $r_{BESD\ counternull}$ for the L-score and r-score data.

$$r_{BESD\ counternull} = \sqrt{\frac{4r_{BESD}^2}{1 + 3r_{BESD}^2}} = \sqrt{\frac{4(.862)^2}{1 + 3(.862)^2}} = .959,$$

with $p = .0041$, for the L-score data and

$$r_{BESD\ counternull} = \sqrt{\frac{4(.785)^2}{1 + 3(.785)^2}} = .930,$$

with $p = 0.15$, for the r-score data. For the L-score and r-score data, it is as likely that the true effect size correlation, r_{BESD}, is equal to .959 or .930, respectively, as that it is equal to .00. Table 5.5 provides an overall summary of the significance level information and the effect size correlations based on the L-score and r-score data.

For the present data, the L-score analyses provide greater statistical significance and larger effect size correlations than do the r-score analyses. The consistencies between the effect size correlations of the two composite scores L and r, however, are far more striking than are their differences in this example. If these were actual data, we would probably want to summarize our results, showing BESDs based on the obtained result, the null result, and the counternull result, as well as the null-counternull interval with the associated p value, as we showed earlier in Table 5.2.

TABLE 5.5
A Comparison of Significance Level Information and Effect Size Correlations Based on the L-Score and r-Score Data in Table 5.3

Significance information	L scores	r scores	Difference
$F_{contrast}$	20.19	11.26	8.93
p level	.0041	.015	−.011
Effect size correlations			
$r_{contrast}$	.878	.808	.070
$r_{alerting}$	.990	.959	.031
$r_{effect\ size}$	.871	.798	.073
r_{BESD}	.862	.785	.077
$r_{BESD\ counternull}$	.959	.930	.029

An Example with Two or More Between-Subjects Factors

If the multiple groups we want to compare are arranged not in a one-way layout, but in a factorial design (e.g., sex × age), we simply apply the procedures of Chapter 4 to the composite scores created for each of our subjects. When all our factors are substantive, all our procedures reduce to exactly those in Chapter 3. When some factors are nonsubstantive, the calculations in Chapter 3 are adjusted as described in Chapter 4.

Table 5.6 shows three repeated measures for female and male subjects at three age levels (8, 9, 10). The general prediction is that there will be no improvement in performance in going from the first to the second measurement, but that there will be noticeable improvement in going from the second to the third measurement with λ weights of −1, −1, +2. The more specific prediction is that this pattern (−1, −1, +2) will be more characteristic of female than of male subjects. This sex difference is predicted for each of the three age levels, so that age is a nonsubstantive factor.

If age had been a substantive factor, we would have treated the six combinations of age and sex as a single factor with six levels and would have proceeded, using the methods of Chapter 3. With age as a nonsubstantive factor, we can compute some of our effect size correlations (e.g., $r_{effect\ size}$ and r_{BESD}) adjusting for the nonsubstantive factor of age as shown in Chapter 4.

Table 5.7 shows the means and analysis of variance of the L scores of Table 5.6 in directly usable form. To illustrate the great simplification introduced by our working directly with L scores, Table 5.8 shows the full three-factor ANOVA of the data in Table 5.6. The contrast of interest, the difference between females and males in the degree to which they show the −1, −1, +2 contrast among the three measurements, is given directly as the main effect of sex in Table 5.7 but is buried in the measurements × sex interaction (with 2 degrees of freedom) in Table 5.8.

TABLE 5.6
Three Repeated Measures for Female and Male Subjects of Three Age Groups

			Measurements			Composite scores	
Sex	Age	Child	1	2	3	Sum	L score
Female	8	1	2	2	4	8	4
		2	2	2	3	7	2
	9	3	2	3	5	10	5
		4	4	4	6	14	4
	10	5	4	4	5	13	2
		6	4	5	8	17	7
Male	8	7	1	2	1	4	−1
		8	2	1	2	5	1
	9	9	2	2	3	7	2
		10	2	3	3	8	1
	10	11	3	2	3	8	1
		12	4	4	5	13	2

TABLE 5.7
Means and Analysis of Variance of the L Scores in Table 5.6

A. Table of means ($n = 2$ per condition)

		Age			Mean
		8	9	10	
Subject sex	Female	3.0	4.5	4.5	4.0
	Male	0.0	1.5	1.5	1.0
	Mean	1.5	3.0	3.0	2.5

B. Analysis of variance of table of means

Source	SS	df	MS	F	p
Between	33	5	6.6	2.20	.18
Sex	27	1	27.0	9.00	.024
Age	6	2	3.0	1.00	.42
Sex × Age	0	2	0.0	0.0	1.00
Within	18	6	3.0		
Total	51	11			

TABLE 5.8
Overall Analysis of Variance of the Data in Table 5.6

Source	SS	df	MS	F	p
Between subjects	57.0	11	5.18	a	
Sex	16.0	1	16.00	9.60	.021
Age	30.5	2	15.25	9.15	.015
Sex × age	0.5	2	0.25	0.15	.86
Subjects (nested in conditions)	10.0	6	1.67		
Within subjects	24	24	1.00	a	
Measurements	12.67	2	6.33	15.20	.00051
Meas. × sex	4.67	2	2.33	5.60	.019
Meas. × age	1.33	4	0.33	0.80	.55
Meas. × sex × age	0.33	4	0.08	0.20	.93
Meas. × subjects	5.00	12	0.42		

[a] No proper F is available, nor would it be of interest.

Obtaining Significance Levels. Part A of Table 5.7 shows that females produce larger L scores than do males, and Part B shows that this difference yields an $F_{contrast}$ of 9.00. This value of $F_{contrast}$ with 1 and 6 degrees of freedom has $p = .024$.

Effect Size Correlation, $r_{contrast}$. As usual, we find $r_{contrast}$ from Equation 3.2. In this example

$$r_{contrast} = \sqrt{\frac{F_{contrast}}{F_{contrast} + df_{within}}} = \sqrt{\frac{9}{9+6}} = .775.$$

Because $r_{contrast}$ is already a maximally partialed r as described in Chapter 4, no further change in it is possible after adjustment for nonsubstantive factors.

Effect Size Correlation, $r_{alerting}$. Because there are only two levels in the factor under investigation, sex of subject, we do not compute $r_{alerting}$, because it can take on values only of +1.00, 0.00, or −1.00.

Effect Size Correlations, $r_{effect\ size}$ and $r_{effect\ size|NS}$. Had there been no nonsubstantive factors, we would have used Equation 3.13 to obtain $r_{effect\ size}$. Had we done that, we would have found

$$r_{effect\ size} = \sqrt{\frac{F_{contrast}}{F_{contrast} + F_{noncontrast}(df_{noncontrast}) + df_{within}}}$$

$$= \sqrt{\frac{9}{9 + 0.50(4) + 6}} = .728.$$

However, because age is a nonsubstantive factor, we use Equation 4.5 to find

$$r_{effect\ size|NS} = \sqrt{\frac{F_{contrast}}{F_{contrast} + F_{NC|NS}(df_{NC|NS}) + df_{within}}}$$

$$= \sqrt{\frac{9}{9 + 0.0(2) + 6}} = .775,$$

a value somewhat larger than the $r_{effect\ size}$ not adjusted for the nonsubstantive factor.

The quantities $F_{NC|NS}$ and $df_{NC|NS}$ are obtained from Equation 4.2 and Equation 4.3, respectively. For the present example,

$$F_{NC|NS} = \frac{(SS_{between} - MS_{contrast} - SS_{NS})/(df_{NC|NS})}{MS_{within}}$$

$$= \frac{(33 - 27 - 6)/(2)}{3.0} = 0.0$$

$df_{NC|NS} = df_{between} - 1 - df_{NS} = 5 - 1 - 2 = 2.$

The reason that $F_{NC|NS}$ is zero, even though $df_{NC|NS}$ is positive, is that all $SS_{between}$ that is due to the substantive factor is explained by our contrast.

Effect Size Correlation, r_{BESD}. In the present example, because age is a nonsubstantive effect, we use Equation 4.6 to find

$$r_{BESD} = \sqrt{\frac{F_{contrast}}{F_{contrast} + F_{NC|NS}(df_{NC|NS} + df_{within})}}$$

$$= \sqrt{\frac{9}{9 + 1.00(2 + 6)}} = .728.$$

Effect Size Correlation, $r_{BESD\ counternull}$. We use Equation 2.16 to compute $r_{BESD\ counternull}$ for the r_{BESD} adjusted for the nonsubstantive effects:

$$r_{BESD\ counternull} = \sqrt{\frac{4r_{BESD}^2}{1 + 3r_{BESD}^2}} = \sqrt{\frac{4(.728)^2}{1 + 3(.728)^2}} = .905,$$

with $p = .024$ from F or $.012$ from one-tailed t. Therefore, the true effect size correlation r_{BESD} is as likely to be equal to .905 as to .00. If these were actual data, we would probably want to summarize our results, showing BESDs based on the obtained result, the null result, and the counternull result as well as the $1 - 2(.012) = 97.6\%$ null-counternull interval, as we showed earlier in Table 5.2.

INTRODUCTION TO NONINTRINSICALLY REPEATED MEASURES STUDIES

The remaining discussion in this chapter concerns nonintrinsically repeated measures designs. In these designs, we will see that for the most part, we can continue to rely on methods already presented. In particular, typically, significance levels and $r_{contrast}$s can be found for contrasts by the use of the techniques just presented for intrinsically repeated measures designs. Also, the other effect size correlations – $r_{alerting}$, $r_{effect\ size}$, r_{BESD}, $r_{BESD\ counternull}$, and $r_{effect\ size|NS}$ – can be found by using the techniques of previous chapters, ignoring the fact that each subject produced more than one score (i.e., pooling all subject effects into an omnibus error term). Only in unusual designs, discussed at the end of the chapter, are any new procedures needed.

NONINTRINSICALLY REPEATED MEASURES STUDIES: SIGNIFICANCE LEVELS AND $r_{contrast}$

The Standard Approach

When our purpose is to obtain significance levels, or $r_{contrast}$ (which is closely tied to significance levels), we typically treat the nonintrinsically repeated measures data as though they were intrinsically repeated measures data. We illustrate with examples drawn from earlier sections of this chapter, where we described procedures applicable to one between-subjects factor with (a) two levels, (b) three or more levels, and (c) two or more between-subjects factors.

One Factor, Two Levels. Table 5.1 showed the comparison of female and male subjects on several composite scores. Suppose one of these, the L score for linear trend, is regarded as a contrast in a nonintrinsically repeated measures design, where different subjects could have been assigned to the first, second, and third measurement. However, for purposes of obtaining significance levels and $r_{contrast}$, we regard the L scores as arising from an intrinsically repeated measure design. Then, using Equation 2.1, we find

$$t = \left(\frac{M_1 - M_2}{S_{within}}\right)\left(\frac{\sqrt{N}}{2}\right) = \frac{3.75 - 3.25}{1.38}\left(\frac{\sqrt{8}}{2}\right) = .26,$$

which, with N – 2 = 8 – 2 = 6 degrees of freedom, has $p = .40$. From Equation 2.3, we find

$$r_{contrast} = \sqrt{\frac{t^2}{t^2 + df_{within}}} = \sqrt{\frac{(.26)^2}{(.26)^2 + 6}} = .11.$$

One Factor, Three or More Levels. Table 5.3 shows several composite scores for each subject of three age groups, including the L score for linear trend, reflecting linearity of practice effects. For purposes of obtaining significance levels and $r_{contrast}$, we regard the L scores as arising from an intrinsically repeated measures design. Then, using Equation 3.1 to obtain $MS_{contrast}$, we find

$$MS_{contrast} = \frac{nL^2}{\Sigma \lambda_i^2} = \frac{3[(2)(-1) + (4)(0) + (7.33)(+1)]^2}{(-1)^2 + (0)^2 + (+1)^2}$$

$$= \frac{3(5.33)^2}{2} = 42.61.$$

Table 5.3 shows that the MS_{within} (or S^2 in Table 5.3) for the L scores is 2.11, so

$$F_{contrast} = \frac{MS_{contrast}}{MS_{within}} = \frac{42.61}{2.11} = 20.19.$$

This value of $F_{contrast}$, with degrees of freedom equal to 1 and 6, has $p = .0041$, showing that the linearity of practice effects grows significantly more pronounced with increasing age: From Equation 3.2, we find

$$r_{contrast} = \sqrt{\frac{F_{contrast}}{F_{contrast} + df_{within}}} = \sqrt{\frac{20.19}{20.19 + 6}} = .878.$$

Two or More Factors. Table 5.6 shows L scores for female and male subjects at each of three age levels. These L scores are based on λ weights of $-1, -1, +2$ reflecting the general prediction that improvement does not occur on the second trial but on the third. For purposes of obtaining significance levels and $r_{contrast}$, we regard the L scores as arising from the intrinsically repeated measures design.

Table 5.7 shows the $F_{contrast}$ comparing the L scores of female and male subjects to be 9.00, which with 1 and 6 degrees of freedom has $p = .024$, indicating that females show significantly better agreement than do males with the predicted pattern of performance: $-1, -1, +2$. From Equation 3.2, we find

$$r_{contrast} = \sqrt{\frac{F_{contrast}}{F_{contrast} + df_{within}}} = \sqrt{\frac{9}{9 + 6}} = .775.$$

Significance Levels for the Average Value of a Repeated Measures Contrast

Table 5.9 shows the results of a 2×2 factorial study in which a treatment medication is compared to a placebo control and, at the same time, a psychotherapeutic treatment is compared to a placebo control. In this particular design, the medication factor is a repeated measures factor. For simplicity, we have assumed that it is well established that there are no order effects (i.e., first vs. second administered condition) and no sequence effects (i.e., treatment then placebo vs. placebo then treatment). This assumption does not affect the basic principle we will be illustrating but prevents our having to introduce additional between-subjects effects of sequence, psychotherapy $\times$ sequence, additional within-subjects effects of order, order $\times$ psychotherapy, order $\times$ sequence, and order $\times$ sequence $\times$ psychotherapy, the last two of which are confounded with the medication treatment effect, and with the medication by psychotherapy interaction, respectively.

The last column of Table 5.9, labeled "Difference," is the medication treatment minus medication placebo difference score. This difference score is the L score computed from Equation 5.1 as

$$L = \Sigma(Y_i \lambda_i) = Y_1(+1) + Y_2(-1).$$

TABLE 5.9
Results of a Study of the Effects of Psychotherapy and Medication

Psychotherapy	Patient	Medication		Mean	Difference[a]
		Treatment	Placebo		
Treatment	1	12	8	10	+4
	2	8	6	7	+2
	3	4	4	4	0
	Mean	8	6	7	+2
	S^2	16	4	9	4
Placebo	4	8	6	7	+2
	5	6	2	4	+4
	6	4	4	4	0
	Mean	6	4	5	+2
	S^2	4	4	3	4
	Grand mean	7	5	6	+2
	S^2_{pooled}	10.0	4.0	6.0	4.0

[a] The treatment minus placebo difference score is the L score computed as
$L = \Sigma(Y_i \lambda_i) = Y_1(+1) + Y_2(-1)$.

If, on average, there were no effect of treatment, the average L score, $\bar{L}$, would be zero. We evaluate the plausibility of this null hypothesis by means of the following t statistic.

The t statistic for $\bar{L}$. Equation 5.2 shows how to obtain t for $\bar{L}$:

$$t = \frac{\bar{L} - \bar{L}_0}{\sqrt{\left(\frac{1}{kn}\right) S^2_{pooled}}}, \qquad (5.2)$$

where in the numerator, $\bar{L}$ is the obtained mean L score (+2.0 for the data in Table 5.9) and $\bar{L}_0$ is the null value of the L score (most often zero, as in the case of the data in Table 5.9); in the denominator, k is the number of levels of the between-groups factor ($k = 2$ for Table 5.9), and n is the number of subjects at each of the k levels of the between-groups factor ($n = 3$ for Table 5.9). Note that $\bar{L}$ is the average of kn individual values or, equivalently, the average of k group means each based on n individual values.

The quantity S^2_{pooled} is obtained from Equation 5.3:

$$S^2_{pooled} = \frac{\Sigma S^2_i}{k}. \qquad (5.3)$$

TABLE 5.10
Repeated Measures Analysis of Variance of the Data in Table 5.9

Source	SS	df	MS	$F_{(1,4)}$	$t_{(4)}$	One-tailed p	$r_{contrast}$
Between subjects	60	5	12				
Psychotherapy	12	1	12	1.00	1.00	.19	.45
(a) Subjects (nested)	48	4	12				
Within subjects	20	6	3.33				
Medication	12	1	12	6.00	2.45	.035	.77
Med. × psych.	0	1	0	0.00	0.00	.50	.00
(b) Med. × subjects	8	4	2				

For the data in Table 5.9, we find

$$S^2_{pooled} = \frac{4+4}{2} = 4.$$

Then, for the data in Table 5.9, Equation 5.2, the t for the repeated measures factor, yields

$$t = \frac{\bar{L} - \bar{L}_0}{\sqrt{\left(\frac{1}{kn}\right)S^2_{pooled}}} = \frac{2-0}{\sqrt{\left(\frac{1}{(2)3}\right)4}} = 2.4495,$$

which, with degrees of freedom = 4, has $p = .035$, one-tailed. We find the degrees of freedom for the t statistic for $\bar{L}$ from Equation 5.4:

$$df = k(n-1), \tag{5.4}$$

which for the data in Table 5.9 yielded

$$df = k(n-1) = 2(3-1) = 4,$$

as noted above.

Table 5.10 shows the analysis of variance of the data in Table 5.9 with F statistics for the between-subjects factor of psychotherapy and the within-subjects factor of medication and the interaction of psychotherapy and medication. We note that the value of F for medication of 6.00 is equal to the value of the t^2 we obtained from Equation 5.2, that is,

$$F = t^2 \quad \text{or} \quad 6.00 = (2.4495)^2.$$

The t Statistic for $\bar{L}$ with Unequal Sample Sizes. For the data in Table 5.9, $n_1 = n_2 = 3$, and so the example of these data used to illustrate the use of Equation 5.2 was an equal-n example. Equation 5.2 can also be used when sample sizes at different levels of the between-subjects factor are unequal.

When sample sizes are unequal, we replace $\bar{L}$ by the mean of the k mean $\bar{L}$s, and we replace n by n_h, the harmonic mean of the sample sizes, and we use an unequal-n version of Equation 5.3. To illustrate, suppose we had computed L scores at three levels of a between-subjects factor with ns of 2, 1, and 4:

					n	Mean	S^2
Level 1:	3,	5			2	4.0	2.0
Level 2:	6				1	6.0	—
Level 3:	1,	1,	3,	3	4	2.0	1.33

The mean of the three mean $\bar{L}$s is $(4 + 6 + 2)/3 = 4.0$, and the harmonic mean of the three sample sizes is obtained from Equation 3.28 as

$$n_h = \frac{k}{\Sigma \frac{1}{n_i}} = \frac{3}{\left(\frac{1}{2} + \frac{1}{1} + \frac{1}{4}\right)} = 1.7143.$$

The unequal-n version of Equation 5.3 is given in Equation 5.5 as

$$S^2_{pooled} = \frac{(n_1 - 1)S_1^2 + (n_2 - 1)S_2^2 + \cdots + (n_k - 1)S_k^2}{(n_1 - 1) + (n_2 - 1) + \cdots + (n_k - 1)}. \qquad (5.5)$$

Then, for the present example, we find

$$S^2_{pooled} = \frac{(2 - 1)2.0 + (1 - 1)0.0 + (4 - 1)1.33}{(2 - 1) + (1 - 1) + (4 - 1)} = 1.50.$$

Therefore, t for these unequal sample sizes is found from the modified Equation 5.2 as follows:

$$t = \frac{\bar{L} - \bar{L}_0}{\sqrt{\left(\frac{1}{kn_h}\right)S^2_{pooled}}} = \frac{4 - 0}{\sqrt{\left(\frac{1}{(3)1.7143}\right)1.50}} = 7.407.$$

The degrees of freedom for this t can be obtained from Equation 5.6, which is the unequal-n version of Equation 5.4:

$$df = \Sigma n_i - k, \qquad (5.6)$$

which, for the present example, we find as

$$df = (2 + 1 + 4) - 3 = 4,$$

so that the p for the t of 7.407 is .00089.

$r_{contrast}$ for the Average Value of a Repeated Measures Contrast

We compute the $r_{contrast}$ associated with the t statistic for $\bar{L}$, as always, using Equation 2.3. Therefore, for the data in Table 5.9, where we found $t = 2.4495$,

$$r_{contrast} = \sqrt{\frac{t^2}{t^2 + df}} = \sqrt{\frac{(2.4495)^2}{(2.4495)^2 + 4}} = .7746.$$

NONINTRINSICALLY REPEATED MEASURES STUDIES: EFFECT SIZE CORRELATIONS OTHER THAN $r_{contrast}$

Rationale for Our Definition of Effect Size Correlations

It is the defining characteristic of nonintrinsically repeated measures studies that the logic of our research does not require that subjects be measured repeatedly. Rather, it is the increased precision and power of the repeated measures design that lead us to use such designs. If large numbers of subjects were available to us at low cost, we typically would be just as happy to use the between-subjects designs described in the preceding chapters. Indeed, with respect to effect size correlations, we would often obtain more generally useful estimates of such correlations if our data entirely comprised observations made only between subjects, a view consistent in spirit with that suggested by Glass, McGaw, and Smith (1981).

Our approach to effect size estimation in a nonintrinsically repeated measures design treats the results as if they arise from a between-subjects design. We return to the example in Table 5.9 to illustrate the rationale underlying our definition of effect size correlations in nonintrinsically repeated measures designs. The example also serves to remind us of the often very arbitrary choice of which factor is to be used as the repeated measures factor.

Table 5.10 shows the analysis of variance of the data in Table 5.9 as a repeated measures design with two distinct error terms: (a) the subjects nested within levels of the psychotherapy factor and (b) the medication × subjects interaction. For the effects of psychotherapy, medication, and their interaction, we list $F_{(1,4)}$, $t_{(4)}$, the one-tailed p associated with t, and $r_{contrast}$. Note that the F for the effect of medication is the square of the t we found for the average value of our repeated measures contrast for the medication effect. The F and t values in Table 5.10 were computed appropriately, using error term (a) for the psychotherapy effect and error term (b) for the medication and medication × psychotherapy effect. Even though there is a 2.0-point advantage of psychotherapy over its control and an identical 2.0-point advantage of medication over its control, the particular choice of design has led to dramatically larger F, t, and $r_{contrast}$ values, and lower p values, for the medication effect than for the psychotherapy effect. Thus the "accident" of the chosen design has led to the "superiority" of one factor over another, as measured by $r_{contrast}$, a superiority that is not at all reflected by an examination of the four means. In principle, we could as well have chosen the psychotherapy factor as the repeated measures factor, a choice that in our example would have led to a reversal of the "results," with psychotherapy showing lower p values and larger values of t, $F_{contrast}$, and $r_{contrast}$.

For effect size correlations other than $r_{contrast}$ in nonintrinsically repeated measures designs, we prefer to treat the results as if they arise from a between-subjects design, and to reanalyze the data pretending each datum arises from a separate subject. Or more quickly, when the full ANOVA is already computed, we can combine the between-subject and within-subject error terms by using Equation 5.7:

$$MS_{error}^{between} = \frac{\Sigma SS_{error}}{\Sigma df_{error}}. \tag{5.7}$$

The superscript *between* serves as a reminder that this error term is identical to the MS_{error} that would be obtained if the data arose from an entirely between-subjects design. Thus, for the analysis of Table 5.10, we find

$$MS_{error}^{between} = \frac{48+8}{4+4} = 7.0, \quad \text{with combined} \quad df = 8.$$

Table 5.11 shows the $F_{(1,8)}^{between}$ and $t_{(8)}^{between}$ obtained using the combined error term of $df = 8$. The effects of medication and of psychotherapy are now equal in terms of t and F, as they are equal in a direct comparison of their means. We should note that Table 5.11 does not give values for p or $r_{contrast}$ based on the combined error term. The reason is that if we wanted to compute p values or $r_{contrast}$ values, we would use the ANOVA in Table 5.10 (i.e., we would analyze the data as if they arose from an intrinsically repeated measures design). The analysis shown in Table 5.11, based on combined error terms, is designed to provide the F statistics used in computing effect size correlations other than $r_{contrast}$.

$r_{alerting}$ and $r_{alerting|NS}$

The four condition means and their associated λ weights examining the effects of medication are as follows:

	Medication		Placebo	
	Mean	λ	Mean	λ
Psychotherapy	8	+1	6	−1
Placebo	6	+1	4	−1

The correlation between the four means and their associated contrast weights is $r_{alerting}$, which for these data has a value of .71. We could also have computed $r_{alerting}$ using the F values in Table 5.11 and Equation 3.17:

$$r_{alerting} = \sqrt{\frac{F_{contrast}}{F_{contrast} + F_{noncontrast}(df_{noncontrast})}}.$$

From Table 5.11, $F_{contrast}$ for medication is 1.71, $F_{noncontrast}$ is obtained from Equation 3.7 as

$$F_{noncontrast} = \frac{F_{between}(df_{between}) - F_{contrast}}{df_{noncontrast}}$$

$$= \frac{1.14(3) - 1.71}{2} = 0.86,$$

and $df_{noncontrast}$ is obtained from Equation 4.1 as

$$df_{noncontrast} = df_{between} - 1 = 3 - 1 = 2.$$

Therefore, we find $r_{alerting}$ to be

$$r_{alerting} = \sqrt{\frac{1.71}{1.71 + 0.86(2)}} = .71.$$

TABLE 5.11

Analysis of Variance of the Data in Table 5.9, Combining the Error Terms of Table 5.10 in Order to Compute Effect Size Correlations Other Than $r_{contrast}$

Source	SS	df	MS	$F^{between}$	$t^{between}_{(8)}$
Between conditions	24	3	8	1.14	—
Psychotherapy	12	1	12	1.71	1.31
Medication	12	1	12	1.71	1.31
Psychoth. × medic.	0	1	0	0.0	0.0
Within-conditions error	56	8	7		

			Effect size correlations					p levels (based on Table 5.10)	
Source	$r_{alerting}$	$r_{alerting|NS}$	$r_{effect\ size}$	$r_{effect\ size|NS}$	r_{BESD}	$r_{BESD\ counternull}$		p	1–2 p
Psychotherapy	.71	1.00	.39	.42	.40	.66		.19	.62
Medication	.71	1.00	.39	.42	.40	.66		.035	.93
Psychoth. × Medic.	.00	.00	.00	.00	.00	.00		.50	.00

Because the value of F for psychotherapy in Table 5.11 is the same value as the F for medication, we would obtain the same $r_{alerting}$ for both contrasts.

The contrast weights for the medication effect $(+1, -1)$ are the same at each level of the psychotherapy factor, however, so that psychotherapy is a nonsubstantive factor with respect to the medication factor. Accordingly, we compute $r_{alerting|NS}$ from Equation 4.7:

$$r_{alerting|NS} = \sqrt{\frac{F_{contrast}}{F_{contrast} + F_{NC|NS}(df_{NC|NS})}}.$$

We find $F_{NC|NS}$ from Equation 4.2 by using the values of F from Table 5.11 as

$$F_{NC|NS} = \frac{(SS_{between} - MS_{contrast} - SS_{NS})/df_{NC|NS}}{MS_{within}}$$

$$= \frac{(24 - 12 - 12)/1}{7} = 0.00,$$

and $df_{NC|NS}$ is obtained from Equation 4.4 as

$$df_{NC|NS} = df_{noncontrast} - df_{NS} = 2 - 1 = 1.$$

Therefore, we find $r_{alerting|NS}$ as

$$r_{alerting|NS} = \sqrt{\frac{1.71}{1.71 + 0.0(1)}} = 1.00,$$

because all substantive between variation is explained by our contrast.

Because the F for psychotherapy is the same as the F for medication, we obtain the same $r_{alerting|NS}$ for both contrasts.

$r_{effect\ size}$ and $r_{effect\ size|NS}$

We compute $r_{effect\ size}$ for the effect of medication from the values of F in Table 5.11 and Equation 3.13:

$$r_{effect\ size} = \sqrt{\frac{F_{contrast}}{F_{contrast} + F_{noncontrast}(df_{noncontrast}) + df_{within}}}$$

$$= \sqrt{\frac{1.71}{1.71 + 0.86(2) + 8}} = .39.$$

Because the F for psychotherapy is the same value as the F for medication in Table 5.11, we obtain the same $r_{effect\ size}$ for both contrasts.

We have already noted that the contrast weights for the medication factor $(+1, -1)$ are the same at each level of the psychotherapy factor, so that psychotherapy is a nonsubstantive factor. Therefore, we prefer to use $r_{effect\ size|NS}$ rather than $r_{effect\ size}$ to measure effect size. We do so from the values in Table 5.11 using Equation 4.5:

$$r_{effect\ size|NS} = \sqrt{\frac{F_{contrast}}{F_{contrast} + F_{NC|NS}(df_{NC|NS}) + df_{within}}}$$

$$= \sqrt{\frac{1.71}{1.71 + 0.0(1) + 8}} = .42.$$

Because the F for psychotherapy is the same value as the F for medication, we obtain the same $r_{effect\ size|NS}$ for both contrasts.

r_{BESD}

The effect size correlation r_{BESD} is defined to adjust for nonsubstantive factors. Therefore, in this example, we find r_{BESD} for the medication effect, given that psychotherapy is a nonsubstantive factor, from the values of F in Table 5.11 and Equation 4.6:

$$r_{BESD} = \sqrt{\frac{F_{contrast}}{F_{contrast} + F_{NC|NS}(df_{NC|NS} + df_{within})}}$$

$$= \sqrt{\frac{1.71}{1.71 + 1.00(1 + 8)}} = .40.$$

Recall that in Equation 4.6, if $F_{NC|NS}$ has a value less than 1.00, we replace that value with 1.00.

Just as in the case of $r_{alerting}$, $r_{alerting|NS}$, $r_{effect\ size}$, and $r_{effect\ size|NS}$, the value of r_{BESD} for the psychotherapy factor is the same as that for the medication factor.

$r_{BESD\ counternull}$

We use Equation 2.16 to compute $r_{BESD\ counternull}$ for the medication effect:

$$r_{BESD\ counternull} = \sqrt{\frac{4r_{BESD}^2}{1 + 3r_{BESD}^2}} = \sqrt{\frac{4(.40)^2}{1 + 3(.40)^2}} = .66.$$

For both the medication and the psychotherapy factors, given their r_{BESD} value of .40 each, it is as likely that the true effect size correlation, r_{BESD}, is equal to .66 as that it is equal to .00. The bottom half of Table 5.11 summarizes these effect size correlations for the effects of medication and of psychotherapy.

Although the null-counternull interval is the same for both the psychotherapy and the medication contrasts (i.e., from .00 to .66), the p levels are different for the two contrasts. The reason is that the greater precision of the repeated measures factor – medication in this example – leads to a smaller p value for it (.035 versus .19, in this example). We calculate the proportion of the distribution covered by the null-counternull interval as 1.00 minus 2 times the one-tailed p value. The last column of the bottom section of Table 5.11 shows these proportions. Because of the greater precision of the medication contrast, we see that the same null-counternull interval (of .00 to .66) covers 93% of the distribution in the case of the medication factor, but only 62% of the distribution in the case of the psychotherapy factor.

REVIEW QUESTIONS

1. Subjects identified as high or low in cognitive complexity are shown a series of film clips of social interactions in which the actions and intentions vary in their degree of complexity from lowest to highest. The subjects describe the actions and intentions using rating scales, and the hypothesis is simply that there will be greater variability of responding among those subjects who are higher (as opposed to lower) in cognitive complexity. Given the following data, what raw ingredients do we need to test this hypothesis and calculate the effect size correlation?

Cognitive complexity	Subjects	Complexity of stimulus		
		Lowest	Medium	Highest
High	1	8	11	13
	2	7	10	14
	3	8	12	16
Low	4	4	5	5
	5	4	4	6
	6	3	5	5

Answer: All we need from the preceding table are the standard deviations (S) for each row and the mean of these values in the high and low row conditions, in order to compute the basic data for a t test:

Cognitive complexity	Subjects	Complexity of stimulus			S
		Lowest	Medium	Highest	
High	1	8	11	13	2.52
	2	7	10	14	3.51
	3	8	12	16	4.00
	Mean S				3.34
Low	4	4	5	5	0.58
	5	4	4	6	1.15
	6	3	5	5	1.15
	Mean S				0.96

First, we compute S^2_{within}, for which we will need the within-group variance of the standard deviations. For the High group, with standard deviations (S_1) of 2.52, 3.51, and 4.00, we find $S_1^2 = 0.568$; for the Low group, with standard deviations (S_2) of 0.58, 1.15, and 1.15, we find $S_2^2 = 0.108$. Substitution gives us:

$$S^2_{within} = \frac{[(n_1-1)S_1^2] + [(n_2-1)S_2^2]}{df_{within}} = \frac{[(3-1)0.568] + [(3-1)0.108]}{(3-1)+(3-1)} = 0.338$$

and

$$t = \left[\frac{M_1 - M_2}{\sqrt{S^2_{within}}}\right]\left[\frac{\sqrt{N}}{2}\right] = \left[\frac{3.34 - 0.96}{\sqrt{0.338}}\right]\left[\frac{\sqrt{6}}{2}\right] = 5.014,$$

which, with $df = (n_1 - 1) + (n_2 - 1) = 4$, has an associated $p = .0037$, one-tailed. The contrast correlation, computed from Equation 2.3, is a comparison of two groups and therefore is the same value as the effect size correlation and the r_{BESD}:

$$r_{contrast} = \sqrt{\frac{t^2}{t^2 + df_{within}}} = \sqrt{\frac{(5.014)^2}{(5.014)^2 + 4}} = .929.$$

2. Given the same set of data, suppose that we had predicted a linear increase in performance scores with increases in the level of stimulus complexity, and that we also predicted that this linear increase would be more marked in the highly complex (as opposed to the less complex) subjects. What data do we need to test this hypothesis?

   Answer: Now we need the contrast scores, or L scores, for the predicted linear trend and also the mean S^2 of the L scores, so our table of raw ingredients would be as follows:

Cognitive complexity	Subjects	Complexity of stimulus			Linear trend (L)
		Lowest	Medium	Highest	
	1	8	11	13	+5
High	2	7	10	14	+7
	3	8	12	16	+8
	Sum				20
	Mean				6.67
	S^2				2.33
	4	4	5	5	+1
Low	5	4	4	6	+2
	6	3	5	5	+2
	Sum				5
	Mean				1.67
	S^2				0.33
Mean S^2					1.33

In Question 1 we worked with composite scores based on the variability (S) of responses because that was what the hypothesis required. Now the hypothesis is different and requires us to work with composite scores based on contrast, or L, scores. From Equation 5.1, we compute these scores for each subject in this situation as

$$L = Y_1\lambda_1 + Y_2\lambda_2 + Y_3\lambda_3,$$

which will be linear trend L scores with contrast weights of $-1, 0, +1$. For example, the L score for Subject 1 is $[(8)(-1)] + [(11)(0)] + [(13)(+1)] = 5$. From Equation 3.1, we compute the $MS_{contrast}$ from the L scores as follows:

$$MS_{contrast} = \frac{nL^2}{\Sigma\lambda_i^2} = \frac{3[(6.67)(+1) + (1.67)(-1)]^2}{(+1)^2 + (-1)^2} = 37.5.$$

The MS_{within} (i.e., S^2_{within}) for L scores is the mean of the two values of S^2 (2.33 and 0.33), or mean $S^2 = 1.33$, and thus

$$F_{contrast} = \frac{MS_{contrast}}{MS_{within}} = \frac{37.5}{1.33} = 28.2,$$

which, with 1 and 4 degrees of freedom, has $p = .006$.

3. In another study, subjects listened to a propaganda message and filled out an opinion questionnaire. A few days later, they heard the same message again and filled out the same questionnaire. Before the study, half the subjects were forewarned about the propagandistic nature of the message, and the other half were not forewarned. The investigator's predictions were (a) that scores would increase from the first to the second measurement and (b) that this increase would be greater for subjects who had not been forewarned. Given the following results, how can we examine these predictions? In this table, the S^2 values in the "Mean" column refer to the three means in that particular group, not to the mean of two S^2s, so the S^2 of 0.75 is the variance of 7.0, 7.0, 5.5.

Forewarned?	Subjects	Presentation of message		Mean	L score
		Time 1	Time 2		
	1	3	4	3.5	+1
Yes	2	1	2	1.5	+1
	3	2	3	2.5	+1
	Mean	2	3	2.5	+1
	S^2	1	1	1.00	0
	4	6	8	7.0	+2
No	5	5	9	7.0	+4
	6	4	7	5.5	+3
	Mean	5	8	6.5	+3
	S^2	1	1	0.75	1
$\bar{L}$					2.0
S^2 pooled					0.5

Answer: The overall increase of scores is examined by Equation 5.2:

$$t = \frac{\bar{L} - \bar{L}_0}{\sqrt{\left(\frac{1}{kn}\right) S^2_{pooled}}} = \frac{2 - 0}{\sqrt{\left(\frac{1}{2(3)}\right) 0.5}} = 6.928,$$

where $\bar{L}$ is the mean of the L scores obtained as in the preceding question, $\bar{L}_0$ is the null hypothesis value of $\bar{L}$, k is the number of levels of the between-groups factor ($k = 2$), and n is the number of subjects at each of the k levels of the between-groups factor ($n = 3$). As shown in the table above, we computed the pooled variance from

$$S^2_{pooled} = \frac{\sum S^2_i}{k} = \frac{0 + 1}{2} = 0.5,$$

so, with $df = k(n - 1) = 4$, our contrast t has $p = .0011$, one-tailed. The excess increase in scores of the not-forewarned subjects is investigated by a t (Equation 2.1) comparing the increase of the forewarned and not-forewarned subjects:

$$t = \left(\frac{M_1 - M_2}{S_{within}}\right)\left(\frac{\sqrt{N}}{2}\right) = \left(\frac{3-1}{\sqrt{0.5}}\right)\left(\frac{\sqrt{6}}{2}\right) = 3.464,$$

which has an associated $p = .013$, one tailed.

4. How shall we calculate and interpret the contrast correlation ($r_{contrast}$) for the result in the previous question, showing the excess increase in scores of the not-forewarned subjects?

   Answer: We compute the contrast correlation as before, that is,

   $$r_{contrast} = \sqrt{\frac{t^2}{t^2 + df}} = \sqrt{\frac{(3.464)^2}{(3.464)^2 + 4}} = .866.$$

   This value represents the correlation between lambda weights of -1 and $+1$ and the L scores of the forewarned and not-forewarned groups.

5. How could we have computed the first contrast in Question 3 if the cells had contained unequal ns?

   Answer: We replace $\bar{L}$ by the mean of the k mean values of $\bar{L}$, and we replace n by the harmonic mean of the sample sizes (n_h), defined for k samples in Equation 3.28 as

   $$n_h = \frac{k}{\sum \frac{1}{n_i}},$$

   and $n_h = n$ when all the sample sizes are equivalent. We calculate the unequal version of the pooled variance (S^2_{pooled}) from Equation 5.5 and substitute in the following modified version of Equation 5.2:

   $$t = \frac{\bar{L} - \bar{L}_0}{\sqrt{\left(\frac{1}{kn_h}\right)S^2_{pooled}}}$$

   with degrees of freedom defined in Equation 5.6 as $df = \Sigma n_i - k$.

CHAPTER 6

Multiple Contrasts

Our emphasis in the first five chapters has been on the computation of an individual contrast, the various effect size correlations associated with an individual contrast, and the significance level associated with it. It is often the case, however, that we want to compute multiple contrasts. Our purpose in this chapter is to address a number of issues arising when computing multiple contrasts.

In the preceding chapters, the emphasis has been on the planning and computation of single contrasts. Here and there in the preceding chapters, we have alluded indirectly to the topic of multiple contrasts, but we continued to treat each of several possible contrasts as though it were the only one being considered (i.e., Chapter 3, pp. 51–52; Chapter 4, pp. 77–79, 98–101; Chapter 5, pp. 133–136, 138–140).

In this chapter, we deal specifically with the situation of multiple contrasts. The major topics addressed include (a) the relationships among contrasts, (b) the comparison of competing contrasts, and (c) the analysis of contrasts that were computed only after we examined the data.

RELATIONSHIPS AMONG CONTRASTS

Orthogonal Contrasts

When two sets of contrasts are uncorrelated with one another, they are said to be *orthogonal*. This orthogonality means that each contrast, as defined by its weights, pertains to a distinctly different prediction. In a set of results based on k conditions, we can compute up to $k-1$ such orthogonal contrasts. Contrasts are orthogonal when the sum of the products of the corresponding weights (λs) is zero. For example, Table 6.1 shows two contrasts that represent six points on a straight line (Contrast 1) and six points on a U-shaped (quadratic) function (Contrast 2). The bottom row shows the results of multiplying the weights of Contrast 1 by the corresponding weights of Contrast 2, and we see that the sum of the products is equal to zero, showing that the two contrasts are orthogonal.

TABLE 6.1
An Example of Orthogonal Lambda Weights (Contrasts 1 and 2) and Their Product

	1	2	3	4	5	6	Sum
Contrast 1	−5	−3	−1	+1	+3	+5	0
Contrast 2	+5	−1	−4	−4	−1	+5	0
(Contrast 1) × (Contrast 2)	−25	+3	+4	−4	−3	+25	0

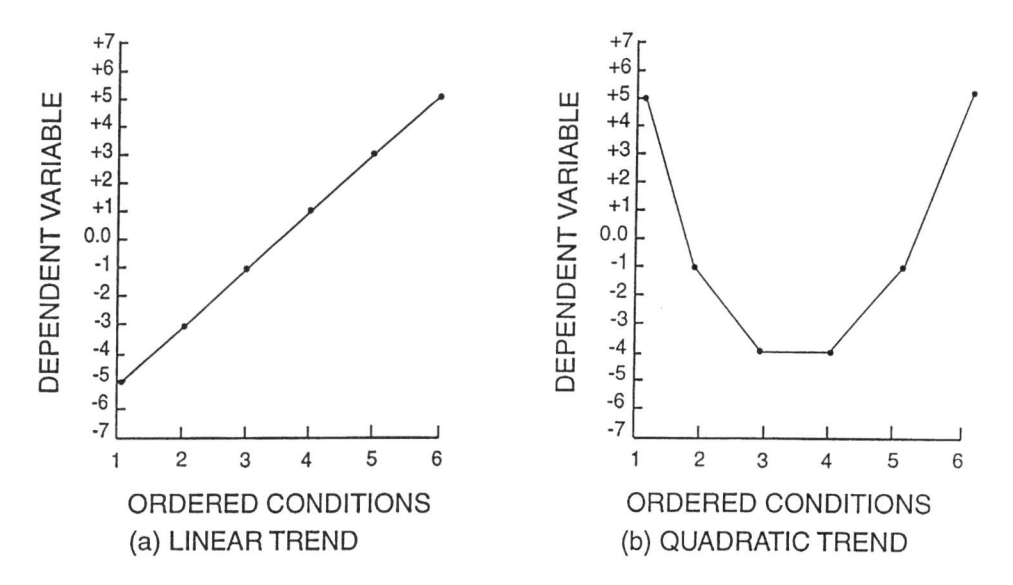

FIGURE 6.1
Displays of (a) data with a perfectly linear and (b) data with a perfectly quadratic trend.

In parts (a) and (b) of Figure 6.1, we see Contrasts 1 and 2 plotted to show what data with pure linear and pure quadratic trends look like. In Figure 6.1, we observe that data with a pure linear trend show a consistent gain, but they could also show a consistent loss. We see that data with a pure quadratic trend show a change in direction from down to up in a U curve, but they could also show a change from up to down in a ∩ curve (an upside-down U).

We can also plot the sum of the contrast weights in Table 6.1 to show what data containing both linear and quadratic trends look like. Figure 6.2 shows these summed trends, that is, data with strong linear and strong quadratic trends. Data in real-life situations usually exhibit combinations of pure trends as opposed to the idealized trends shown in Figure 6.1.

The weights for pure linear and quadratic trends are listed in Table 6.2 for $k = 2$ up to $k = 10$ conditions. The linear and quadratic orthogonal weights in Table 6.2 are especially appropriate whenever the k conditions of the study can be arranged from the smallest to the largest levels of the independent variable, as is the case

TABLE 6.2
Weights for Orthogonal Polynomial-Based Contrasts

k^*	Polynomial†	Ordered conditions									
		1	2	3	4	5	6	7	8	9	10
2	Linear	−1	+1								
3	Linear	−1	0	+1							
	Quadratic	+1	−2	+1							
4	Linear	−3	−1	+1	+3						
	Quadratic	+1	−1	−1	+1						
5	Linear	−2	−1	0	+1	+2					
	Quadratic	+2	−1	−2	−1	+2					
6	Linear	−5	−3	−1	+1	+3	+5				
	Quadratic	+5	−1	−4	−4	−1	+5				
7	Linear	−3	−2	−1	0	+1	+2	+3			
	Quadratic	+5	0	−3	−4	−3	0	+5			
8	Linear	−7	−5	−3	−1	+1	+3	+5	+7		
	Quadratic	+7	+1	−3	−5	−5	−3	+1	+7		
9	Linear	−4	−3	−2	−1	0	+1	+2	+3	+4	
	Quadratic	+28	+7	−8	−17	−20	−17	−8	+7	+28	
10	Linear	−9	−7	−5	−3	−1	+1	+3	+5	+7	+9
	Quadratic	+6	+2	−1	−3	−4	−4	−3	−1	+2	+6

* Number of conditions.
† Shape of trend.

when age levels, dosage levels, learning trials, pretest score levels, or other ordered levels comprise the independent variable.

When our orthogonal contrasts consume the available degrees of freedom (that is, when the number of contrasts is $k-1$), then the total sum of squares across the contrasts will add up to the total sum of squares among the conditions. For example, if we had $k = 4$ conditions, we could compute three orthogonal contrasts, each based on a different trend; for example, linear, quadratic, and (the much less frequently useful) cubic. The sums of squares of these three orthogonal contrasts would add up to the total between sum of squares among the four conditions.

Sets of Orthogonal Contrasts

Although in a study with k groups there are $k-1$ mutually orthogonal contrasts in a set (such as those based on orthogonal polynomials), there is an infinite number of *sets* of contrasts that could be computed, each of which is made up of $k-1$ orthogonal contrasts. Table 6.3 illustrates this idea by showing five sets of contrasts, each set containing three contrasts (labeled 1, 2, 3) among four conditions,

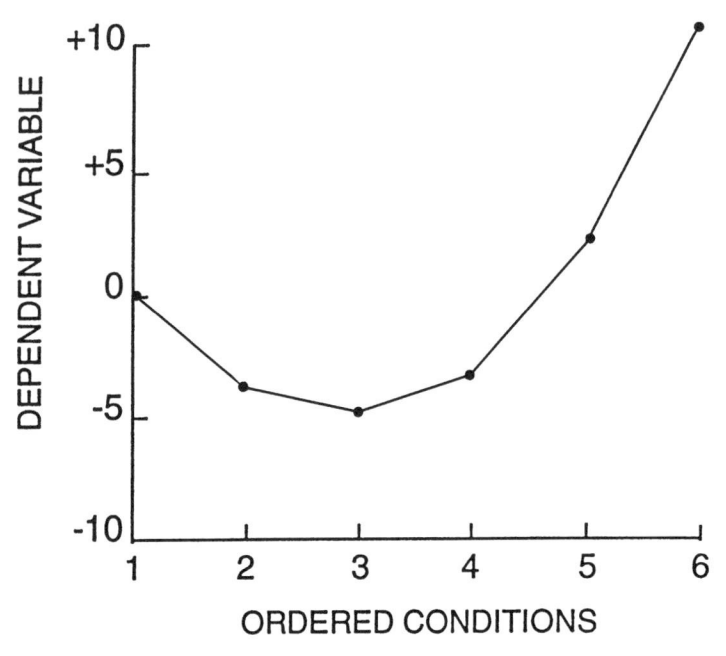

FIGURE 6.2
Data showing both linear and quadratic components, based on summing the Contrast 1 and Contrast 2 weights of Table 6.1. Because the variance of the quadratic weights for six conditions ($\sigma^2 = 14.00$) is greater than the variance of the linear weights for six conditions ($\sigma^2 = 11.67$), the trend created by simply adding weights is somewhat more quadratic than it is linear. The correlation of the combined contrast with the quadratic weights is .74. The correlation of the combined contrast with the linear weights is .67. Note that the ratio of

$$\frac{\sigma_1}{\sigma_2} = \frac{r_1}{r_2} = 1.10 \text{ in this example.}$$

Should we want to combine any number of sets of weights so that each will contribute an exactly equal share to the total, we need only z-score the weights defining each contrast before combining them.

A, B, C, and D, which could represent, for example, no treatment, medication only, psychotherapy only, and both medication and psychotherapy, respectively. Within each set, the three contrasts are orthogonal; that is, Contrast 1 is uncorrelated with Contrast 2 and Contrast 3, and Contrast 2 is uncorrelated with Contrast 3. However, none of the three contrasts in any of the five sets is orthogonal to all of the three contrasts of any of the other sets.

Set I is the familiar one in which there is a linear trend (Contrast 1), a quadratic trend (Contrast 2), and a leftover trend (Contrast 3), which is a cubic trend in this example of four conditions.

Set II represents the situation in which one condition, D, is compared to the mean of the other three (Contrast 1); one of those three, C, is compared to the mean of the remaining two (Contrast 2); and the remaining two, A and B, are compared to each other (Contrast 3). This set reflects a prediction that D represents the largest

TABLE 6.3
Five Examples of Sets of Orthogonal Contrasts

Set I	A	B	C	D
Contrast 1	−3	−1	+1	+3
Contrast 2	+1	−1	−1	+1
Contrast 3	−1	+3	−3	+1

Set II	A	B	C	D
Contrast 1	−1	−1	−1	+3
Contrast 2	−1	−1	+2	0
Contrast 3	−1	+1	0	0

Set III	A	B	C	D
Contrast 1	−1	−1	−1	+3
Contrast 2	−1	0	+1	0
Contrast 3	−1	+2	−1	0

Set IV	A	B	C	D
Contrast 1	+1	+1	−1	−1
Contrast 2	+1	−1	0	0
Contrast 3	0	0	+1	−1

Set V	A	B	C	D
Contrast 1	+1	+1	−1	−1
Contrast 2	+1	−1	+1	−1
Contrast 3	+1	−1	−1	+1

effect (Contrast 1); that among the remaining conditions, psychotherapy is better than no psychotherapy (Contrast 2); and that medication alone is better than no treatment (Contrast 3).

Note that adding the weights of Contrasts 1, 2, and 3 of Set II yields the linear trend, Contrast 1 of Set I. The three contrasts, 1, 2, and 3 of Set II contribute to their sum (Contrast 1 of Set I) in proportion to their variances, 3.0, 1.5, and 0.5, respectively. Therefore, the squared correlations of the orthogonal Contrasts 1, 2, and 3 of Set II with Contrast 1 of Set I are .60, .30, and .10, respectively (i.e., directly proportional to their variances).

Contrast 1 of Set III has the same contrast weights as does Contrast 1 of Set II, but Sets II and III have different second contrasts. To see how the weights of Set III might arise, consider a study of sensitivity to nonverbal cues where four exposure lengths are employed: 1, 3, 9, and 27 frames equivalent to 1/24, 3/24, 9/24, and 27/24 of a second. The longest exposure is predicted to yield the greatest accuracy scores (Contrast 1). However, the remaining three lengths are linearly arrayed (in the logs of 1, 3, 9), leading to the weights of Contrast 2 in which the $\lambda = 0$ of Condition B is regarded as a number, whereas the $\lambda = 0$ of Condition D is regarded as indicating a set-aside condition. The weights of Contrast 3 of Set III may be best viewed as a residual (like the cubic trend of Set I) rather than as a realistic prediction in this case (Rosenthal, Hall, DiMatteo, Rogers, & Archer, 1979, Chapter 5).

Set IV reflects the situation in which the average of two conditions of one type are predicted to be better than the average of two conditions of another type (i.e., Contrast 1). But in addition, for each of the two types of conditions, a follow-up contrast addresses a question designed to help differentiate between the two conditions within type. Suppose that Conditions A and B receive psychotherapy, whereas C and D do not: Contrast 1 examines the psychotherapy effect. Further suppose that Conditions A and C receive medication, whereas Conditions B and D do not: Contrast 2 examines the benefit of medication among those receiving psychotherapy, whereas Contrast 3 examines the benefit of medication among those not receiving psychotherapy.

Set V reflects a situation of the following type: In a study of female and male therapists treating female and male patients, suppose that Condition A has females treating females, B has males treating females, C has females treating males, and D has males treating males. Then Contrast 1 examines the sex-of-patient effect, Contrast 2 examines the sex-of-therapist effect, and Contrast 3 is probably seen, not as a residual contrast, but as an examination of the important factor of same versus opposite-sexedness of the treatment dyads.

Nonorthogonal Contrasts

Although there are often some benefits in employing orthogonal contrasts, there is no rule that says we *must* or even should do so. The benefits are (a) that each orthogonal contrast addresses a nonoverlapping, (i.e., statistically uncorrelated) question, and (b) that the sum of the $k - 1$ orthogonal contrasts' individual sums of squares add up to the total $SS_{between}$. However, we always want to use contrast weights that specifically address the scientific questions of interest. Doing so often calls for nonorthogonal contrasts, particularly if we are interested in comparing plausible rival hypotheses. Such a situation is represented in Table 6.4, in which the top row shows the mean cognitive performance scores of ten children each in Grades 2, 5, 8, and 11. Prediction 1 shows one plausible hypothesis, which is a constant rate of improvement with age, as in Contrast 1 of Set I of Table 6.3. Prediction 2 shows a plausible rival hypothesis, which is that only those in Grade 11 will differ from all younger children, as in Contrast 1 of Set II of Table 6.3.

Table 6.5 shows the analysis of variance of the four means of Table 6.4 with a within sum of squares equal to 84 on 12 degrees of freedom. In addition to the usual quantities, Table 6.5 shows, for each of the four predictions or contrasts, the values of $SS_{noncontrast}$, $MS_{noncontrast}$, and $F_{noncontrast}$. From the quantities provided in Table 6.5, therefore, we can compute the four rs and the $r_{BESD\ counternull}$ for each of the four predictions or contrasts in Table 6.4.

TABLE 6.4
Hypothetical Results of Research on Cognitive Performance with Four Nonorthogonal Predictions

	Grade 2 ($n = 10$)	Grade 5 ($n = 10$)	Grade 8 ($n = 10$)	Grade 11 ($n = 10$)
Means	3	5	6	8
Prediction 1	−3	−1	+1	+3
Prediction 2	−1	−1	−1	+3
Prediction 3	−1	0	0	+1
Prediction 4	−1	−1	+1	+1

TABLE 6.5
Analysis of Variance of Data in Table 6.4

Source	SS	df	MS	F	p	$SS_{noncontrast}$ ($SS_{between} - SS_{contrast}$)	$MS_{noncontrast}$ ($SS_{noncontrast}/df_{noncontrast}$)[a]	$F_{noncontrast}$ ($MS_{noncontrast}/MS_{within}$)	p
Between	130	3	43.33	6.19	.0087				
Predictions									
1	128	1	128	18.29	.0011	2.00	1.00	0.14	.87
2	83.33	1	83.33	11.90	.0048	46.67	23.33	3.33	.07
3	125	1	125	17.86	.0012	5.00	2.50	0.36	.70
4	90	1	90	12.86	.0037	40.00	20.00	2.86	.10
Within	84	12	7						

[a] Where $df_{noncontrast} = df_{between} - 1$, which is $3 - 1 = 2$ in this case.

For Prediction 1, we can compute $r_{alerting}$ directly as the correlation between the four means (3, 5, 6, 8) and their corresponding contrast weights (−3, −1, +1, +3), which yields an $r_{alerting}$ of .992. Alternatively, we can compute $r_{alerting}$ from Equation 3.17,

$$r_{alerting} = \sqrt{\frac{F_{contrast}}{F_{contrast} + F_{noncontrast}(df_{noncontrast})}}$$

$$= \sqrt{\frac{18.29}{18.29 + 0.14(2)}} = .992,$$

the same value we obtained from direct computation of $r_{alerting}$, as indeed it must

Relationships among Contrasts

be. We obtain $r_{contrast}$ from Equation 3.2,

$$r_{contrast} = \sqrt{\frac{F_{contrast}}{F_{contrast} + df_{within}}}$$

$$= \sqrt{\frac{18.29}{18.29 + 12}} = .777,$$

and $r_{effect\ size}$ from Equation 3.13,

$$r_{effect\ size} = \sqrt{\frac{F_{contrast}}{F_{contrast} + F_{noncontrast}(df_{noncontrast}) + df_{within}}}$$

$$= \sqrt{\frac{18.29}{18.29 + 0.14(2) + 12}} = .773.$$

We obtain r_{BESD} from Equation 3.15,

$$r_{BESD} = \sqrt{\frac{F_{contrast}}{F_{contrast} + F_{noncontrast}(df_{noncontrast} + df_{within})}}$$

$$= \sqrt{\frac{18.29}{18.29 + 1.00(2 + 12)}} = .753,$$

remembering that when $F_{noncontrast}$ is less than 1.00, as it is in this case (0.14), it is entered as 1.00 when we are computing r_{BESD}.

Finally, we compute $r_{BESD\ counternull}$ from Equation 2.16,

$$r_{BESD\ counternull} = \sqrt{\frac{4r_{BESD}^2}{1 + 3r_{BESD}^2}}$$

$$= \sqrt{\frac{4(.753)^2}{1 + 3(.753)^2}} = .916.$$

These correlations for Prediction 1 are summarized in the first column of Table 6.6. The second column of Table 6.6 shows the analogous correlations for Prediction 2. Both predictions are well supported by the data, but Prediction 1 does noticeably better. That the two predictions both fared well should not surprise us too much, because they are similar (nonorthogonal) contrasts. Indeed the correlation between the weights representing the two hypotheses is quite substantial ($r = .775$).

Now consider the third hypothesis, Prediction 3 in Table 6.4, which states that second-graders and eleventh-graders will differ most, but that fifth- and eighth-graders will not differ from one another. That prediction can be expressed by lambda weights of $-1, 0, 0, +1$, and is correlated .95 with Prediction 1 and .82 with Prediction 2. Table 6.6 shows the analogous five correlations for this prediction, a prediction that did just about as well as Prediction 1.

TABLE 6.6
The Four rs and $r_{BESD\ counternull}$ for the Four Predictions in Table 6.4 and for Two Difference Contrasts

Correlations	Predictions				Comparisons between predictions	
	1	2	3	4	1 vs. 2	3 vs. 4
$r_{alerting}$	.992	.801	.981	.832	.284	.191
$r_{contrast}$	.777	.706	.773	.719	.332	.230
$r_{effect\ size}$	.773	.624	.764	.649	.221	.148
r_{BESD}	.753	.451	.749	.493	.111	.073
$r_{BESD\ counternull}$	.916	.711	.915	.750	.218	.145

Finally, consider Prediction 4, which is similar to Prediction 2 in expecting a steplike rather than a gradual increase with age. Prediction 4, however, expects the step to occur between the fifth and eighth grades, whereas Prediction 2 expects the step to occur between the eighth and eleventh grades. The fourth column of correlations of Table 6.6 shows that Prediction 4 did slightly better than Prediction 2.

We have now computed p levels and effect size correlations for the four predictions in Table 6.4, with results displayed in Tables 6.5 and 6.6. Suppose we want now to summarize the size of, and compute the p level of, the difference between any two of these contrasts (e.g., Predictions 1 and 2). How can we do it?

EXAMINING THE DIFFERENCE BETWEEN CONTRASTS

The basic strategy for comparing two contrasts is simply to subtract the weights of one contrast from the corresponding weights of the other contrast to create a new difference contrast. This new contrast examines the difference between the accuracy or predictive power of the two contrasts. Whenever contrast weights are subtracted (or added), however, the resulting contrast is more influenced by the contrast whose weights have greater variance. Therefore, in order to be sure that the comparison is fair (i.e., not simply reflecting the contrast with greater variance), the weights of each contrast should be divided by the standard deviation of its weights as defined in Equation 3.16:

$$\sigma_\lambda = \sqrt{\frac{\Sigma \lambda^2}{k}}.$$

Formally, standardizing the contrast weights of the competing contrasts before creating the difference contrast not only makes the difference contrast equally correlated with both original contrasts (positively for one, negatively for the other) but also makes the difference contrast orthogonal to the average of the two original standardized contrasts. Intuitively, this orthogonality separates the question of whether one theory is better than another from the question of whether the average of the theories has any merit.

The values of σ_λ for Predictions 1 and 2 are 2.24 and 1.73, respectively. Therefore their standardized weights are

$$(-3, -1, +1, +3)/2.24 \quad \text{for Prediction 1}$$
$$\text{and} \quad (-1, -1, -1, +3)/1.73 \quad \text{for Prediction 2,}$$
$$\text{yielding} \quad (-1.34, -.45, +.45, +1.34) \quad \text{for Prediction 1}$$
$$\text{and} \quad (-.58, -.58, -.58, +1.73) \quad \text{for Prediction 2.}$$

Subtracting the standardized weights of Prediction 2 from the corresponding standardized weights of Prediction 1 yields the following contrast weights:

$$(-.76, +.13, +1.03, -.39).$$

Using these weights for the difference contrast, we find $r_{alerting} = .284$, $SS_{contrast} = 10.460$, $F_{contrast} = 1.49$, $p = .25$, $F_{noncontrast} = 8.54$, $r_{contrast} = .332$, $r_{effect\ size} = .221$, $r_{BESD} = .111$, and $r_{BESD\ counternull} = .218$. Although Prediction 1 was noticeably better than Prediction 2, based on the positive sign of $r_{alerting}$ and the other effect size correlations, the difference was associated with a modest p value (.25). The linear trend in the relationship between cognitive performance and grade level was noticeably greater than the difference between eleventh-graders and the younger children, though not at conventional levels of significance.

The Mean of Compared Contrasts as a Nonsubstantive Contrast

When we examine the difference between two contrasts, we often already know that there is some validity to both the contrasts being compared; we want to learn only about the difference between the levels of validity of the two contrasts. In such cases, it will not provide a great deal of new information to learn that the contrast constructed as the mean of the (standardized) contrast weights (i.e., their "common ground") shows some degree of validity. Accordingly, the contrast based on the mean of the two contrasts being compared can typically be regarded as a nonsubstantive contrast, nonsubstantive in the sense of not being under scrutiny. Nonsubstantive contrasts are treated as in Chapter 4, where we introduced the idea of nonsubstantive factors.

We illustrate the application of the mean of two contrasts as a nonsubstantive contrast in our comparison of Predictions 1 and 2 in Table 6.4. The original contrast weights were

$$-3, -1, +1, +3 \quad \text{for Prediction 1}$$
$$\text{and} \quad -1, -1, -1, +3 \quad \text{for Prediction 2.}$$

Dividing each of these sets of contrast weights by their respective standard deviations (σ_λ) of 2.24 and 1.73 yields

$$-1.34, -.45, +.45, +1.34 \quad \text{for Prediction 1}$$
$$\text{and} \quad -.58, -.58, -.58, +1.73 \quad \text{for Prediction 2.}$$

The mean of these two sets of contrast weights is $-.96, -.52, -.06, +1.54$.

With these weights defining the mean contrast, we find $r_{alerting} = .952$, $SS_{contrast} = 117.712$, $F_{contrast} = 16.82$, $p = .0015$, $F_{noncontrast} = 0.88$, $r_{contrast} = .764$, $r_{effect\ size} = .742$, $r_{BESD} = .739$, and $r_{BESD\ counternull} = .910$. Although this is a very "successful" contrast with substantial effect size correlations and a low p value, it carries no surprises and is of no substantive interest when we are considering which of the two predictions is better. Accordingly, we treat this mean contrast as nonsubstantive, using the procedures in Chapter 4.

We begin by computing, $F_{NC|NS}$ for our difference contrast from Equation 4.2:

$$F_{NC|NS} = \frac{(SS_{between} - MS_{contrast} - SS_{NS})/df_{NC|NS}}{MS_{within}}$$

$$= \frac{(130 - 10.460 - 117.712)/(1)}{7} = 0.26.$$

This value is very small because almost all the between sum of squares is explained by the difference contrast under study and the nonsubstantive sum contrast. Note that we obtained $df_{NC|NS}$ from Equation 4.3:

$$df_{NC|NS} = df_{between} - 1 - df_{NS}$$

$$= 3 - 1 - 1 = 1.$$

Treating our mean contrast as nonsubstantive has no effect on $r_{contrast}$ ($r_{contrast} = .332$), which is always tied directly to our significance level. However, treating our mean contrast as nonsubstantive will tend to increase the magnitude of the remaining effect size correlations as well as the $r_{BESD\ counternull}$, as we now illustrate.

We obtain $r_{effect\ size}$ adjusted for the nonsubstantive contrast from Equation 4.5,

$$r_{effect\ size|NS} = \sqrt{\frac{F_{contrast}}{F_{contrast} + F_{NC|NS}(df_{NC|NS}) + df_{within}}}$$

$$= \sqrt{\frac{1.49}{1.49 + (0.26)(1) + 12}} = .329,$$

a value noticeably larger than the value of the original $r_{effect\ size}$ of .221 before adjustment for the nonsubstantive contrast.

We obtain r_{BESD} adjusted for the nonsubstantive contrast from Equation 4.6,

$$r_{BESD} = \sqrt{\frac{F_{contrast}}{F_{contrast} + F_{NC|NS}(df_{NC|NS} + df_{within})}}$$

$$= \sqrt{\frac{1.49}{1.49 + 1.00(1 + 12)}} = .321,$$

a value even more noticeably larger than the value of the original r_{BESD} of .111. Note that in Equation 4.6, the value of $F_{NC|NS}$ is always entered as 1.00 if the computed value of $F_{NC|NS}$ is less than 1.00, as it is in this case (where $F_{NC|NS} = 0.26$).

As usual, we compute $r_{BESD\ counternull}$ from Equation 2.16 as

$$r_{BESD\ counternull} = \sqrt{\frac{4r^2}{1+3r^2}}$$

$$= \sqrt{\frac{4(.321)^2}{1+3(.321)^2}} = .561,$$

a value substantially larger than the value of the original $r_{BESD\ counternull}$ of .218.

Should we want to adjust $r_{alerting}$ for the nonsubstantive contrast, we use Equation 4.7,

$$r_{alerting|NS} = \sqrt{\frac{F_{contrast}}{F_{contrast} + F_{NC|NS}(df_{NC|NS})}}$$

$$= \sqrt{\frac{1.49}{1.49 + (0.26)(1)}} = .923$$

(reflecting the very accurate prediction of the means from the sum and difference contrasts), compared to the value of the unadjusted $r_{alerting}$ of .284. We should not make too much of this very large value of $r_{alerting|NS}$, however, because of the very small number of degrees of freedom between conditions after we subtract df_{NS} from $df_{noncontrast}$ (i.e., 1).

Examining the Difference between Contrasts in Two-Way Designs with a Nonsubstantive Factor

Many of the contrasts we want to compare will occur in the context of a two-way design. When, for each of the contrasts to be compared, the same contrast weights occur at all levels of one of the factors, that factor is defined as nonsubstantive (see Chapter 4). In this section, we illustrate the comparison of contrasts in two-factor designs where one of the factors is nonsubstantive. (If both factors were substantive, the two factors would be treated as a one-way design and the contrasts would be compared as already described in this chapter.)

Consider the data in Table 6.7, which were collected to address the comparison of two theories predicting that health would be improved (A) linearly, as the number of weekly treatments increased from 0 to 3, or (B) if, and only if, three treatments were given weekly. The contrast weights representing Theory A were

	0	1	2	3
Mild	−3	−1	+1	+3
Moderate	−3	−1	+1	+3
Severe	−3	−1	+1	+3

with a σ_λ of 2.24, and the contrast weights representing Theory B were

	0	1	2	3
Mild	−1	−1	−1	+3
Moderate	−1	−1	−1	+3
Severe	−1	−1	−1	+3

with a σ_λ of 1.73.

TABLE 6.7
Means and Analysis of Variance of a 3 × 4 Factorial Design

A. Table of means (n = 10 per condition)

		Number of treatments weekly				
		0	1	2	3	Mean
Severity	Mild	3	10	9	12	8.5
of	Moderate	1	4	8	9	5.5
illness	Severe	1	4	6	5	4.0
	Mean	1.67	6.00	7.67	8.67	6.0

B. Analysis of variance of table of means

Source	SS	df	MS	F	p
Between	1420	11	129.09	5.16	.000002
Treatments	860	3	286.67	11.47	.000002
Severity	420	2	210.00	8.40	.0004
Treat. × severity	140	6	23.33	0.93	.47
Within	2700	108	25.00		
Total	4120	119			

Dividing each of the sets of contrast weights by their respective σ_λ yields, for Theory A,

	0	1	2	3
Mild	−1.34	−.45	+.45	+1.34
Moderate	−1.34	−.45	+.45	+1.34
Severe	−1.34	−.45	+.45	+1.34

and for Theory B,

	0	1	2	3
Mild	−.58	−.58	−.58	+1.73
Moderate	−.58	−.58	−.58	+1.73
Severe	−.58	−.58	−.58	+1.73

The set of contrast weights examining the superiority of Theory A over Theory B is given by the difference between these two sets of contrast weights, subtracting weights for Set B from those of Set A:

	0	1	2	3
Mild	−.76	+.13	+1.03	−.39
Moderate	−.76	+.13	+1.03	−.39
Severe	−.76	+.13	+1.03	−.39

To compute $r_{alerting}$, we correlate these twelve weights with their corresponding means in Table 6.7 and find $r_{alerting} = .4292$. Multiplying $r^2_{alerting}$ (.1842 in this example) by the $SS_{between}$ in Table 6.7 (1,420 in this example) yields the $MS_{contrast}$ value of 261.60. We then find $F_{contrast} = 261.60/25 = 10.46$, $p = .0016$, $F_{noncontrast} = 4.63$, $r_{contrast} = .297$, $r_{effect\ size} = .252$, $r_{BESD} = .137$, and $r_{BESD\ counternull} = .267$. These values support the superiority of Theory A over Theory B, both in terms of the various effect size correlations and in terms of significance level. What we have not yet done, however, is to adjust $r_{alerting}$, $r_{effect\ size}$, r_{BESD}, or $r_{BESD\ counternull}$ for our nonsubstantive factor of severity of illness or for our nonsubstantive contrast defined as the mean of our two competing contrasts.

Obtaining the SS_{NS} for the Mean Contrast. The mean contrast weights for Theories A and B are

	0	1	2	3
Mild	−.96	−.52	−.06	+1.54
Moderate	−.96	−.52	−.06	+1.54
Severe	−.96	−.52	−.06	+1.54

From these weights and their corresponding means given in Table 6.7A, we find $r_{alerting} = .6285$. Multiplying $r^2_{alerting}$ (.3950 in this example) by the $SS_{between}$ in Table 6.7 (1,420 in this example) yields the value of the sum of squares for this mean contrast: 560.90. We will use this quantity to adjust our estimates of most of our effect size correlations.

Obtaining the SS_{NS} for the Nonsubstantive Factor. In the two-factor design of Table 6.7, severity of illness is a nonsubstantive factor, so that the sum of squares for severity, 420, is associated with the nonsubstantive factor. We add this quantity to the sum of squares associated with the nonsubstantive contrast to find the total nonsubstantive sum of squares:

$$SS_{NS} = 420 + 560.90 = 980.90.$$

We are now able to compute $F_{NC|NS}$ from Equation 4.2 as

$$F_{NC|NS} = \frac{(SS_{between} - MS_{contrast} - SS_{NS})/df_{NC|NS}}{MS_{within}}$$

$$= \frac{(1420 - 261.60 - 980.90)/7}{25} = 1.01.$$

Note that we obtained $df_{NC|NS}$ from Equation 4.3,

$$df_{NC|NS} = df_{between} - 1 - df_{NS}$$
$$= 11 - 1 - 3 = 7,$$

where df_{NS} was composed of the 1 df for the mean contrast and the 2 df for the severity factor. We now use $F_{NC|NS}$ in computing our effect size correlations adjusted for the nonsubstantive contrast (the mean contrast) and the nonsubstantive factor of severity.

We obtain $r_{\text{effect size}|NS}$ from Equation 4.5,

$$r_{\text{effect size}|NS} = \sqrt{\frac{F_{\text{contrast}}}{F_{\text{contrast}} + F_{NC|NS}(df_{NC|NS}) + df_{\text{within}}}}$$

$$= \sqrt{\frac{10.46}{10.46 + 1.01(7) + 108}} = .289,$$

a value somewhat larger than the value of the unadjusted $r_{\text{effect size}}$ of .252.

We obtain r_{BESD} adjusted for both the nonsubstantive factor and the mean contrast from Equation 4.6,

$$r_{BESD} = \sqrt{\frac{F_{\text{contrast}}}{F_{\text{contrast}} + F_{NC|NS}(df_{NC|NS} + df_{\text{within}})}}$$

$$= \sqrt{\frac{10.46}{10.46 + 1.01(7 + 108)}} = .287,$$

a value appreciably larger than the value of the unadjusted r_{BESD} of .137.

We compute $r_{BESD\ counternull}$ from Equation 2.16 as

$$r_{BESD\ counternull} = \sqrt{\frac{4r_{BESD}^2}{1 + 3r_{BESD}^2}}$$

$$= \sqrt{\frac{4(.287)^2}{1 + 3(.287)^2}} = .514,$$

a value substantially larger than the value of the original unadjusted $r_{BESD\ counternull}$ of .267.

Because of the larger number of degrees of freedom (11) associated with the SS_{between} and with the $df_{NC|NS}$ (7) than are often available, the computation of the adjusted value of r_{alerting} is informative. From Equation 4.7, we have

$$r_{\text{alerting}|NS} = \sqrt{\frac{F_{\text{contrast}}}{F_{\text{contrast}} + F_{NC|NS}(df_{NC|NS})}}$$

$$= \sqrt{\frac{10.46}{10.46 + 1.01(7)}} = .772,$$

a value substantially greater than the value of the unadjusted r_{alerting} of .429.

Comparing Contrasts in Repeated Measures

We have discussed the comparison of two contrasts in the context of between-subjects designs with and without nonsubstantive factors. We use the same techniques to compare contrasts in repeated measures designs, the case in Chapter 5. We can do so because we treat repeated measures designs by using techniques already developed for between-subjects designs. We illustrate with the data in Table 6.8.

TABLE 6.8
Four Repeated Measures with Associated Composite Scores

	Measurements					Composite scores	
	1	2	3	4	Sum	$L_1{}^a$	$L_2{}^b$
Females							
Child 1	2	4	4	8	18	18	6
Child 2	1	5	6	7	19	19	6
Child 3	3	5	4	8	20	14	5
Child 4	2	6	6	9	23	21	7
Sum	8	20	20	32	80	72	24
Mean	2	5	5	8	20	18	6
S^2						8.67	0.67
Males							
Child 5	1	5	5	6	17	15	5
Child 6	3	5	3	7	18	10	4
Child 7	2	4	3	7	16	14	5
Child 8	2	6	5	8	21	17	6
Sum	8	20	16	28	72	56	20
Mean	2	5	4	7	18	14	5
S^2						8.67	0.67

[a] λs of $-3, -1, +1, +3$ ($\sigma_\lambda = 2.236$).
[b] λs of $-1, 0, 0, +1$ ($\sigma_\lambda = 0.707$).

Table 6.8 shows four measurements of scholastic achievement made on each of eight children, four girls and four boys. The first two measures were taken in the fall and spring terms of the fourth grade, and the latter two measures were taken in the fall and spring terms of the fifth grade. There are two competing theories about the patterning of performance scores over these four occasions. The first theory is age-based, predicting that performance improves linearly with age, with associated contrast weights of $-3, -1, +1, +3$. The second theory is school-year-based, predicting that performance improves from fall to spring but that, because of summer vacation, there is essentially no improvement from spring of the fourth grade to fall of the fifth grade, with contrast weights of $-1, 0, 0, +1$. Our goal is to learn how well each theory does and to evaluate the degree to which one does better than the other. We note that the two sets of contrast weights have quite a lot in common; indeed, the correlation of the two sets of contrast weights is .95.

Table 6.8 shows, for each child, the L score (L_1) based on the weights $-3, -1, +1, +3$, and the L score (L_2) based on the weights $-1, 0, 0, +1$. We compute the t statistic for each of these contrasts – that is, the t statistic for the mean L-score

($\bar{L}$) – from Equation 5.2,

$$t = \frac{\bar{L} - \bar{L}_0}{\sqrt{\left(\frac{1}{kn}\right) S^2_{pooled}}},$$

where $\bar{L}$ is the obtained mean L score, $\bar{L}_0$ is the null value of the L score (most often zero, as in this case), k is the number of levels of the between groups factor (two in this case), and n is the number of subjects at each of the k levels (four in this case). Note that $\bar{L}$ is the average of the k group means, each based on n values. The quantity S^2_{pooled} is the average of the kS^2s, as shown in Equation 5.3. We find the degrees of freedom for t from Equation 5.4,

$$df = k(n-1),$$

which for the data in Table 6.8 yields $df = 2(4-1) = 6$.

For L_1, the first set of contrast weights, we then find

$$t_{(6)} = \frac{16 - 0}{\sqrt{\left(\frac{1}{(2)(4)}\right) 8.67}} = 15.37, \; p = .0000024, \text{ one-tailed},$$

and from Equation 2.3 we find

$$r_{contrast} = \sqrt{\frac{t^2}{t^2 + df}} = \sqrt{\frac{(15.37)^2}{(15.37)^2 + 6}} = .988.$$

For L_2, the second set of contrast weights, we find

$$t_{(6)} = \frac{5.5 - 0}{\sqrt{\left(\frac{1}{(2)(4)}\right) 0.67}} = 19.05, \; p = .00000068, \text{ one-tailed},$$

and

$$r_{contrast} = \sqrt{\frac{(19.05)^2}{(19.05)^2 + 6}} = .992.$$

In order to compare directly contrasts based on (a) weights of $-3, -1, +1, +3$ (with $\sigma_\lambda = 2.236$) with (b) weights of $-1, 0, 0, +1$ (with $\sigma_\lambda = 0.707$), we first standardize each set of weights by dividing each weight by its σ_λ. The first set of weights then becomes $-1.34, -.45, +.45, +1.34$ ($\sigma_\lambda = 1.00$) and the second set of weights becomes $-1.41, .00, .00, +1.41$ ($\sigma_\lambda = 1.00$).

Table 6.9 shows the standardized L scores for each child for Contrasts 1 and 2. The final column of Table 6.9 shows the difference between the two standardized L scores for each child. The t statistic for this difference score and the associated

TABLE 6.9
Standardized Composite Scores and Their Differences for the Data in Table 6.8

	Standardized L scores (λ/σ_λ)		
	$L_1{}^a$	$L_2{}^b$	$L_2 - L_1$
Females			
Child 1	8.04	8.49	.45
Child 2	8.49	8.49	.00
Child 3	6.25	7.07	.82
Child 4	9.38	9.90	.52
Sum	32.16	33.95	1.79
Mean	8.04	8.49	.45
S^2	1.73	1.33	.11
Males			
Child 5	6.70	7.07	.37
Child 6	4.46	5.66	1.20
Child 7	6.25	7.07	.82
Child 8	7.59	8.49	.90
Sum	25.00	28.29	3.29
Mean	6.25	7.07	.82
S^2	1.73	1.33	.12

[a] λs of $-1.34, -0.45, +0.45, +1.34$ ($\sigma_\lambda = 1.00$).
[b] λs of $-1.41, 0, 0, +1.41$ ($\sigma_\lambda = 1.00$).

$r_{contrast}$ directly evaluate the superiority of one contrast over the other. For the data in Table 6.9

$$t = \frac{(\bar{L}_2 - \bar{L}_1) - 0}{\sqrt{\left(\frac{1}{kn}\right) S^2_{(L_2-L_1)} pooled}} = \frac{.635 - 0}{\sqrt{\left(\frac{1}{(2)(4)}\right) 0.115}} = 5.30,$$

$p = .00092$, one-tailed, and

$$r_{contrast} = \sqrt{\frac{(5.30)^2}{(5.30)^2 + 6}} = .908.$$

The results of our analyses so far show that in terms of p values and $r_{contrast}$, both our contrasts did very well, but that in a direct comparison, the contrast with weights $-1, 0, 0, +1$, did substantially better than the contrast with weights $-3, -1, +1, +3$.

Thus far in our analysis of the data in Tables 6.8 and 6.9, we have focused on the t statistic and the $r_{contrast}$ for each of our repeated measures contrasts: L_1, L_2, and their difference, $L_2 - L_1$. But we might well wonder whether girls and boys differ with respect to these three contrasts, and we can ask for effect sizes for these differences.

We begin by computing a between-groups t statistic for each of our L scores (L_1 and L_2) and their difference score ($L_2 - L_1$), along with their associated $r_{contrast}$s.

For the standardized composite scores of L_1, shown in Table 6.9, we find from Equation 2.1 that

$$t = \left(\frac{M_1 - M_2}{S_{within}}\right)\left(\frac{\sqrt{N}}{2}\right) = \left(\frac{8.04 - 6.25}{\sqrt{1.73}}\right)\left(\frac{\sqrt{8}}{2}\right) = 1.92,$$

which, with degrees of freedom = 6, has $p = .051$, one-tailed, and from Equation 3.2 has

$$r_{contrast} = \sqrt{\frac{t^2}{t^2 + df}} = \sqrt{\frac{(1.92)^2}{(1.92)^2 + 6}} = .62,$$

showing that girls' linearity of improvement was greater, and with fairly low p, than that of boys.

The analogous computations for L_2 yield

$$t_{(6)} = \frac{8.49 - 7.07}{\sqrt{1.33}}\left(\frac{\sqrt{8}}{2}\right) = 1.74, \ p = .066, \text{ one-tailed,}$$

and

$$r_{contrast} = \sqrt{\frac{(1.74)^2}{(1.74)^2 + 6}} = .58,$$

showing that girls' L_2 scores were higher than those of boys (i.e., girls learned more between the first occasion and the last occasion).

Finally, the analogous computations for the difference between the L_1 scores and the L_2 scores yields

$$t_{(6)} = \frac{.45 - .82}{\sqrt{.115}}\left(\frac{\sqrt{8}}{2}\right) = -1.54, \ p = .087, \text{ one-tailed,}$$

and

$$r_{contrast} = \sqrt{\frac{(1.54)^2}{(1.54)^2 + 6}} = -.53,$$

showing that the superiority of L_2 over L_1, the summer vacation slowdown effect, was smaller for girls than for boys. Note that because only two groups are being compared (i.e., boys with girls), the value of $r_{contrast}$ equals the value of the other effect size correlations, $r_{effect\ size}$ and r_{BESD}.

Intrinsically and Nonintrinsically Repeated Measures Designs

In Chapter 5, we distinguished between intrinsically and nonintrinsically repeated measures designs. The former are those that could not have been conducted at all without the use of repeated measures. The latter are those that could logically be carried out entirely as between-subjects designs, although a repeated measures design was used to increase precision and power.

The type of research we have been discussing could be regarded as either an intrinsically or a nonintrinsically repeated measures design. If we had in mind a specifically longitudinal developmental design, we would have *had* to measure each child four times. If, however, we could just as well have used different children at each of our four occasions of measurement (i.e., using a cross-sectional development design – to avoid the carryover effect of previous testing, for example), we would want to regard our study as a nonintrinsically repeated measures design. The distinction between intrinsically and nonintrinsically repeated measures designs has no effect on the value of the t statistic or $r_{contrast}$, but it can have a substantial effect on the value of effect size correlations other than $r_{contrast}$. All the analyses we have presented so far for the data in Tables 6.8 and 6.9 have treated the design as an intrinsically repeated measures design with the L scores for each of the children serving as composite scores. In the section that follows, we show the effect size correlations other than $r_{contrast}$ that would be obtained if we regarded our study as a nonintrinsically repeated measures design.

Effect Size Correlations Other Than $r_{contrast}$

Table 6.10 shows the analysis of variance of the data in Table 6.8 regarded as resulting from a nonintrinsically repeated measures design. The table displays all the quantities required to compute the effect size correlations in Table 6.11, which identifies the equations used to compute each of the effect size correlations. In these tables, the factor "sex of research participant" was regarded as nonsubstantive because L_1, L_2, and $L_2 - L_1$ have the same λ weights for both females and males. Thus, Table 6.11 includes correlations adjusted for that nonsubstantive source of variation.

UNPLANNED CONTRASTS

Throughout this book our emphasis has been on planned contrasts – a priori, well-specified predictions for how the data should look. In this section, we discuss contrasts that were not planned but simply noticed during the course of the data analysis. Such contrasts are more likely to appear when more factors are used.

We encourage investigators to study their results closely and to compute contrasts that were not planned but that seemed to "jump out of the data." Such "data snooping" has, in the past, been discouraged by some psychological researchers as poor data-analytic practice. If it is done carefully, however, snooping can lead to learning a great deal that is new and important about the phenomena being investigated. "Careful" snooping involves a recognition that valid p values

TABLE 6.10
Analysis of Variance of the Data in Table 6.8 Disregarding the Repeated Measures Structure (i.e., Treating the Data as a Nonintrinsically Repeated Measures Design)

Source	SS	df	MS	$F^{between}$	p
Between conditions	126.0	7	18.00	21.60	$1/10^8$
Occasions	122.0	3	40.67	48.80	$1/10^9$
Contrast L_1	102.4	1	102.40	122.88	$1/10^{10}$
Contrast L_2	121.0	1	121.00	145.20	$1/10^{11}$
Contrast $L_2 - L_1$	7.2	1	7.20	8.61	.007
Sex	2.0	1	2.00	2.40	.13
Occasions × sex	2.0	3	0.67	0.80	.51
Contrast (L_1 × sex)	1.6	1	1.60	1.92	.18
Contrast (L_2 × sex)	1.0	1	1.00	1.20	.28
Contrast ($L_2 - L_1$ × sex)	0.7	1	0.70	0.84	.37
Within-conditions error	20	24	0.83		

TABLE 6.11
Effect Size Correlations for L_1, L_2, and $L_2 - L_1$, and Their Interaction with Sex; the Contrasts of Tables 6.8, 6.9, and 6.10, Disregarding the Repeated Measures Structure (i.e., Treating the Data as a Nonintrinsically Repeated Measures Design)

Correlations	Equation	Female plus male (average)			Female minus male		
		L_1	L_2	$L_2 - L_1$	L_1	L_2	$L_2 - L_1$
$r_{alerting}$	3.17	.901	.980	.239	.113	.089	−.074
$r_{alerting|NS}$	4.7	.909	.988	.241	.114	.090	−.075
$r_{contrast}$[a]	3.2	.988	.992	.908	.617	.579	−.532
$r_{effect\ size}$	3.13	.837	.910	.222	.105	.083	−.069
$r_{effect\ size|NS}$	4.5	.843	.917	.223	.105	.083	−.070
r_{BESD}	3.15	.671	.913	.102	.051	.040	−.033
$r_{BESD\ counternull}$	2.16	.875	.976	.202	.101	.080	−.066

[a] From the repeated measures analysis of L scores; not from the ANOVA in Table 6.10.

obtained for unplanned, or post hoc, or snooped, contrasts are not the same as if they were planned. The same caveat applies to valid effect size estimation. After discussing an example of an unplanned contrast, we will present some simple procedures for adjusting significance levels for unplanned contrasts. We also indicate how effect size estimates can be modified.

TABLE 6.12
Means in a 2 × 3 × 4 Factorial Design

	Sex of patient					
	Female			Male		
	Degree of chronicity			Degree of chronicity		
Dosage level	High	Medium	Low	High	Medium	Low
300 mg	3	3	18	3	3	4
200 mg	2	3	4	2	4	3
100 mg	2	2	3	1	2	2
0 mg	1	1	2	1	2	3

Note: There are ten patients in each of the twenty-four conditions.

TABLE 6.13
Analysis of Variance of the Means in Table 6.12

Source	SS	df	MS	F	p
Between	2,518.33	23	109.49	1.12	.33
Dosage	591.67	3	197.22	2.01	.11
Chronicity	400.83	2	200.42	2.05	.13
Sex of patient	81.67	1	81.67	0.83	.36
Dosage × chronicity	515.83	6	85.97	0.88	.51
Dosage × sex	258.33	3	86.11	0.88	.45
Chronicity × sex	205.83	2	102.92	1.05	.35
Dosage × chron. × sex	464.18	6	77.36	0.79	.58
Within	21,168	216	98.00		
Total	23,686.33	239			

An Example of an Unplanned Contrast

For our example, we consider a 2 × 3 × 4 factorial design in which female and male patients at high, medium, or low levels of chronicity of illness are randomly assigned to one of four levels of medication dosage. The outcome variable is degree of healthy functioning. Table 6.12 presents the means for each of the twenty-four conditions or cells of this study, and Table 6.13 presents the standard analysis of variance for this design. Inspection of the means of Table 6.12 shows that one cell of the 2 × 3 × 4 design – the cell with female patients, with the least degree of chronicity of illness, and with the highest dosage level of medication – has a mean (18) that is very far from all the other means. We will explore that result by means of an unplanned contrast, but first we consider the contrasts we had planned.

Contrasts Planned for the Present Example. For the present example, suppose that we had planned three basic contrasts: (a) a linear trend in dosage level with weights $-3, -1, +1, +3$, with the best outcome predicted for the highest level; (b) a linear trend in chronicity with weights $+1, 0, -1$, with the best outcome predicted for the lowest level of chronicity; and (c) a "linear trend" in sex of patient with weights of $+1$ and -1 for females and males, respectively.

We also had a fourth contrast made up of additive components of these first three basic contrasts. Table 6.14 shows the allocation of points to each of the twenty-four conditions for the fourth contrast. Each entry in Part A is simply the sum (i.e., addition) of the points contributed by the dosage factor (1, 2, 3, or 4 points), the chronicity factor (1, 2, or 3 points), and the sex factor (1 or 2 points). Thus the upper left cell of the design was allocated 4 points for dosage level, 1 point for chronicity level, and 2 points for being female, for a total of 7 points. The predicted points in Part A of Table 6.14 are not contrast weights because they do not add to zero. However, they can be made into contrast weights by subtracting the mean of the twenty-four predicted values (6.0) from each prediction, with the results shown in Table 6.14, Part B.

The Unplanned Contrast. Table 6.15, Part A, shows the contrast weights required to investigate the unplanned contrast in which a single cell of the design was to be compared to the remaining twenty-three cells. Whenever a single cell of

TABLE 6.14
Allocation of Points to the Twenty-four Conditions in Table 6.12 to Generate an Additive Prediction (A) and Conversion of These Points to Contrast Weights (B)

A. Point allocations

Sex of subject	(points)		(2)	(2)	(2)	(1)	(1)	(1)
Chronicity	(points)		(1)	(2)	(3)	(1)	(2)	(3)
		(4)	7	8	9	6	7	8
Dosage (points)		(3)	6	7	8	5	6	7
		(2)	5	6	7	4	5	6
		(1)	4	5	6	3	4	5

B. Points converted to contrast weights

			2	2	2	1	1	1
			1	2	3	1	2	3
		4	+1	+2	+3	0	+1	+2
		3	0	+1	+2	−1	0	+1
		2	−1	0	+1	−2	−1	0
		1	−2	−1	0	−3	−2	−1

TABLE 6.15
Contrast Weights for Unplanned (Post Hoc) Comparison of One Cell against All Others (A) and Analysis of Variance of These Contrast Weights (B)

A. Contrast weights

Sex of subject			2	2	2	1	1	1
Chronicity			1	2	3	1	2	3
		4	−1	−1	+23	−1	−1	−1
Dosage		3	−1	−1	−1	−1	−1	−1
		2	−1	−1	−1	−1	−1	−1
		1	−1	−1	−1	−1	−1	−1

Source	SS	df	MS
Between	552	23	24
Dosage	72	3	24
Chronicity	48	2	24
Sex of patient	24	1	24
Dosage × chronicity	144	6	24
Dosage × sex	72	3	24
Chronicity × sex	48	2	24
Dosage × chronicity × sex	144	6	24

a set of k cells is to be compared to the remaining cells, the single cell has weight (λ) = $k - 1$ (or $1 - k$) and the remaining $k - 1$ cells each have weight -1 (or $+1$). Part B of Table 6.15 shows the analysis of variance of the $2 \times 3 \times 4$ arrangement of the contrast weights (λs) in Part A. The results of the analysis of variance illustrate that when a single cell value differs from the cell values of all others, which do not differ from each other, all main effects and all interactions have the same mean square; 24 in this example.

Table 6.16 shows for the planned and unplanned contrasts the values of $MS_{contrast}$, $F_{contrast}$, p, and $r_{contrast}$. Table 6.16 shows that our planned additive contrast has a smaller p and a larger $r_{contrast}$ than did any of the three linear trend contrasts, but that the unplanned contrast has a substantially smaller p value and a larger $r_{contrast}$ than did even the additive planned contrast. But how are we to interpret this p value given that we chose the unplanned contrast after the fact simply because it "looked big"?

Adjusting for Unplanned Contrasts

There are a great many procedures available for adjusting significance levels for unplanned contrasts (Miller, 1981; Rosenthal & Rosnow, 1985). Here we present only an old (Tippett, 1931), simple, all-purpose conservative procedure, the Bonferroni adjustment ($p_{adjusted}$) of the obtained p, or $p_{obtained}$ (Rosenthal &

TABLE 6.16
Planned and Unplanned Contrasts for the Data in Table 6.12

	$MS_{contrast}$	$F_{contrast}$	p	$r_{contrast}$
Planned contrasts				
Linear trend in dosage	507.00	5.17	.024	.15
Linear trend in chronicity	360.00	3.67	.057	.13
Linear trend in sex of patient	81.67	0.83	.36	.06
Additive contrast	942.31	9.62	.0022	.21
Unplanned contrast				
One cell versus all others	2321.81	23.69	.0000022	.31

Rubin, 1983, 1984). To make this adjustment, we simply multiply $p_{obtained}$ by the number of contrasts examined to arrive at the unplanned contrast we finally computed. In practice, the "number of contrasts examined" may not be precisely stated or known and so is often implicit. We will label this number $C_{implicit}$. The Bonferroni adjusted p value, $p_{adjusted}$, is then

$$p_{adjusted} = p_{obtained} \times C_{implicit}. \tag{6.1}$$

The value of $C_{implicit}$ reflects the procedure used to sift through other contrasts to find the unplanned contrast being examined. For example, suppose we decided to compare the largest obtained mean with all others. Then, with twenty-four means, we would make twenty-four implicit comparisons to find the largest one, and so, from Equation 6.1 we find

$$p_{adjusted} = .0000022 \times 24 = .000053.$$

It could be argued, however, that we would have found it equally striking if one of our twenty-four means had been dramatically *lower* than the remaining twenty-three means. If we had considered the most extreme low mean, as well as the most extreme high mean, we would have computed $24 + 24 = 48$ implicit contrasts. Then

$$p_{adjusted} = .0000022 \times 48 = .00011.$$

It is also possible that in our examination of the data, we would not have restricted ourselves to looking for highest or lowest means. We might, for example, compare each mean to every other. In a set of k means, there are $[k(k-1)]/2$ possible pairwise comparisons. For the present example, with $k = 24$, we have $[24(23)]/2 = 276$ possible comparisons. If we had chosen our contrast from among the 276 pairwise comparisons plus the 48 most-extreme-means-against-all-others, we would have had 324 implicit contrasts. Then,

$$p_{adjusted} = .0000022 \times 324 = .00071.$$

In the present example, therefore, even a very conservatively adjusted p value is still very extreme.

Tolerance for Implicit Contrasts. Sometimes it is difficult to state precisely the number of implicit contrasts that were computed to arrive at our unplanned contrast. In such situations, it may be useful to compute the number of implicit contrasts that could have been computed without the adjusted p value exceeding some alpha level, usually .05. This value, "the tolerance for implicit contrasts," T_{ic}, is readily computed from Equation 6.2:

$$T_{ic} = \frac{\alpha}{p_{obtained}}, \tag{6.2}$$

which for $\alpha = .05$, and the value for our unplanned contrast of Table 6.16, $p = .0000022$, yields

$$T_{ic} = \frac{.05}{.0000022} = 22{,}727,$$

which is interpreted as our having been able to compute over 22,000 implicit contrasts to obtain our unplanned contrast before our $p_{adjusted}$ would exceed $p = .05$ (Rosenthal, 1979).

Adjusting Significance Levels for Planned Contrasts

In most research applications, the number of planned contrasts is modest (e.g., half a dozen or fewer), so that only a minor adjustment of significance levels results. However, if the number of planned contrasts is large (e.g., ten or more), we may want to adjust the obtained p values by the same procedures described for the case of unplanned contrasts. In addition, in the case of multiple planned contrasts, we can use procedures that are statistically more powerful. The details of one such simple procedure are given elsewhere (Rosenthal & Rubin, 1984); briefly, the procedure requires that we assign to each contrast a weight that is proportional to the theoretical importance of that contrast. This procedure "puts our power where the theory is," giving a greater allocation of power to our more important contrasts. In this procedure we find the adjusted p value from

$$p_{adjusted} = p_{obtained} \times \frac{\Sigma W}{W_{contrast}}, \tag{6.3}$$

where $W_{contrast}$ is the importance weight of the contrast for which we want to adjust the p value, and ΣW is the sum of all the importance weights assigned to the contrasts in the set of contrasts.

Table 6.17 illustrates the use of Equation 6.3. To each of ten planned contrasts, an importance weight is assigned (before the results of the study are known) indicating the relative importance of each contrast. In Table 6.17 the contrasts are listed in decreasing order of importance. For each contrast, the value of $p_{obtained}$ is given along with the value of the quantity $\Sigma W / W_{contrast}$, the inverse of the relative importance of the contrast. The final column gives the resulting values of $p_{adjusted}$, the product of $p_{obtained}$, and the inverse of the relative importance. As we would

TABLE 6.17
Adjusted p Values for a Hypothetical Set of Ten Planned Contrasts Weighted by Importance with Associated Hypothetical $p_{obtained}$ Values

Contrast	Weight ($W_{contrast}$)	$p_{obtained}$	$\Sigma W/W_{contrast}$	$p_{adjusted}$
1	60	.023	1.67	.038
2	15	.10	6.67	.67
3	9	.0053	11.11	.059
4	5	.22	20.00	1.00[a]
5	4	.0011	25.00	.028
6	2	.14	50.00	1.00[a]
7	2	.42	50.00	1.00[a]
8	1	.00014	100.00	.014
9	1	.062	100.00	1.00[a]
10	1	.11	100.00	1.00[a]
	ΣW 100			

[a] Values exceeding 1.00 are interpreted as 1.00.

expect, the value of $p_{adjusted}$ is always larger than the value of $p_{obtained}$, and the more so for the contrasts regarded as less important. Overall, the median $p_{obtained}$ was .081, and the median $p_{adjusted}$ was .83.

If we want to weight our contrasts equally or are unable to distinguish among them, we assign a weight of 1 to each contrast, so that Equation 6.3 simplifies to

$$p_{adjusted} = p_{obtained} \times \Sigma W, \qquad (6.4)$$

where ΣW is simply the number of contrasts examined, so that Equation 6.4 is formally the same as Equation 6.1, which gives the very simple Bonferroni adjustment with $C_{implicit} = \Sigma W$.

Adjusting Effect Sizes: A Preliminary Note

It is often informative to adjust the effect size estimates associated with unplanned contrasts or with multiple planned contrasts to make them consistent with the significance level that has been adjusted for the number of such contrasts. If we have examined 100 effect size estimates and focus on the largest, this estimate is likely to be larger than the true effect size underlying it. An analogy is tossing 100 coins, each 10 times, and finding one with 10 heads out of its 10 tosses; clearly, it is not certain that this coin has two heads! Yet the simple effect size estimate and standard error associated with this particular coin ($p = 10/10, SE = \sqrt{P(1-P)}$) would suggest that.

One simple way to adjust effect sizes for the number of contrasts is to find $F_{contrast\ (adjusted)}$ from $p_{adjusted}$, and (referring again to Table 3.6) to apply

Equation 3.2 to find $r_{contrast\ (adjusted)}$ and, for example, Equations 3.13 and 3.15 to find $r_{effect\ size\ (adjusted)}$ and $r_{BESD\ (adjusted)}$, respectively.

For the example of an unplanned contrast we have been discussing, the contrast was associated with $F_{contrast} = 23.69$, $p = .0000022$, and $r_{contrast} = .31$, as shown in Table 6.16. If we adjusted our obtained p of .0000022 for 324 implicit contrasts, we would find $p_{adjusted}$ from Equation 6.1 to be

$$p_{adjusted} = p_{obtained} \times C_{implicit}$$
$$p_{adjusted} = .0000022 \times 324 = .00071.$$

From tables (on paper, in calculators, or computers), we find $p_{adjusted}$ of .00071 to be associated with an $F_{contrast\ (adjusted)}$ of 11.80 with 1 and 216 degrees of freedom. Then, from Equation 3.2, we find $r_{contrast\ (adjusted)}$

$$r_{contrast(adjusted)} = \sqrt{\frac{F_{contrast(adjusted)}}{F_{contrast(adjusted)} + df_{within}}}$$

$$= \sqrt{\frac{11.80}{11.80 + 216}} = .23.$$

Computation of other effect size indices proceeds analogously by the use of any of the equations given in Chapters 3 and 4, but with $F_{contrast}$ replaced by $F_{contrast\ (adjusted)}$. The methods applicable to the one-way designs of Chapter 3 are identical to those applicable to the factorial designs of Chapter 4 when all the factors are substantive. However, when there are nonsubstantive factors, the same level of significance is usually associated with a larger effect size estimate than when all factors are substantive.

Bayesian Methods

The methods described above for adjusting for many comparisons are all quite simple and often useful. Yet we have mentioned only a very few of the myriad of alternatives discussed, for example, by Rupert Miller (1981), in computational detail, and in broad conceptual terms by John Tukey (1991). Truly appropriate methods can be substantially more complex but can provide more satisfactory answers. We believe that the best of these are based on Bayesian methods for data analysis as described in Gelman, Carlin, Stern, and Rubin (1995). Using them requires fairly sophisticated computing software, which is not yet generally accessible. Consequently, the details are currently beyond the scope of our discussion.

REVIEW QUESTIONS

1. Researcher A predicts that firstborns should be higher in need for achievement than later-borns. Researcher B argues that males in general, no matter whether they are first- or later-born, should be higher in need for achievement. Are these two predictions orthogonal or nonorthogonal to one another?

Answer: We can formulate these two predictions as two contrasts, with the dependent variable being the subjects' scores on a test of need achievement:

Contrasts	Firstborn		Later-born		Sum
	Males	Females	Males	Females	
Researcher A	+1	+1	−1	−1	0
Researcher B	+1	−1	+1	−1	0
Product	+1	−1	−1	+1	0

Because the sum of the multiplied weights is zero, the two predictions are orthogonal (i.e., uncorrelated).

2. Two researchers (A and B) collaborate on an investigation to improve children's attention span by using attention-enhancing training. The researchers randomly assign 20 children to 0, 1, 2, or 3 hours of enhancement training and afterward test them using a specific psychological instrument on which higher scores mean greater ability to attend. Researcher A predicts a linear increase in attention span, which she denotes by lambda weights of −3, −1, +1, +3 for 0, 1, 2, and 3 hours of training, respectively. Researcher B predicts that a threshold of 2 hours of training is needed to improve children's attention spans, but that additional hours of training will not result in further gains, a prediction he denotes by lambda weights of −1, −1, +1, +1 for 0, 1, 2, and 3 hours of training, respectively.

The researchers' experiment results in the following scores, with the overall analysis of variance and contrasts addressed to each researcher's prediction shown below. Compute the alerting r, contrast r, effect size r, BESD r, and BESD counternull r, and interpret the results.

	Condition 1 (0 hours)	Condition 2 (1 hour)	Condition 3 (2 hours)	Condition 4 (3 hours)
	4	2	10	8
	4	2	10	8
	3	1	9	7
	2	0	8	6
	2	0	8	6
Sum	15	5	45	35
Mean	3	1	9	7
s^2	1.0	1.0	1.0	1.0

Source	SS	df	MS	F	p value
Between	200	3	66.67	66.67	$3/10^9$
Predictions					
A: −3, −1, +1, +3	100	1	100.00	100.00	$3/10^8$
B: −1, −1, +1, +1	180	1	180.00	180.00	$4/10^{10}$
Within	16	16	1.00		

Answer: Using Equation 3.17 for Prediction A gives us

$$r_{alerting} = \sqrt{\frac{F_{contrast}}{F_{contrast} + F_{noncontrast}(df_{noncontrast})}}$$

$$= \sqrt{\frac{100}{100 + 50(2)}} = .707,$$

a value we could also have gotten by correlating the four means (3, 1, 9, 7) with their corresponding contrast weights (−3, −1, +1, +3).

For Prediction B, using the same approach,

$$r_{alerting} = \sqrt{\frac{180}{180 + 10(2)}} = .949,$$

a value also obtained by correlating the four means (3, 1, 9, 7) with their corresponding contrast weights (−1, −1, +1, +1).

Equation 3.2 for Prediction A gives us

$$r_{contrast} = \sqrt{\frac{F_{contrast}}{F_{contrast} + df_{within}}}$$

$$= \sqrt{\frac{100}{100 + 16}} = .928,$$

and for Prediction B, using the same equation,

$$r_{contrast} = \sqrt{\frac{180}{180 + 16}} = .958.$$

Equation 3.13 for Prediction A gives us

$$r_{effect\ size} = \sqrt{\frac{F_{contrast}}{F_{contrast} + F_{noncontrast}(df_{noncontrast}) + df_{within}}}$$

$$= \sqrt{\frac{100}{100 + 50(2) + 16}} = .680,$$

and for Prediction B, using the same equation,

$$r_{effect\ size} = \sqrt{\frac{180}{180 + 10(2) + 16}} = .913.$$

Equation 3.15 for Prediction A gives us

$$r_{BESD} = \sqrt{\frac{F_{contrast}}{F_{contrast} + F_{noncontrast}(df_{noncontrast} + df_{within})}}$$

$$= \sqrt{\frac{100}{100 + 50(2 + 16)}} = .316,$$

and for Prediction B, using the same equation,

$$r_{BESD} = \sqrt{\frac{180}{180 + 10(2 + 16)}} = .707.$$

Equation 2.16 for Prediction A gives us

$$r_{BESD\ counternull} = \sqrt{\frac{4r_{BESD}^2}{1 + 3r_{BESD}^2}}$$

$$= \sqrt{\frac{4(.316)^2}{1 + 3(.316)^2}} = .554,$$

and for Prediction B, using the same equation,

$$r_{BESD\ counternull} = \sqrt{\frac{4(.707)^2}{1 + 3(.707)^2}} = .894.$$

Summarizing our calculations as follows, we see that B fared better than A:

Correlation	Prediction A	Prediction B
$r_{alerting}$	.707	.949
$r_{contrast}$	.928	.958
$r_{effect\ size}$	.680	.913
r_{BESD}	.316	.707
$r_{BESD\ counternull}$	.554	.894

Squaring the alerting r tells us the proportion of the between-conditions sum of squares that was accounted for by each of the two contrasts, and we find that Prediction A accounted for 50 % of the variability between conditions, whereas Prediction B did a better job (accounting for 90 % of this variability). Contrast correlations refer to the partial correlations between sets of lambda weights and individual scores with all of the noncontrast between-groups variation removed, and both A and B contrasts had similar contrast rs. The effect size correlation, which refers to the unpartialed correlation between the lambda weights and the individual scores, was much more impressive in the case of B than A. The BESD correlations allow us to translate the results into binomial effect size displays, and the BESD counternull correlations tell us the value of the BESD correlation greater than the r_{BESD} obtained that is just as likely as the null value of r_{BESD} (i.e., $r_{BESD} = .00$).

3. Using a repeated measures design, each of four subjects experiences three sessions of treatment in the same sequence (A, B, and C), with the following results:

Subject	Session A	Session B	Session C	Mean	Sum	L_1	L_2
1	0	7	3	3.33	10	3	11
2	1	7	4	4.00	12	3	9
3	3	8	5	5.33	16	2	8
4	4	8	6	6.00	18	2	6
Sum	8	30	18	18.66	56	10	34
Mean	2.0	7.5	4.5	4.67	14	2.5	8.5
S^2						0.33	4.33

Source	SS	df	MS	F	p value
Between subjects	13.33	3	4.44		
Within					
Sessions	60.67	2	30.33	68.93	.000073
Sessions × Subjects	2.67	6	0.44		

One theory predicts that subjects' performance will improve from Session A to Session C (i.e., −1, 0, +1), whereas a second theory predicts that performance will improve from Session A to Session B but then in Session C will revert back to the rate in Session A (i.e., −1, +2, −1). Correlating the lambda weights of the first theory with the session means gives us $r_{alerting} = .454$, which when squared tells us that the first prediction accounts for 21 % of the variability between sessions. Doing the same with the lambdas for the second theory gives us $r_{alerting} = .891$, which when squared accounts for 79 % of the variability between sessions. Although we see that the second theory fares better than the first theory, when we submit the results in an article, the editor insists that we also compare these theories by a significance test. Do this, and then interpret the result for the editor.

Answer: In order to compare the two contrasts, we first have to standardize each set of weights by dividing them by their σ_λ, where $\sigma_{\lambda_1} = 0.816$ (Theory 1) and $\sigma_{\lambda_2} = 1.414$ (Theory 2). When we divide these values into the respective lambdas $(-1, 0, +1,$ or $-1, +2, -1)$, the standardized weights for Theory 1 are $-1.225, 0, +1.225$, and for Theory 2 are $-0.707, 1.414, -0.707$. The standardized L scores and the difference score for each subject for these two contrasts are

	L_1	L_2	$L_2 - L_1$
Subject 1	3.676	7.779	4.103
Subject 2	3.676	6.365	2.689
Subject 3	2.451	5.658	3.207
Subject 4	2.451	4.243	1.792
Sum	12.254	24.045	11.791
Mean	3.064	6.011	2.948
S^2	0.500	2.167	0.935

The t test that addresses the superiority of one contrast over another gives us

$$t = \frac{2.948}{\sqrt{\left(\frac{1}{4}\right)(0.935)}} = 6.10,$$

which, with $df = 3$, has an associated $p = .0044$, one-tailed.

4. Suppose that a 2 × 3 factorial design was used in a study of a new drug, in which rows represent the sex of the subjects and columns represent three dosage levels (no drug, 10 mg, and 20 mg, respectively). The researcher predicts an improvement in the subjects' performance at 10 mg, but no further improvement is predicted, and the contrast weights for dosage levels are the same in rows 1 and 2 (i.e., sex is defined as a nonsubstantive factor). However, another researcher disagrees with this prediction and instead predicts that only men will show this threshold effect, and that women, while showing more modest benefits at 10 mg, will show further improvement with increased dosage. In other words, the two sets of predictions are as follows:

	Researcher A:			Researcher B:		
	0 mg	10 mg	20 mg	0 mg	10 mg	20 mg
Men	−2	+1	+1	−2	+1	+1
Women	−2	+1	+1	−1	0	+1

How can we obtain $r_{effect\ size}$ in light of the assumptions made by the researchers?

Answer: For Researcher A, because the contrast weights imply the same trend across dosage levels for both men and women, we could subtract the mean performance score for each row from the score earned by each subject in that row. We could correlate these row de-meaned scores and their associated lambda weights (i.e., the effect size correlation controlling for the nonsubstantive factor of subjects' sex) to get the adjusted $r_{effect\ size}$. An alternative procedure, without de-meaning the data, would be to use Equation 4.5 to obtain effect size correlation ($r_{effect\ size|NS}$) adjusted for the nonsubstantive factor.

Researcher B views sex of subjects and dosage levels as two substantive factors. To address this prediction, we can simply conceptualize this view of the two factors as a one-way design (i.e., a 1 × 6 design), and $r_{effect\ size}$ can be computed from Equation 3.13.

5. A researcher is interested in the relationship between need for social approval and compliance with task-orienting cues in an experiment. The researcher is also interested in testing the effect of manipulated expectancies on subjects' compliance with the same task-orienting cues. The researcher uses a 3 × 3 between-groups factorial design:

Need for social approval	Manipulated expectancy		
	Positive	None	Negative
High	A	B	C
Moderate	D	E	F
Low	G	H	I

Despite the elaborate design, the researcher makes only two predictions. One prediction is that subjects higher in the need for social approval will be more compliant than subjects lower in the need for social approval (i.e., A = B = C > D = E = F > G = H = I). The second prediction is that positive and negative expectancies will be equally effective in increasing compliance when compared with the no-expectancy condition (i.e., A = C = D = F = G = I > B = E = H). However, after inspection of the results, another hypothesis occurs to the researcher, which is that subjects in the high-need-for-approval group with positive expectancy should be the most compliant and subjects in the low-need-for-approval group with negative expectancy cues should be the least compliant (A > B = C = D = E = F = G = H > I). This researcher is troubled about the accuracy of his p value in reporting the unplanned contrast. How might the researcher adjust the p value for the unplanned contrast?

Answer: One approach would be to estimate how many implicit contrasts comparing the largest with the smallest mean are possible and then to multiply this number by the obtained p value for the unplanned contrast. With nine means, there are $n(n-1)/2 = 36$ possible pairwise comparisons, so by Equation 6.1, we find $p_{adjusted}$ to be $(p_{obtained}) \times (36)$.

6. After submitting his results, the above researcher hears from the journal editor that a reviewer complained that "only an adjustment for the p value had been made." The editor asks whether it is possible to add some adjustment for the effect size correlations as well. How can the researcher respond?

Answer: The researcher can report the effect size correlations adjusted for the number of implicit contrasts computed by replacing the quantity $F_{contrast}$ with the quantity $F_{contrast\ (adjusted)}$ in Equations 3.2, 3.13, 3.15, and 3.17. The value of $F_{contrast\ (adjusted)}$ is found from $p_{adjusted}$ and the degrees of freedom for F, as illustrated at the end of this chapter.

APPENDIX A

List of Equations

CHAPTER 2

(2.1) $$t = \left(\frac{M_1 - M_2}{S_{within}}\right)\left(\frac{\sqrt{N}}{2}\right)$$ (p. 8)

(2.2) $$S^2_{within} = \frac{(n_1 - 1)S_1^2 + (n_2 - 1)S_2^2}{df_{within}}$$ (p. 8)

(2.3) $$r = \sqrt{\frac{t^2}{t^2 + df_{within}}} = \frac{t}{\sqrt{t^2 + df_{within}}}$$ (p. 9)

(2.4) $$r_{xy} = \frac{\Sigma Z_x Z_y}{N}$$ (p. 10)

(2.5) $$r = \sqrt{\frac{F}{F + df_{within}}}$$ (p. 10)

(2.6) $$r = \sqrt{\frac{SS_{contrast}}{SS_{contrast} + SS_{within}}}$$ (p. 11)

(2.7) $$d = \frac{M_1 - M_2}{\sigma_{within}}$$ (p. 11)

(2.8) $$d = \frac{2t}{\sqrt{df_{within}}}$$ (p. 11)

(2.9) $$g = \frac{M_1 - M_2}{S_{within}}$$ (p. 11)

(2.10) $$g = \frac{2t}{\sqrt{N}}$$ (p. 12)

(2.11) $$d = g\sqrt{\frac{N}{df_{within}}}$$ (p. 12)

(2.12) $$g = d\sqrt{\frac{df_{within}}{N}}$$ (p. 12)

(2.13) $$r = \frac{g}{\sqrt{g^2 + 4\left(\frac{df_{within}}{N}\right)}}$$ (p. 12)

(2.14) $$r = \frac{d}{\sqrt{d^2 + 4}}$$ (p. 13)

(2.15) $$ES_{counternull} = 2ES_{obtained} - ES_{null}$$ (p. 13)

(2.16) $$r_{counternull} = \sqrt{\frac{4r^2}{1 + 3r^2}}$$ (p. 14)

(2.17) $$\chi^2(1) = \Sigma \frac{(Obs - Exp)^2}{Exp}$$ (p. 19)

(2.18) $$r_{counternull} = \frac{2r}{\sqrt{1 + 3r^2}}$$ (p. 20)

(2.19) $$r_\phi = \sqrt{\frac{\chi^2(1)}{N}}$$ (p. 23)

(2.20) $$t = \left(\frac{M_1 - M_2}{S_{within}}\right)\left(\frac{\sqrt{N}}{2}\right)\sqrt{\frac{n_h}{\bar{n}}}$$ (p. 30)

(2.21) $$n_h = \frac{1}{\frac{1}{2}\left(\frac{1}{n_1} + \frac{1}{n_2}\right)}$$ (p. 30)

(2.22) $$g = \frac{2t}{\sqrt{N}}\sqrt{\frac{\bar{n}}{n_h}}$$ (p. 31)

(2.23) $$d = \frac{2t}{\sqrt{df_{within}}}\sqrt{\frac{\bar{n}}{n_h}}$$ (p. 31)

(2.24) $$r = \frac{d}{\sqrt{d^2 + 4\left(\frac{\bar{n}}{n_h}\right)}}$$ (p. 32)

(2.25) $$r = \frac{g}{\sqrt{g^2 + 4\left(\frac{\bar{n}}{n_h}\right)\left(\frac{df}{N}\right)}}$$ (p. 32)

(2.26) $$r_{BESD} = \sqrt{\frac{t^2}{t^2 + df_{within}\left(\frac{n_h}{\bar{n}}\right)}}$$ (p. 33)

(2.27) $$t = \frac{M_1 - M_2}{\sqrt{\frac{S_1^2}{n_1} + \frac{S_2^2}{n_2}}}$$ (p. 34)

(2.28) $$df_{satterthwaite} = \left[\frac{S_1^2}{n_1} + \frac{S_2^2}{n_2}\right]^2 \bigg/ \left[\frac{(S_1^2/n_1)^2}{n_1 - 1} + \frac{(S_2^2/n_2)^2}{n_2 - 1}\right]$$ (p. 34)

CHAPTER 3

(3.1) $$MS_{contrast} = SS_{contrast} = \frac{nL^2}{\Sigma \lambda_i^2}$$ (p. 37)

(3.2) $$r_{contrast} = \sqrt{\frac{F_{contrast}}{F_{contrast} + df_{within}}}$$ (p. 38)

(3.3) $$MS_{contrast} = r_{alerting}^2 \times SS_{between}$$ (p. 40)

(3.4) $$SS_{between} = \Sigma[n(M_i - \bar{M})^2]$$ (p. 40)

(3.5) $$r_{alerting}^2 = \frac{F_{contrast}}{F_{contrast} + F_{noncontrast}(df_{noncontrast})}$$ (p. 40)

(3.6) $$F_{noncontrast} = \frac{(SS_{between} - MS_{contrast})/df_{noncontrast}}{MS_{within}}$$ (p. 40)

(3.7) $$F_{noncontrast} = \frac{F_{between}(df_{between}) - F_{contrast}}{df_{noncontrast}}$$ (p. 40)

(3.8) $$df_{noncontrast} = df_{between} - 1$$ (p. 41)

(3.9) $$r_{alerting}^2 = \frac{SS_{contrast}}{SS_{between}}$$ (p. 41)

(3.10) $$t_{contrast} = \frac{\Sigma(M_i \lambda_i)}{\sqrt{MS_{within}\left(\Sigma \frac{\lambda_i^2}{n}\right)}} = \frac{L}{\sqrt{MS_{within}\left(\Sigma \frac{\lambda_i^2}{n}\right)}}$$ (p. 41)

(3.11) $$b_{contrast} = \sqrt{\frac{MS_{contrast}}{n\Sigma \lambda_i^2}} = \frac{L}{\Sigma \lambda_i^2}$$ (p. 42)

(3.12) $$\text{Adjusted observation} = \text{Residual} + \bar{M} + (\lambda_i b_{contrast})$$ (p. 43)

(3.13) $$r_{effect\ size} = \sqrt{\frac{F_{contrast}}{F_{contrast} + F_{noncontrast}(df_{noncontrast}) + df_{within}}}$$ (p. 46)

(3.14) $$r_{effect\ size} = \frac{r_{contrast}}{\sqrt{1 - r_{contrast}^2 + \frac{r_{contrast}^2}{r_{alerting}^2}}}$$ (p. 46)

(3.15) $$r_{BESD} = \sqrt{\frac{F_{contrast}}{F_{contrast} + F_{noncontrast}(df_{noncontrast} + df_{within})}}$$ (p. 48)

(3.16) $$\sigma_\lambda = \sqrt{\frac{\Sigma \lambda^2}{k}}$$ (p. 49)

(3.17) $$r_{alerting} = \sqrt{\frac{F_{contrast}}{F_{contrast} + F_{noncontrast}(df_{noncontrast})}}$$ (p. 51)

(3.18) $$F_{noncontrast}^* = \frac{(SS_{between}^* - MS_{contrast})/df_{noncontrast}^*}{MS_{within}}$$ (p. 57)

(3.19) $$F_{noncontrast}^* = \frac{F_{between}^*(df_{between}^*) - F_{contrast}}{df_{noncontrast}^*}$$ (p. 57)

(3.20) $$r_{alerting} = \sqrt{\frac{F_{contrast}(MS_{within})}{MS_{between}(df_{between})}}$$ (p. 62)

(3.21) $$r_{alerting} = \sqrt{\frac{F_{contrast}}{F_{between}(df_{between})}}$$ (p. 62)

(3.22) $$r_{effect\ size} = \sqrt{\frac{F_{contrast}}{F_{between}(df_{between}) + df_{within}}}$$ (p. 62)

(3.23) $$F_{noncontrast} = \frac{F_{between}(df_{between}) - F_{contrast}}{df_{between} - 1}$$ (p. 63)

(3.24) $$F_{contrast} = \frac{[\Sigma(M_i\lambda_i)]^2}{MS_{within}} \left[\frac{1}{\Sigma\frac{\lambda_i^2}{n_i}}\right]$$ (p. 63)

(3.25) $$F_{contrast} = \bar{F}_{contrast}(n_h^\lambda/\bar{n})$$ (p. 64)

(3.26) $$\bar{F}_{contrast} = \frac{[\Sigma(M_i\lambda_i)]^2}{MS_{within}} \left[\frac{1}{(\Sigma\lambda_i^2)/\bar{n}}\right]$$ (p. 64)

(3.27) $$n_h^\lambda = \frac{\Sigma\lambda_i^2}{\Sigma(\lambda_i^2/n_i)}$$ (p. 64)

(3.28) $$n_h = \frac{k}{\Sigma\frac{1}{n_i}}$$ (p. 64)

(3.29) $$t_{contrast} = \frac{\Sigma(M_i\lambda_i)}{\sqrt{MS_{within}\left(\Sigma\frac{\lambda_i^2}{n_i}\right)}}$$ (p. 64)

(3.30) $$\bar{F}_{contrast} = F_{contrast}(\bar{n}/n_h^\lambda)$$ (p. 65)

CHAPTER 4

(4.1) $$df_{noncontrast} = df_{between} - 1$$ (p. 80)

(4.2) $$F_{NC|NS} = \frac{(SS_{between} - MS_{contrast} - SS_{NS})/df_{NC|NS}}{MS_{within}}$$ (p. 81)

(4.3) $$df_{NC|NS} = df_{between} - 1 - df_{NS}$$ (p. 81)

(4.4) $$df_{NC|NS} = df_{noncontrast} - df_{NS}$$ (p. 81)

(4.5) $$r_{effect\ size|NS} = \sqrt{\frac{F_{contrast}}{F_{contrast} + F_{NC|NS}(df_{NC|NS}) + df_{within}}}$$ (p. 81)

(4.6) $$r_{BESD} = \sqrt{\frac{F_{contrast}}{F_{contrast} + F_{NC|NS}(df_{NC|NS} + df_{within})}}$$ (p. 93)

(4.7) $$r_{alerting|NS} = \sqrt{\frac{F_{contrast}}{F_{contrast} + F_{NC|NS}(df_{NC|NS})}}$$ (p. 106)

(4.8) $$\bar{F}_{contrast} = \frac{\bar{n}L^2/\Sigma\lambda_i^2}{MS_{within}}$$ (p. 115)

CHAPTER 5

(5.1) $$L = \Sigma(Y_i\lambda_i) = Y_1\lambda_1 + Y_2\lambda_2 + \cdots + Y_k\lambda_k$$ (p. 129)

(5.2) $$t = \frac{\bar{L} - \bar{L}_0}{\sqrt{\left(\frac{1}{kn}\right)S_{pooled}^2}}$$ (p. 139)

(5.3) $$S_{pooled}^2 = \frac{\Sigma S_i^2}{k}$$ (p. 139)

(5.4) $$df = k(n-1)$$ (p. 140)

(5.5) $$S_{pooled}^2 = \frac{(n_1-1)S_1^2 + (n_2-1)S_2^2 + \cdots + (n_k-1)S_k^2}{(n_1-1) + (n_2-1) + \cdots + (n_k-1)}$$ (p. 141)

(5.6) $$df = \Sigma n_i - k$$ (p. 141)

(5.7) $$MS_{error}^{between} = \frac{\Sigma SS_{error}}{\Sigma df_{error}}$$ (p. 142)

CHAPTER 6

(6.1) $$p_{adjusted} = p_{obtained} \times C_{implicit}$$ (p. 175)

(6.2) $$T_{ic} = \frac{\alpha}{p_{obtained}}$$ (p. 176)

(6.3) $$p_{adjusted} = p_{obtained} \times \frac{\Sigma W}{W_{contrast}}$$ (p. 176)

(6.4) $$p_{adjusted} = p_{obtained} \times \Sigma W$$ (p. 177)

APPENDIX B

Statistical Tables

TABLE B.1
Table of Standard Normal Deviates (Z)

	Second digit of Z									
Z	.00	.01	.02	.03	.04	.05	.06	.07	.08	.09
.0	.5000	.4960	.4920	.4880	.4840	.4801	.4761	.4721	.4681	.4641
.1	.4602	.4562	.4522	.4483	.4443	.4404	.4364	.4325	.4286	.4247
.2	.4207	.4168	.4129	.4090	.4052	.4013	.3974	.3936	.3897	.3859
.3	.3821	.3783	.3745	.3707	.3669	.3632	.3594	.3557	.3520	.3483
.4	.3446	.3409	.3372	.3336	.3300	.3264	.3228	.3192	.3156	.3121
.5	.3085	.3050	.3015	.2981	.2946	.2912	.2877	.2843	.2810	.2776
.6	.2743	.2709	.2676	.2643	.2611	.2578	.2546	.2514	.2483	.2451
.7	.2420	.2389	.2358	.2327	.2296	.2266	.2236	.2206	.2177	.2148
.8	.2119	.2090	.2061	.2033	.2005	.1977	.1949	.1922	.1894	.1867
.9	.1841	.1814	.1788	.1762	.1736	.1711	.1685	.1660	.1635	.1611
1.0	.1587	.1562	.1539	.1515	.1492	.1469	.1446	.1423	.1401	.1379
1.1	.1357	.1335	.1314	.1292	.1271	.1251	.1230	.1210	.1190	.1170
1.2	.1151	.1131	.1112	.1093	.1075	.1056	.1038	.1020	.1003	.0985
1.3	.0968	.0951	.0934	.0918	.0901	.0885	.0869	.0853	.0838	.0823
1.4	.0808	.0793	.0778	.0764	.0749	.0735	.0721	.0708	.0694	.0681
1.5	.0668	.0655	.0643	.0630	.0618	.0606	.0594	.0582	.0571	.0559
1.6	.0548	.0537	.0526	.0516	.0505	.0495	.0485	.0475	.0465	.0455
1.7	.0446	.0436	.0427	.0418	.0409	.0401	.0392	.0384	.0375	.0367
1.8	.0359	.0351	.0344	.0336	.0329	.0322	.0314	.0307	.0301	.0294
1.9	.0287	.0281	.0274	.0268	.0262	.0256	.0250	.0244	.0239	.0233
2.0	.0228	.0222	.0217	.0212	.0207	.0202	.0197	.0192	.0188	.0183
2.1	.0179	.0174	.0170	.0166	.0162	.0158	.0154	.0150	.0146	.0143
2.2	.0139	.0136	.0132	.0129	.0125	.0122	.0119	.0116	.0113	.0110
2.3	.0107	.0104	.0102	.0099	.0096	.0094	.0091	.0089	.0087	.0084
2.4	.0082	.0080	.0078	.0075	.0073	.0071	.0069	.0068	.0066	.0064

(continued)

TABLE B.1
(continued)

	Second digit of Z								
Z	.00	.01	.02	.03	.04	.05	.06	.07	.08	.09
2.5	.0062	.0060	.0059	.0057	.0055	.0054	.0052	.0051	.0049	.0048
2.6	.0047	.0045	.0044	.0043	.0041	.0040	.0039	.0038	.0037	.0036
2.7	.0035	.0034	.0033	.0032	.0031	.0030	.0029	.0028	.0027	.0026
2.8	.0026	.0025	.0024	.0023	.0023	.0022	.0021	.0021	.0020	.0019
2.9	.0019	.0018	.0018	.0017	.0016	.0016	.0015	.0015	.0014	.0014
3.0	.0013	.0013	.0013	.0012	.0012	.0011	.0011	.0011	.0010	.0010
3.1	.0010	.0009	.0009	.0009	.0008	.0008	.0008	.0008	.0007	.0007
3.2	.0007									
3.3	.0005									
3.4	.0003									
3.5	.00023									
3.6	.00016									
3.7	.00011									
3.8	.00007									
3.9	.00005									
4.0*	.00003									

* Additional values of Z are found in the bottom row of Table B.2, since t values for $df = \infty$ are also Z values.

Note: All p values are one-tailed in this table. Reproduced from *Nonparametric Statistics* (p. 247), by S. Siegel, 1956, New York: McGraw-Hill, with the permission of the publisher.

TABLE B.2
Extended Table of t

df \ p	.25	.10	.05	.025	.01	.005	.0025	.001
1	1.000	3.078	6.314	12.706	31.821	63.657	127.321	318.309
2	.816	1.886	2.920	4.303	6.965	9.925	14.089	22.327
3	.765	1.638	2.353	3.182	4.541	5.841	7.453	10.214
4	.741	1.533	2.132	2.776	3.747	4.604	5.598	7.173
5	.727	1.476	2.015	2.571	3.365	4.032	4.773	5.893
6	.718	1.440	1.943	2.447	3.143	3.707	4.317	5.208
7	.711	1.415	1.895	2.365	2.998	3.499	4.029	4.785
8	.706	1.397	1.860	2.306	2.896	3.355	3.833	4.501
9	.703	1.383	1.833	2.262	2.821	3.250	3.690	4.297
10	.700	1.372	1.812	2.228	2.764	3.169	3.581	4.144

df \ p	.25	.10	.05	.025	.01	.005	.0025	.001
11	.697	1.363	1.796	2.201	2.718	3.106	3.497	4.025
12	.695	1.356	1.782	2.179	2.681	3.055	3.428	3.930
13	.694	1.350	1.771	2.160	2.650	3.012	3.372	3.852
14	.692	1.345	1.761	2.145	2.624	2.977	3.326	3.787
15	.691	1.341	1.753	2.131	2.602	2.947	3.286	3.733
16	.690	1.337	1.746	2.120	2.583	2.921	3.252	3.686
17	.689	1.333	1.740	2.110	2.567	2.898	3.223	3.646
18	.688	1.330	1.734	2.101	2.552	2.878	3.197	3.610
19	.688	1.328	1.729	2.093	2.539	2.861	3.174	3.579
20	.687	1.325	1.725	2.086	2.528	2.845	3.153	3.552
21	.686	1.323	1.721	2.080	2.518	2.831	3.135	3.527
22	.686	1.321	1.717	2.074	2.508	2.819	3.119	3.505
23	.685	1.319	1.714	2.069	2.500	2.807	3.104	3.485
24	.685	1.318	1.711	2.064	2.492	2.797	3.090	3.467
25	.684	1.316	1.708	2.060	2.485	2.787	3.078	3.450
26	.684	1.315	1.706	2.056	2.479	2.779	3.067	3.435
27	.684	1.314	1.703	2.052	2.473	2.771	3.057	3.421
28	.683	1.313	1.701	2.048	2.467	2.763	3.047	3.408
29	.683	1.311	1.699	2.045	2.462	2.756	3.038	3.396
30	.683	1.310	1.697	2.042	2.457	2.750	3.030	3.385
35	.682	1.306	1.690	2.030	2.438	2.724	2.996	3.340
40	.681	1.303	1.684	2.021	2.423	2.704	2.971	3.307
45	.680	1.301	1.679	2.014	2.412	2.690	2.952	3.281
50	.679	1.299	1.676	2.009	2.403	2.678	2.937	3.261
55	.679	1.297	1.673	2.004	2.396	2.668	2.925	3.245
60	.679	1.296	1.671	2.000	2.390	2.660	2.915	3.232
70	.678	1.294	1.667	1.994	2.381	2.648	2.899	3.211
80	.678	1.292	1.664	1.990	2.374	2.639	2.887	3.195
90	.677	1.291	1.662	1.987	2.368	2.632	2.878	3.183
100	.677	1.290	1.660	1.984	2.364	2.626	2.871	3.174
200	.676	1.286	1.652	1.972	2.345	2.601	2.838	3.131
500	.675	1.283	1.648	1.965	2.334	2.586	2.820	3.107
1,000	.675	1.282	1.646	1.962	2.330	2.581	2.813	3.098
2,000	.675	1.282	1.645	1.961	2.328	2.578	2.810	3.094
10,000	.675	1.282	1.645	1.960	2.327	2.576	2.808	3.091
∞	.674	1.282	1.645	1.960	2.326	2.576	2.807	3.090

Note: All *p* values are one-tailed in this table.

TABLE B.2
(continued)

df \ p	.0005	.00025	.0001	.00005	.000025	.00001
1	636.619	1,273.239	3,183.099	6,366.198	12,732.395	31,830.989
2	31.598	44.705	70.700	99.992	141.416	223.603
3	12.924	16.326	22.204	28.000	35.298	47.928
4	8.610	10.306	13.034	15.544	18.522	23.332
5	6.869	7.976	9.678	11.178	12.893	15.547
6	5.959	6.788	8.025	9.082	10.261	12.032
7	5.408	6.082	7.063	7.885	8.782	10.103
8	5.041	5.618	6.442	7.120	7.851	8.907
9	4.781	5.291	6.010	6.594	7.215	8.102
10	4.587	5.049	5.694	6.211	6.757	7.527
11	4.437	4.863	5.453	5.921	6.412	7.098
12	4.318	4.716	5.263	5.694	6.143	6.756
13	4.221	4.597	5.111	5.513	5.928	6.501
14	4.140	4.499	4.985	5.363	5.753	6.287
15	4.073	4.417	4.880	5.239	5.607	6.109
16	4.015	4.346	4.791	5.134	5.484	5.960
17	3.965	4.286	4.714	5.044	5.379	5.832
18	3.922	4.233	4.648	4.966	5.288	5.722
19	3.883	4.187	4.590	4.897	5.209	5.627
20	3.850	4.146	4.539	4.837	5.139	5.543
21	3.819	4.110	4.493	4.784	5.077	5.469
22	3.792	4.077	4.452	4.736	5.022	5.402
23	3.768	4.048	4.415	4.693	4.972	5.343
24	3.745	4.021	4.382	4.654	4.927	5.290
25	3.725	3.997	4.352	4.619	4.887	5.241
26	3.707	3.974	4.324	4.587	4.850	5.197
27	3.690	3.954	4.299	4.558	4.816	5.157
28	3.674	3.935	4.275	4.530	4.784	5.120
29	3.659	3.918	4.254	4.506	4.756	5.086
30	3.646	3.902	4.234	4.482	4.729	5.054
35	3.591	3.836	4.153	4.389	4.622	4.927
40	3.551	3.788	4.094	4.321	4.544	4.835
45	3.520	3.752	4.049	4.269	4.485	4.766
50	3.496	3.723	4.014	4.228	4.438	4.711
55	3.476	3.700	3.986	4.196	4.401	4.667
60	3.460	3.681	3.962	4.169	4.370	4.631
70	3.435	3.651	3.926	4.127	4.323	4.576
80	3.416	3.629	3.899	4.096	4.288	4.535
90	3.402	3.612	3.878	4.072	4.261	4.503
100	3.390	3.598	3.862	4.053	4.240	4.478
200	3.340	3.539	3.789	3.970	4.146	4.369
500	3.310	3.504	3.747	3.922	4.091	4.306
1,000	3.300	3.492	3.733	3.906	4.073	4.285
2,000	3.295	3.486	3.726	3.898	4.064	4.275
10,000	3.292	3.482	3.720	3.892	4.058	4.267
∞	3.291	3.481	3.719	3.891	4.056	4.265

Note: All *p* values are one-tailed in this table.

df \ p	.000005	.0000025	.000001	.0000005	.00000025	.0000001
1	63,661.977	127,323.954	318,309.886	636,619.772	1,273,239.545	3,183,098.862
2	316.225	447.212	707.106	999.999	1,414.213	2,236.068
3	60.397	76.104	103.299	130.155	163.989	222.572
4	27.771	33.047	41.578	49.459	58.829	73.986
5	17.807	20.591	24.771	28.477	32.734	39.340
6	13.555	15.260	17.830	20.047	22.532	26.286
7	11.215	12.437	14.241	15.764	17.447	19.932
8	9.782	10.731	12.110	13.257	14.504	16.320
9	8.827	9.605	10.720	11.637	12.623	14.041
10	8.150	8.812	9.752	10.516	11.328	12.492
11	7.648	8.227	9.043	9.702	10.397	11.381
12	7.261	7.780	8.504	9.085	9.695	10.551
13	6.955	7.427	8.082	8.604	9.149	9.909
14	6.706	7.142	7.743	8.218	8.713	9.400
15	6.502	6.907	7.465	7.903	8.358	8.986
16	6.330	6.711	7.233	7.642	8.064	8.645
17	6.184	6.545	7.037	7.421	7.817	8.358
18	6.059	6.402	6.869	7.232	7.605	8.115
19	5.949	6.278	6.723	7.069	7.423	7.905
20	5.854	6.170	6.597	6.927	7.265	7.723
21	5.769	6.074	6.485	6.802	7.126	7.564
22	5.694	5.989	6.386	6.692	7.003	7.423
23	5.627	5.913	6.297	6.593	6.893	7.298
24	5.566	5.845	6.218	6.504	6.795	7.185
25	5.511	5.783	6.146	6.424	6.706	7.085
26	5.461	5.726	6.081	6.352	6.626	6.993
27	5.415	5.675	6.021	6.286	6.553	6.910
28	5.373	5.628	5.967	6.225	6.486	6.835
29	5.335	5.585	5.917	6.170	6.426	6.765
30	5.299	5.545	5.871	6.119	6.369	6.701
35	5.156	5.385	5.687	5.915	6.143	6.447
40	5.053	5.269	5.554	5.768	5.983	6.266
45	4.975	5.182	5.454	5.659	5.862	6.130
50	4.914	5.115	5.377	5.573	5.769	6.025
55	4.865	5.060	5.315	5.505	5.694	5.942
60	4.825	5.015	5.264	5.449	5.633	5.873
70	4.763	4.946	5.185	5.363	5.539	5.768
80	4.717	4.896	5.128	5.300	5.470	5.691
90	4.682	4.857	5.084	5.252	5.417	5.633
100	4.654	4.826	5.049	5.214	5.376	5.587

(continued)

TABLE B.2
(continued)

df \ p	.000005	.0000025	.000001	.0000005	.00000025	.0000001
200	4.533	4.692	4.897	5.048	5.196	5.387
500	4.463	4.615	4.810	4.953	5.094	5.273
1,000	4.440	4.590	4.781	4.922	5.060	5.236
2,000	4.428	4.578	4.767	4.907	5.043	5.218
10,000	4.419	4.567	4.756	4.895	5.029	5.203
∞	4.417	4.565	4.753	4.892	5.026	5.199

Note: All p values are one-tailed in this table.

Standard normal deviates (Z) corresponding to t can be estimated quite accurately from

$$Z = \left[df \, \log_e \left(1 + \frac{t^2}{df} \right) \right]^{1/2} \left[1 - \frac{1}{2df} \right]^{1/2}$$

Reproduced from "Extended tables of the percentage points of Student's t-distribution," by E. T. Federighi, 1959, *Journal of the American Statistical Association*, pp. 683–688, with the permission of the publisher.

TABLE B.3
Table of F

df_2	df_1 \ p	1	2	3	4	5	6	8	12	24	∞
1	.001	405284	500000	540379	562500	576405	585937	598144	610667	623497	636619
	.005	16211	20000	21615	22500	23056	23437	23925	24426	24940	25465
	.01	4052	4999	5403	5625	5764	5859	5981	6106	6234	6366
	.025	647.79	799.50	864.16	899.58	921.85	937.11	956.66	976.71	997.25	1018.30
	.05	161.45	199.50	215.71	224.58	230.16	233.99	238.88	243.91	249.05	254.32
	.10	39.86	49.50	53.59	55.83	57.24	58.20	59.44	60.70	62.00	63.33
	.20	9.47	12.00	13.06	13.73	14.01	14.26	14.59	14.90	15.24	15.58
2	.001	998.5	999.0	999.2	999.2	999.3	999.3	999.4	999.4	999.5	999.5
	.005	198.50	199.00	199.17	199.25	199.30	199.33	199.37	199.42	199.46	199.51
	.01	98.49	99.00	99.17	99.25	99.30	99.33	99.36	99.42	99.46	99.50
	.025	38.51	39.00	39.17	39.25	39.30	39.33	39.37	39.42	39.46	39.50
	.05	18.51	19.00	19.16	19.25	19.30	19.33	19.37	19.41	19.45	19.50
	.10	8.53	9.00	9.16	9.24	9.29	9.33	9.37	9.41	9.45	9.49
	.20	3.56	4.00	4.16	4.24	4.28	4.32	4.36	4.40	4.44	4.48
3	.001	167.5	148.5	141.1	137.1	134.6	132.8	130.6	128.3	125.9	123.5
	.005	55.55	49.80	47.47	46.20	45.39	44.84	44.13	43.39	42.62	41.83
	.01	34.12	30.81	29.46	28.71	28.24	27.91	27.49	27.05	26.60	26.12
	.025	17.44	16.04	15.44	15.10	14.89	14.74	14.54	14.34	14.12	13.90
	.05	10.13	9.55	9.28	9.12	9.01	8.94	8.84	8.74	8.64	8.53
	.10	5.54	5.46	5.39	5.34	5.31	5.28	5.25	5.22	5.18	5.13
	.20	2.68	2.89	2.94	2.96	2.97	2.97	2.98	2.98	2.98	2.98

df_2 \ df_1	p	1	2	3	4	5	6	8	12	24	∞
4	.001	74.14	61.25	56.18	53.44	51.71	50.53	49.00	47.41	45.77	44.05
	.005	31.33	26.28	24.26	23.16	22.46	21.98	21.35	20.71	20.03	19.33
	.01	21.20	18.00	16.69	15.98	15.52	15.21	14.80	14.37	13.93	13.46
	.025	12.22	10.65	9.98	9.60	9.36	9.20	8.98	8.75	8.51	8.26
	.05	7.71	6.94	6.59	6.39	6.26	6.16	6.04	5.91	5.77	5.63
	.10	4.54	4.32	4.19	4.11	4.05	4.01	3.95	3.90	3.83	3.76
	.20	2.35	2.47	2.48	2.48	2.48	2.47	2.47	2.46	2.44	2.43
5	.001	47.04	36.61	33.20	31.09	29.75	28.84	27.64	26.42	25.14	23.78
	.005	22.79	18.31	16.53	15.56	14.94	14.51	13.96	13.38	12.78	12.14
	.01	16.26	13.27	12.06	11.39	10.97	10.67	10.29	9.89	9.47	9.02
	.025	10.01	8.43	7.76	7.39	7.15	6.98	6.76	6.52	6.28	6.02
	.05	6.61	5.79	5.41	5.19	5.05	4.95	4.82	4.68	4.53	4.36
	.10	4.06	3.78	3.62	3.52	3.45	3.40	3.34	3.27	3.19	3.10
	.20	2.18	2.26	2.25	2.24	2.23	2.22	2.20	2.18	2.16	2.13
6	.001	35.51	27.00	23.70	21.90	20.81	20.03	19.03	17.99	16.89	15.75
	.005	18.64	14.54	12.92	12.03	11.46	11.07	10.57	10.03	9.47	8.88
	.01	13.74	10.92	9.78	9.15	8.75	8.47	8.10	7.72	7.31	6.88
	.025	8.81	7.26	6.60	6.23	5.99	5.82	5.60	5.37	5.12	4.85
	.05	5.99	5.14	4.76	4.53	4.39	4.28	4.15	4.00	3.84	3.67
	.10	3.78	3.46	3.29	3.18	3.11	3.05	2.98	2.90	2.82	2.72
	.20	2.07	2.13	2.11	2.09	2.08	2.06	2.04	2.02	1.99	1.95
7	.001	29.22	21.69	18.77	17.19	16.21	15.52	14.63	13.71	12.73	11.69
	.005	16.24	12.40	10.88	10.05	9.52	9.16	8.68	8.18	7.65	7.08
	.01	12.25	9.55	8.45	7.85	7.46	7.19	6.84	6.47	6.07	5.65
	.025	8.07	6.54	5.89	5.52	5.29	5.12	4.90	4.67	4.42	4.14
	.05	5.59	4.74	4.35	4.12	3.97	3.87	3.73	3.57	3.41	3.23
	.10	3.59	3.26	3.07	2.96	2.88	2.83	2.75	2.67	2.58	2.47
	.20	2.00	2.04	2.02	1.99	1.97	1.96	1.93	1.91	1.87	1.83
8	.001	25.42	18.49	15.83	14.39	13.49	12.86	12.04	11.19	10.30	9.34
	.005	14.69	11.04	9.60	8.81	8.30	7.95	7.50	7.01	6.50	5.95
	.01	11.26	8.65	7.59	7.01	6.63	6.37	6.03	5.67	5.28	4.86
	.025	7.57	6.06	5.42	5.05	4.82	4.65	4.43	4.20	3.95	3.67
	.05	5.32	4.46	4.07	3.84	3.69	3.58	3.44	3.28	3.12	2.93
	.10	3.46	3.11	2.92	2.81	2.73	2.67	2.59	2.50	2.40	2.29
	.20	1.95	1.98	1.95	1.92	1.90	1.88	1.86	1.83	1.79	1.74
9	.001	22.86	16.39	13.90	12.56	11.71	11.13	10.37	9.57	8.72	7.81
	.005	13.61	10.11	8.72	7.96	7.47	7.13	6.69	6.23	5.73	5.19
	.01	10.56	8.02	6.99	6.42	6.06	5.80	5.47	5.11	4.73	4.31
	.025	7.21	5.71	5.08	4.72	4.48	4.32	4.10	3.87	3.61	3.33
	.05	5.12	4.26	3.86	3.63	3.48	3.37	3.23	3.07	2.90	2.71
	.10	3.36	3.01	2.81	2.69	2.61	2.55	2.47	2.38	2.28	2.16
	.20	1.91	1.94	1.90	1.87	1.85	1.83	1.80	1.76	1.72	1.67

(continued)

TABLE B.3
(continued)

df_2 \ df_1	p	1	2	3	4	5	6	8	12	24	∞
10	.001	21.04	14.91	12.55	11.28	10.48	9.92	9.20	8.45	7.64	6.76
	.005	12.83	9.43	8.08	7.34	6.87	6.54	6.12	5.66	5.17	4.64
	.01	10.04	7.56	6.55	5.99	5.64	5.39	5.06	4.71	4.33	3.91
	.025	6.94	5.46	4.83	4.47	4.24	4.07	3.85	3.62	3.37	3.08
	.05	4.96	4.10	3.71	3.48	3.33	3.22	3.07	2.91	2.74	2.54
	.10	3.28	2.92	2.73	2.61	2.52	2.46	2.38	2.28	2.18	2.06
	.20	1.88	1.90	1.86	1.83	1.80	1.78	1.75	1.72	1.67	1.62
11	.001	19.69	13.81	11.56	10.35	9.58	9.05	8.35	7.63	6.85	6.00
	.005	12.23	8.91	7.60	6.88	6.42	6.10	5.68	5.24	4.76	4.23
	.01	9.65	7.20	6.22	5.67	5.32	5.07	4.74	4.40	4.02	3.60
	.025	6.72	5.26	4.63	4.28	4.04	3.88	3.66	3.43	3.17	2.88
	.05	4.84	3.98	3.59	3.36	3.20	3.09	2.95	2.79	2.61	2.40
	.10	3.23	2.86	2.66	2.54	2.45	2.39	2.30	2.21	2.10	1.97
	.20	1.86	1.87	1.83	1.80	1.77	1.75	1.72	1.68	1.63	1.57
12	.001	18.64	12.97	10.80	9.63	8.89	8.38	7.71	7.00	6.25	5.42
	.005	11.75	8.51	7.23	6.52	6.07	5.76	5.35	4.91	4.43	3.90
	.01	9.33	6.93	5.95	5.41	5.06	4.82	4.50	4.16	3.78	3.36
	.025	6.55	5.10	4.47	4.12	3.89	3.73	3.51	3.28	3.02	2.72
	.05	4.75	3.88	3.49	3.26	3.11	3.00	2.85	2.69	2.50	2.30
	.10	3.18	2.81	2.61	2.48	2.39	2.33	2.24	2.15	2.04	1.90
	.20	1.84	1.85	1.80	1.77	1.74	1.72	1.69	1.65	1.60	1.54
13	.001	17.81	12.31	10.21	9.07	8.35	7.86	7.21	6.52	5.78	4.97
	.005	11.37	8.19	6.93	6.23	5.79	5.48	5.08	4.64	4.17	3.65
	.01	9.07	6.70	5.74	5.20	4.86	4.62	4.30	3.96	3.59	3.16
	.025	6.41	4.97	4.35	4.00	3.77	3.60	3.39	3.15	2.89	2.60
	.05	4.67	3.80	3.41	3.18	3.02	2.92	2.77	2.60	2.42	2.21
	.10	3.14	2.76	2.56	2.43	2.35	2.28	2.20	2.10	1.98	1.85
	.20	1.82	1.83	1.78	1.75	1.72	1.69	1.66	1.62	1.57	1.51
14	.001	17.14	11.78	9.73	8.62	7.92	7.43	6.80	6.13	5.41	4.60
	.005	11.06	7.92	6.68	6.00	5.56	5.26	4.86	4.43	3.96	3.44
	.01	8.86	6.51	5.56	5.03	4.69	4.46	4.14	3.80	3.43	3.00
	.025	6.30	4.86	4.24	3.89	3.66	3.50	3.29	3.05	2.79	2.49
	.05	4.60	3.74	3.34	3.11	2.96	2.85	2.70	2.53	2.35	2.13
	.10	3.10	2.73	2.52	2.39	2.31	2.24	2.15	2.05	1.94	1.80
	.20	1.81	1.81	1.76	1.73	1.70	1.67	1.64	1.60	1.55	1.48
15	.001	16.59	11.34	9.34	8.25	7.57	7.09	6.47	5.81	5.10	4.31
	.005	10.80	7.70	6.48	5.80	5.37	5.07	4.67	4.25	3.79	3.26
	.01	8.68	6.36	5.42	4.89	4.56	4.32	4.00	3.67	3.29	2.87
	.025	6.20	4.77	4.15	3.80	3.58	3.41	3.20	2.96	2.70	2.40
	.05	4.54	3.68	3.29	3.06	2.90	2.79	2.64	2.48	2.29	2.07
	.10	3.07	2.70	2.49	2.36	2.27	2.21	2.12	2.02	1.90	1.76
	.20	1.80	1.79	1.75	1.71	1.68	1.66	1.62	1.58	1.53	1.46
16	.001	16.12	10.97	9.00	7.94	7.27	6.81	6.19	5.55	4.85	4.06
	.005	10.58	7.51	6.30	5.64	5.21	4.91	4.52	4.10	3.64	3.11
	.01	8.53	6.23	5.29	4.77	4.44	4.20	3.89	3.55	3.18	2.75
	.025	6.12	4.69	4.08	3.73	3.50	3.34	3.12	2.89	2.63	2.32
	.05	4.49	3.63	3.24	3.01	2.85	2.74	2.59	2.42	2.24	2.01
	.10	3.05	2.67	2.46	2.33	2.24	2.18	2.09	1.99	1.87	1.72
	.20	1.79	1.78	1.74	1.70	1.67	1.64	1.61	1.56	1.51	1.43

df_2 \ df_1	p	1	2	3	4	5	6	8	12	24	∞
17	.001	15.72	10.66	8.73	7.68	7.02	6.56	5.96	5.32	4.63	3.85
	.005	10.38	7.35	6.16	5.50	5.07	4.78	4.39	3.97	3.51	2.98
	.01	8.40	6.11	5.18	4.67	4.34	4.10	3.79	3.45	3.08	2.65
	.025	6.04	4.62	4.01	3.66	3.44	3.28	3.06	2.82	2.56	2.25
	.05	4.45	3.59	3.20	2.96	2.81	2.70	2.55	2.38	2.19	1.96
	.10	3.03	2.64	2.44	2.31	2.22	2.15	2.06	1.96	1.84	1.69
	.20	1.78	1.77	1.72	1.68	1.65	1.63	1.59	1.55	1.49	1.42
18	.001	15.38	10.39	8.49	7.46	6.81	6.35	5.76	5.13	4.45	3.67
	.005	10.22	7.21	6.03	5.37	4.96	4.66	4.28	3.86	3.40	2.87
	.01	8.28	6.01	5.09	4.58	4.25	4.01	3.71	3.37	3.00	2.57
	.025	5.98	4.56	3.95	3.61	3.38	3.22	3.01	2.77	2.50	2.19
	.05	4.41	3.55	3.16	2.93	2.77	2.66	2.51	2.34	2.15	1.92
	.10	3.01	2.62	2.42	2.29	2.20	2.13	2.04	1.93	1.81	1.66
	.20	1.77	1.76	1.71	1.67	1.64	1.62	1.58	1.53	1.48	1.40
19	.001	15.08	10.16	8.28	7.26	6.61	6.18	5.59	4.97	4.29	3.52
	.005	10.07	7.09	5.92	5.27	4.85	4.56	4.18	3.76	3.31	2.78
	.01	8.18	5.93	5.01	4.50	4.17	3.94	3.63	3.30	2.92	2.49
	.025	5.92	4.51	3.90	3.56	3.33	3.17	2.96	2.72	2.45	2.13
	.05	4.38	3.52	3.13	2.90	2.74	2.63	2.48	2.31	2.11	1.88
	.10	2.99	2.61	2.40	2.27	2.18	2.11	2.02	1.91	1.79	1.63
	.20	1.76	1.75	1.70	1.66	1.63	1.61	1.57	1.52	1.46	1.39
20	.001	14.82	9.95	8.10	7.10	6.46	6.02	5.44	4.82	4.15	3.38
	.005	9.94	6.99	5.82	5.17	4.76	4.47	4.09	3.68	3.22	2.69
	.01	8.10	5.85	4.94	4.43	4.10	3.87	3.56	3.23	2.86	2.42
	.025	5.87	4.46	3.86	3.51	3.29	3.13	2.91	2.68	2.41	2.09
	.05	4.35	3.49	3.10	2.87	2.71	2.60	2.45	2.28	2.08	1.84
	.10	2.97	2.59	2.38	2.25	2.16	2.09	2.00	1.89	1.77	1.61
	.20	1.76	1.75	1.70	1.65	1.62	1.60	1.56	1.51	1.45	1.37
21	.001	14.59	9.77	7.94	6.95	6.32	5.88	5.31	4.70	4.03	3.26
	.005	9.83	6.89	5.73	5.09	4.68	4.39	4.01	3.60	3.15	2.61
	.01	8.02	5.78	4.87	4.37	4.04	3.81	3.51	3.17	2.80	2.36
	.025	5.83	4.42	3.82	3.48	3.25	3.09	2.87	2.64	2.37	2.04
	.05	4.32	3.47	3.07	2.84	2.68	2.57	2.42	2.25	2.05	1.81
	.10	2.96	2.57	2.36	2.23	2.14	2.08	1.98	1.88	1.75	1.59
	.20	1.75	1.74	1.69	1.65	1.61	1.59	1.55	1.50	1.44	1.36
22	.001	14.38	9.61	7.80	6.81	6.19	5.76	5.19	4.58	3.92	3.15
	.005	9.73	6.81	5.65	5.02	4.61	4.32	3.94	3.54	3.08	2.55
	.01	7.94	5.72	4.82	4.31	3.99	3.76	3.45	3.12	2.75	2.31
	.025	5.79	4.38	3.78	3.44	3.22	3.05	2.84	2.60	2.33	2.00
	.05	4.30	3.44	3.05	2.82	2.66	2.55	2.40	2.23	2.03	1.78
	.10	2.95	2.56	2.35	2.22	2.13	2.06	1.97	1.86	1.73	1.57
	.20	1.75	1.73	1.68	1.64	1.61	1.58	1.54	1.49	1.43	1.35

(continued)

TABLE B.3
(continued)

df_2 \ df_1	p	1	2	3	4	5	6	8	12	24	∞
23	.001	14.19	9.47	7.67	6.69	6.08	5.65	5.09	4.48	3.82	3.05
	.005	9.63	6.73	5.58	4.95	4.54	4.26	3.88	3.47	3.02	2.48
	.01	7.88	5.66	4.76	4.26	3.94	3.71	3.41	3.07	2.70	2.26
	.025	5.75	4.35	3.75	3.41	3.18	3.02	2.81	2.57	2.30	1.97
	.05	4.28	3.42	3.03	2.80	2.64	2.53	2.38	2.20	2.00	1.76
	.10	2.94	2.55	2.34	2.21	2.11	2.05	1.95	1.84	1.72	1.55
	.20	1.74	1.73	1.68	1.63	1.60	1.57	1.53	1.49	1.42	1.34
24	.001	14.03	9.34	7.55	6.59	5.98	5.55	4.99	4.39	3.74	2.97
	.005	9.55	6.66	5.52	4.89	4.49	4.20	3.83	3.42	2.97	2.43
	.01	7.82	5.61	4.72	4.22	3.90	3.67	3.36	3.03	2.66	2.21
	.025	5.72	4.32	3.72	3.38	3.15	2.99	2.78	2.54	2.27	1.94
	.05	4.26	3.40	3.01	2.78	2.62	2.51	2.36	2.18	1.98	1.73
	.10	2.93	2.54	2.33	2.19	2.10	2.04	1.94	1.83	1.70	1.53
	.20	1.74	1.72	1.67	1.63	1.59	1.57	1.53	1.48	1.42	1.33
25	.001	13.88	9.22	7.45	6.49	5.88	5.46	4.91	4.31	3.66	2.89
	.005	9.48	6.60	5.46	4.84	4.43	4.15	3.78	3.37	2.92	2.38
	.01	7.77	5.57	4.68	4.18	3.86	3.63	3.32	2.99	2.62	2.17
	.025	5.69	4.29	3.69	3.35	3.13	2.97	2.75	2.51	2.24	1.91
	.05	4.24	3.38	2.99	2.76	2.60	2.49	2.34	2.16	1.96	1.71
	.10	2.92	2.53	2.32	2.18	2.09	2.02	1.93	1.82	1.69	1.52
	.20	1.73	1.72	1.66	1.62	1.59	1.56	1.52	1.47	1.41	1.32
26	.001	13.74	9.12	7.36	6.41	5.80	5.38	4.83	4.24	3.59	2.82
	.005	9.41	6.54	5.41	4.79	4.38	4.10	3.73	3.33	2.87	2.33
	.01	7.72	5.53	4.64	4.14	3.82	3.59	3.29	2.96	2.58	2.13
	.025	5.66	4.27	3.67	3.33	3.10	2.94	2.73	2.49	2.22	1.88
	.05	4.22	3.37	2.98	2.74	2.59	2.47	2.32	2.15	1.95	1.69
	.10	2.91	2.52	2.31	2.17	2.08	2.01	1.92	1.81	1.68	1.50
	.20	1.73	1.71	1.66	1.62	1.58	1.56	1.52	1.47	1.40	1.31
27	.001	13.61	9.02	7.27	6.33	5.73	5.31	4.76	4.17	3.52	2.75
	.005	9.34	6.49	5.36	4.74	4.34	4.06	3.69	3.28	2.83	2.29
	.01	7.68	5.49	4.60	4.11	3.78	3.56	3.26	2.93	2.55	2.10
	.025	5.63	4.24	3.65	3.31	3.08	2.92	2.71	2.47	2.19	1.85
	.05	4.21	3.35	2.96	2.73	2.57	2.46	2.30	2.13	1.93	1.67
	.10	2.90	2.51	2.30	2.17	2.07	2.00	1.91	1.80	1.67	1.49
	.20	1.73	1.71	1.66	1.61	1.58	1.55	1.51	1.46	1.40	1.30
28	.001	13.50	8.93	7.19	6.25	5.66	5.24	4.69	4.11	3.46	2.70
	.005	9.28	6.44	5.32	4.70	4.30	4.02	3.65	3.25	2.79	2.25
	.01	7.64	5.45	4.57	4.07	3.75	3.53	3.23	2.90	2.52	2.06
	.025	5.61	4.22	3.63	3.29	3.06	2.90	2.69	2.45	2.17	1.83
	.05	4.20	3.34	2.95	2.71	2.56	2.44	2.29	2.12	1.91	1.65
	.10	2.89	2.50	2.29	2.16	2.06	2.00	1.90	1.79	1.66	1.48
	.20	1.72	1.71	1.65	1.61	1.57	1.55	1.51	1.46	1.39	1.30

df_2 \ df_1	p	1	2	3	4	5	6	8	12	24	∞
29	.001	13.39	8.85	7.12	6.19	5.59	5.18	4.64	4.05	3.41	2.64
	.005	9.23	6.40	5.28	4.66	4.26	3.98	3.61	3.21	2.76	2.21
	.01	7.60	5.42	4.54	4.04	3.73	3.50	3.20	2.87	2.49	2.03
	.025	5.59	4.20	3.61	3.27	3.04	2.88	2.67	2.43	2.15	1.81
	.05	4.18	3.33	2.93	2.70	2.54	2.43	2.28	2.10	1.90	1.64
	.10	2.89	2.50	2.28	2.15	2.06	1.99	1.89	1.78	1.65	1.47
	.20	1.72	1.70	1.65	1.60	1.57	1.54	1.50	1.45	1.39	1.29
30	.001	13.29	8.77	7.05	6.12	5.53	5.12	4.58	4.00	3.36	2.59
	.005	9.18	6.35	5.24	4.62	4.23	3.95	3.58	3.18	2.73	2.18
	.01	7.56	5.39	4.51	4.02	3.70	3.47	3.17	2.84	2.47	2.01
	.025	5.57	4.18	3.59	3.25	3.03	2.87	2.65	2.41	2.14	1.79
	.05	4.17	3.32	2.92	2.69	2.53	2.42	2.27	2.09	1.89	1.62
	.10	2.88	2.49	2.28	2.14	2.05	1.98	1.88	1.77	1.64	1.46
	.20	1.72	1.70	1.64	1.60	1.57	1.54	1.50	1.45	1.38	1.28
40	.001	12.61	8.25	6.60	5.70	5.13	4.73	4.21	3.64	3.01	2.23
	.005	8.83	6.07	4.98	4.37	3.99	3.71	3.35	2.95	2.50	1.93
	.01	7.31	5.18	4.31	3.83	3.51	3.29	2.99	2.66	2.29	1.80
	.025	5.42	4.05	3.46	3.13	2.90	2.74	2.53	2.29	2.01	1.64
	.05	4.08	3.23	2.84	2.61	2.45	2.34	2.18	2.00	1.79	1.51
	.10	2.84	2.44	2.23	2.09	2.00	1.93	1.83	1.71	1.57	1.38
	.20	1.70	1.68	1.62	1.57	1.54	1.51	1.47	1.41	1.34	1.24
60	.001	11.97	7.76	6.17	5.31	4.76	4.37	3.87	3.31	2.69	1.90
	.005	8.49	5.80	4.73	4.14	3.76	3.49	3.13	2.74	2.29	1.69
	.01	7.08	4.98	4.13	3.65	3.34	3.12	2.82	2.50	2.12	1.60
	.025	5.29	3.93	3.34	3.01	2.79	2.63	2.41	2.17	1.88	1.48
	.05	4.00	3.15	2.76	2.52	2.37	2.25	2.10	1.92	1.70	1.39
	.10	2.79	2.39	2.18	2.04	1.95	1.87	1.77	1.66	1.51	1.29
	.20	1.68	1.65	1.59	1.55	1.51	1.48	1.44	1.38	1.31	1.18
120	.001	11.38	7.31	5.79	4.95	4.42	4.04	3.55	3.02	2.40	1.56
	.005	8.18	5.54	4.50	3.92	3.55	3.28	2.93	2.54	2.09	1.43
	.01	6.85	4.79	3.95	3.48	3.17	2.96	2.66	2.34	1.95	1.38
	.025	5.15	3.80	3.23	2.89	2.67	2.52	2.30	2.05	1.76	1.31
	.05	3.92	3.07	2.68	2.45	2.29	2.17	2.02	1.83	1.61	1.25
	.10	2.75	2.35	2.13	1.99	1.90	1.82	1.72	1.60	1.45	1.19
	.20	1.66	1.63	1.57	1.52	1.48	1.45	1.41	1.35	1.27	1.12
∞	.001	10.83	6.91	5.42	4.62	4.10	3.74	3.27	2.74	2.13	1.00
	.005	7.88	5.30	4.28	3.72	3.35	3.09	2.74	2.36	1.90	1.00
	.01	6.64	4.60	3.78	3.32	3.02	2.80	2.51	2.18	1.79	1.00
	.025	5.02	3.69	3.12	2.79	2.57	2.41	2.19	1.94	1.64	1.00
	.05	3.84	2.99	2.60	2.37	2.21	2.09	1.94	1.75	1.52	1.00
	.10	2.71	2.30	2.08	1.94	1.85	1.77	1.67	1.55	1.38	1.00
	.20	1.64	1.61	1.55	1.50	1.46	1.43	1.38	1.32	1.23	1.00

Note: Reproduced from *Design and Analysis of Experiments in Psychology and Education* (pp. 41–44), by E. F. Lindquist, 1953, Boston: Houghton Mifflin, with the permission of the publisher.

TABLE B.4
Table of χ^2

df	.99	.98	.95	.90	.80	.70	.50	.30	.20	.10	.05	.02	.01	.001
1	.00016	.00063	.00393	.0158	.0642	.148	.455	1.074	1.642	2.706	3.841	5.412	6.635	10.827
2	.0201	.0404	.103	.211	.446	.713	1.386	2.408	3.219	4.605	5.991	7.824	9.210	13.815
3	.115	.185	.352	.584	1.005	1.424	2.366	3.665	4.642	6.251	7.815	9.837	11.345	16.268
4	.297	.429	.711	1.064	1.649	2.195	3.357	4.878	5.989	7.779	9.488	11.668	13.277	18.465
5	.554	.752	1.145	1.610	2.343	3.000	4.351	6.064	7.289	9.236	11.070	13.388	15.086	20.517
6	.872	1.134	1.635	2.204	3.070	3.828	5.348	7.231	8.558	10.645	12.592	15.033	16.812	22.457
7	1.239	1.564	2.167	2.833	3.822	4.671	6.346	8.383	9.803	12.017	14.067	16.622	18.475	24.322
8	1.646	2.032	2.733	3.490	4.594	5.527	7.344	9.524	11.030	13.362	15.507	18.168	20.090	26.125
9	2.088	2.532	3.325	4.168	5.380	6.393	8.343	10.656	12.242	14.684	16.919	19.679	21.666	27.877
10	2.558	3.059	3.940	4.865	6.179	7.267	9.342	11.781	13.442	15.987	18.307	21.161	23.209	29.588
11	3.053	3.609	4.575	5.578	6.989	8.148	10.341	12.899	14.631	17.275	19.675	22.618	24.725	31.264
12	3.571	4.178	5.226	6.304	7.807	9.034	11.340	14.011	15.812	18.549	21.026	24.054	26.217	32.909
13	4.107	4.765	5.892	7.042	8.634	9.926	12.340	15.119	16.985	19.812	22.362	25.472	27.688	34.528
14	4.660	5.368	6.571	7.790	9.467	10.821	13.339	16.222	18.151	21.064	23.685	26.873	29.141	36.123
15	5.229	5.985	7.261	8.547	10.307	11.721	14.339	17.322	19.311	22.307	24.996	28.259	30.578	37.697
16	5.812	6.614	7.962	9.312	11.152	12.624	15.338	18.418	20.465	23.542	26.296	29.633	32.000	39.252
17	6.408	7.255	8.672	10.085	12.002	13.531	16.338	19.511	21.615	24.769	27.587	30.995	33.409	40.790
18	7.015	7.906	9.390	10.865	12.857	14.440	17.338	20.601	22.760	25.989	28.869	32.346	34.805	42.312
19	7.633	8.567	10.117	11.651	13.716	15.352	18.338	21.689	23.900	27.204	30.144	33.687	36.191	43.820
20	8.260	9.237	10.851	12.443	14.578	16.266	19.337	22.775	25.038	28.412	31.410	35.020	37.566	45.315

df	.99	.98	.95	.90	.80	.70	.50	.30	.20	.10	.05	.02	.01	.001
21	8.897	9.915	11.591	13.240	15.445	17.182	20.337	23.858	26.171	29.615	32.671	36.343	38.932	46.797
22	9.542	10.600	12.338	13.041	16.314	18.101	21.337	24.939	27.301	30.813	33.924	37.659	40.289	48.268
23	10.196	11.293	13.091	14.848	17.187	19.021	22.337	26.018	28.429	32.007	35.172	38.968	41.638	49.728
24	10.856	11.992	13.848	15.659	18.062	19.943	23.337	27.096	29.553	33.196	36.415	40.270	42.980	51.179
25	11.524	12.697	14.611	16.473	18.940	20.867	24.337	28.172	30.675	34.382	37.652	41.566	44.314	52.620
26	12.198	13.409	15.379	17.292	19.820	21.792	25.336	29.246	31.795	35.563	38.885	42.856	45.642	54.052
27	12.879	14.125	16.151	18.114	20.703	22.719	26.336	30.319	32.912	36.741	40.113	44.140	46.963	55.476
28	13.565	14.847	16.928	18.939	21.588	23.647	27.336	31.391	34.027	37.916	41.337	45.419	48.278	56.893
29	14.256	15.574	17.708	19.768	22.475	24.577	28.336	32.461	35.139	39.087	42.557	46.693	49.588	58.302
30	14.953	16.306	18.493	20.599	23.364	25.508	29.336	33.530	36.250	40.256	43.773	47.962	50.892	59.703

Note: For larger values of df, the expression $\sqrt{2\chi^2} - \sqrt{2df - 1}$ may be used as a normal deviate with unit variance, remembering that the probability for χ^2 corresponds with that of a single tail of the normal curve. Reproduced from *Design and Analysis of Experiments in Psychology and Education* (p. 29), by E. F. Lindquist, 1953, Boston: Houghton Mifflin, with the permission of the publisher.

References

Abelson, R. P. (1962). *Testing a priori hypotheses in the analysis of variance*. Unpublished manuscript, Yale University, New Haven, CT.

Abelson, R. P. (1985). A variance explanation paradox: When a little is a lot. *Psychological Bulletin, 97,* 129–133.

Bakan, D. (1966). The test of significance in psychological research. *Psychological Bulletin, 66,* 1–29.

Boring, E. G. (1950). *A history of experimental psychology* (2nd ed.). New York: Appleton-Century-Crofts.

Box, G. E. P., Hunter, W. G., & Hunter, J. S. (1978). *Statistics for experimenters*. New York: Wiley.

Brewer, J. K. (1972). On the power of statistical tests in the American Educational Research Journal. *American Educational Research Journal, 9,* 391–401.

Canadian Multicentre Transplant Study Group. (1983). A randomized clinical trial of cyclosporine in cadaveric renal transplantation. *New England Journal of Medicine, 309,* 809–815.

Centers for Disease Control Vietnam Experience Study. (1988). Health status of Vietnam veterans: 1. Psychosocial characteristics. *Journal of the American Medical Association, 259,* 2701–2707.

Chase, L. J., & Chase, R. B. (1976). A statistical power analysis of applied psychological research. *Journal of Applied Psychology, 61,* 234–237.

Cohen, J. (1962). The statistical power of abnormal-social psychological research: A review. *Journal of Abnormal and Social Psychology, 65,* 145–153.

Cohen, J. (1965). Some statistical issues in psychological research. In B. B. Wolman (Ed.), *Handbook of clinical psychology* (pp. 95–121). New York: McGraw-Hill.

Cohen, J. (1973). Statistical power analysis and research results. *American Educational Research Journal, 10,* 225–229.

Cohen, J. (1977). *Statistical power analysis for the behavioral sciences* (Rev. ed.). New York: Academic Press.

Cohen, J. (1988). *Statistical power analysis for the behavioral sciences* (2nd ed.). Hillsdale, NJ: Erlbaum.

Cohen, J. (1990). Things I have learned (so far). *American Psychologist, 45,* 1304–1312.

Gelman, A., Carlin, J., Stern, H., & Rubin, D. B. (1995). *Bayesian data analysis*. New York: Chapman & Hall.

Gigerenzer, G. (1993). The superego, the ego, and the id in statistical reasoning. In G. Keren & C. Lewis (Eds.), *A handbook for data analysis in the behavioral sciences: Methodological issues* (pp. 311–339). Hillsdale, NJ: Erlbaum.

Gigerenzer, G., & Murray, D. J. (1987). *Cognition as intuitive statistics*. Hillsdale, NJ: Erlbaum.

Glass, G. V. (1976, April). Primary, secondary, and meta-analysis of research. Paper presented at the meeting of the American Educational Research Association, San Francisco, CA.

Glass, G. V, McGaw, B., & Smith, M. L. (1981). *Meta-analysis in social research*. Beverly Hills, CA: Sage.

Guilford, J. P. (1956). *Fundamental statistics in psychology and education* (6th ed.). New York: McGraw-Hill.

Haase, R. F., Waechter, D. M., & Solomon, G. S. (1982). How significant is a significant difference? Average effect size of research in counseling psychology. *Journal of Counseling Psychology, 29,* 58–65.

Hallahan, M., & Rosenthal, R. (1996). Contrast analysis in educational research. *Journal of Research in Education. 6,* 3–17.

Hedges, L. V., & Olkin, I. (1985). *Statistical methods for meta-analysis*. New York: Academic Press.

Huberty, C. J., & Morris, J. D. (1989). Multivariate analysis versus multiple univariate analyses. *Psychological Bulletin, 105,* 302–308.

Kolata, G. B. (1981). Drug found to help heart attack survivors. *Science, 214,* 774–775.

Meehl, P. E. (1978). Theoretical risks and tabular asterisks: Sir Karl, Sir Ronald and the slow progress of soft psychology. *Journal of Consulting and Clinical Psychology, 46,* 806–834.

Miller, R. G., Jr. (1981). *Simultaneous statistical inference* (2nd ed.). New York: Springer Verlag.

Nelson, N., Rosenthal, R., & Rosnow, R. L. (1986). Interpretation of significance levels and effect sizes by psychological researchers. *American Psychologist, 41,* 1299–1301.

Ozer, D. J. (1985). Correlation and the coefficient of determination. *Psychological Bulletin, 97,* 307–315.

Rosenthal, R. (1966). *Experimenter effects in behavioral research*. New York: Appleton-Century-Crofts.

Rosenthal, R. (1976). *Experimenter effects in behavioral research* (Enlarged ed.). New York: Halstead Press.

Rosenthal, R. (1979). The "file drawer problem" and tolerance for null results. *Psychological Bulletin, 86,* 638–641.

Rosenthal, R. (1986). Media violence, antisocial behavior, and the social consequences of small effects. *Journal of Social Issues, 42,* 141–154.

Rosenthal, R. (1990). How are we doing in soft psychology? *American Psychologist, 45,* 775–777.

Rosenthal, R. (1991a). Effect sizes: Pearson's correlation, its display via the BESD, and alternative indices. *American Psychologist, 46,* 1086–1087.

Rosenthal, R. (1991b). *Meta-analytic procedures for social research* (Rev. ed.). Newbury Park, CA: Sage.

Rosenthal, R. (1994). Interpersonal expectancy effects: A 30-year perspective. *Current Directions in Psychological Science, 3,* 176–179.

Rosenthal, R., & Gaito, J. (1963). The interpretation of levels of significance by psychological researchers. *Journal of Psychology, 55,* 33–38.

Rosenthal, R., Hall, J. A., DiMatteo, M. R., Rogers, P. L., & Archer, D. (1979). *Sensitivity to nonverbal communication: The PONS Test*. Baltimore: Johns Hopkins University Press.

Rosenthal, R., & Rosnow, R. L. (1985). *Contrast analysis in behavioral research: Focused comparisons in the analysis of variance*. New York: Cambridge University Press.

Rosenthal, R., & Rosnow, R. L. (1991). *Essentials of behavioral research: Methods and data analysis* (2nd ed.). New York: McGraw-Hill.

Rosenthal, R., & Rubin, D. B. (1978). Interpersonal expectancy effects: The first 345 studies. *Behavioral and Brain Sciences, 3,* 377–386.

Rosenthal, R., & Rubin, D. B. (1979). A note on percent variance explained as a measure of the importance of effects. *Journal of Applied Social Psychology, 9,* 395–396.

Rosenthal, R., & Rubin, D. B. (1982). A simple general purpose display of magnitude of experimental effect. *Journal of Educational Psychology, 74,* 166–169.

Rosenthal, R., Rubin, D. B. (1983). Ensemble-adjusted *p* values. *Psychological Bulletin, 94,* 540–541.

Rosenthal, R., & Rubin, D. B. (1984). Multiple contrasts and ordered Bonferroni procedures. *Journal of Educational Psychology, 76,* 1028–1034.

Rosenthal, R., & Rubin, D. B. (1989). Effect size estimation for one-sample multiple-choice-type data: Design, analysis, and meta-analysis. *Psychological Bulletin, 106,* 332–337.

Rosenthal, R., & Rubin, D. B. (1991). Further issues in effect size estimation for one-sample multiple-choice-type data. *Psychological Bulletin, 109,* 351–352.

Rosenthal, R., & Rubin, D. B. (1992–1993). An effect size estimator for parapsychological research. *European Journal of Parapsychology, 9,* 1–11.

Rosenthal, R., & Rubin, D. B. (1994). The counternull value of an effect size: A new statistic. *Psychological Science, 5,* 329–334.

Rosenthal, R., & Rubin, D. B. (1998). *Standardized effect sizes for tables of counts.* Unpublished manuscript, Harvard University, Cambridge, MA.

Rosnow, R. L., & Rosenthal, R. (1988). Focused tests of significance and effect size estimation in counseling psychology. *Journal of Counseling Psychology, 35,* 203–208.

Rosnow, R. L., & Rosenthal, R. (1989). Statistical procedures and the justification of knowledge in psychological science. *American Psychologist, 44,* 1276–1284.

Rosnow, R. L., & Rosenthal, R. (1996a). Computing contrasts, effect sizes, and counternulls on other people's published data: General procedures for research consumers. *Psychological Methods, 1,* 331–340.

Rosnow, R. L., & Rosenthal, R. (1996b). Contrasts and interactions redux: Five easy pieces. *Psychological Science, 7,* 253–257.

Rosnow, R. L., & Rosenthal, R. (1997). *People studying people: Artifacts and ethics in behavioral research.* New York: W. H. Freeman.

Schmidt, F. L. (1996). Statistical significance testing and cumulative knowledge in psychology: Implications for training of researchers. *Psychological Methods, 2,* 115–129.

Sedlmeier, P., & Gigerenzer, G. (1989). Do studies of statistical power have an impact on the power of studies? *Psychological Bulletin, 105,* 309–316.

Smith, M. L., & Glass, G. V. (1977). Meta-analysis of psychotherapy outcome studies. *American Psychologist, 32,* 752–760.

Snedecor, G. W., & Cochran, W. G. (1989). *Statistical methods* (8th ed.). Ames: Iowa State University Press.

Steering Committee of the Physicians' Health Study Research Group. (1988). Preliminary report: Findings from the aspirin component of the ongoing physicians' health study. *New England Journal of Medicine, 318,* 262–264.

Tippett, L. H. C. (1931). *The methods of statistics.* London: Williams & Norgate.

Tukey, J. W. (1977). *Exploratory data analysis.* Reading, MA: Addison-Wesley.

Tukey, J. W. (1991). The philosophy of multiple comparisons. *Statistical Science, 6,* 100–116.

Yates, F. (1990). Foreword. In R. A. Fisher, *Statistical methods, experimental design, and scientific inference* (pp. vii–xxxii). Oxford: Oxford University Press.

Zuckerman, M., Hodgins, H. S., Zuckerman, A., & Rosenthal, R. (1993). Contemporary issues in the analysis of data: A survey of 551 psychologists. *Psychological Science, 4,* 49–53.

Index

Abelson, R. P., ix–x, 5, 16, 205
Alcoholism study (as example), 27–28
Alerting correlation ($r_{alerting}$), 2–4, 50–51
   and factorial designs, 71–73, 102, 106–107, 110–112, 116, 120–121
   and $F_{contrast}$, 40–41
   and meta-analysis, 61–63
   and multiple contrasts, 157, 159–162, 164–165, 171
   and point-biserial r, 9
   and $r^2_{alerting}$, 45–46
   and $r_{contrast}$, 44–47
   and $r_{effect\ size}$, 44–47
   and repeated measures, 135–137, 143–145
   and zero λs, 56
Archer, D., 156, 206
Aspirin study (as example), 25–28

Bakan, D., 5, 205
Bayesian methods, 178
$b_{contrast}$ (regression coefficient), 42–43, 74
BESD correlation (r_{BESD})
   and counternull values, 52–56, 68
   and factorial designs, 93–103, 106, 109–11, 116, 121
   and four-factor design, 92–102
   and meta-analysis, 61–63
   and multiple contrasts, 158–161, 164–165, 169, 171, 178
   and one-dimensional designs, 48–49, 51–56, 61–63, 67–68
   and repeated measures, 132–137, 146
   and two-sample comparisons, 33
   and zero λs, 56
Binomial effect size display (BESD). *See also* BESD correlation
   and chi square (χ^2), 19–20
   and counternull, 20–21
   and dichotomous outcome variables, 21–23
   and odds ratio (*OR*), 23–25
   and r, 17–28
   and relative risk (*RR*), 23–25
   and repeated measures, 127–128
   and risk difference (*RD*), 23–25
   and significance levels, 22–23
   and sum of squares (*SS*), 19
   and three or more groups, 47–50
   and unequal sample sizes, 33
Bonferroni adjusted *p*, 174–177
Boring, E. G., 5, 205
Box, G. E. P., 33, 205
Brewer, J. K., 29, 205

Canadian Multicentre Transplant Study Group, 27, 205
Carlin, J., 178, 205
Centers for Disease Control Vietnam Experience Study, 27, 205
Chase, L. J., 29, 205
Chase, R. B., 29, 205
Chi square (χ^2)
   and BESD, 19–20
   and effect size estimation, 23
   and *Z* statistic, 22–23
Cochran, W. G., 34, 207
Coefficient of determination (r^2), 16–19
Cohen, J., 5, 15, 28–29, 205
Cohen's *d*, 11
   and counternull value, 13–15
   and Hedges's *g*, 12
   and Pearson *r*, 13, 15–16
   and unequal-sample sizes, 30–33
Combining contrasts, 52
Comparing contrasts
   nonsubstantive factors, 160–165
   repeated-measures designs, 165–170
   two-way designs, 162–165
   using standardized weights, 159–160
Confidence intervals, 13
Contrast correlation ($r_{contrast}$), 50–51
   and factorial designs, 74–79, 109, 112, 116, 120
   and $F_{contrast}$, 38–39
   and four-factor design, 88
   and meta-analysis, 61–63

Contrast correlation ($r_{contrast}$) (cont.)
  and multiple contrasts, 158–161, 164, 167–171, 174, 178
  and one-way designs, 42–48, 50–52, 61–63, 67
  and partial r, 42
  and repeated measures, 127, 131, 135–138, 141–142
  and zero λs, 56
Correlation effect size (r), 9, 50–51
  and Cohen's d, 13, 15–16, 32
  and factorial designs, 79–91, 109, 112, 116, 121
  and four-factor design, 90–91
  and Hedges's g, 12, 32
  and meta-analysis, 61–63
  and multiple contrasts, 158–161, 164–165, 169, 171, 178
  and one-dimensional designs, 44–47, 50–52, 61–63, 67
  and point-biserial r, 9–10, 14, 42
  and $r_{alerting}$, 44–47
  and r_{BESD}, 49–50
  and $r_{contrast}$, 44–47
  and repeated measures, 131–137, 145–146
  and transformations, 12–13, 32–33
  and two-sample comparisons, 9–13, 15–16, 25–28, 32
  and zero λs, 56
Counternull, 13
  and BESD, 20–21, 52–61
  and Cohen's d, 13–15
  and correlation ($r_{counternull}$), 13–15, 20–21
  and correlation indices, 13–15
  and four-factor design, 98–102, 116
  and Hedges's g, 13
  and repeated measures, 127, 132, 136, 146
  and set-aside conditions, 59–61
Cyclosporine study (as example), 27–28

Data snooping. *See* Unplanned contrasts
$d_{counternull}$, 15
DiMatteo, M. R., 156, 206

Effect sizes
  and BESD, 15–20, 17–28
  and Cohen's d, 11–13, 15–16
  and correlational (r) indices, 6, 9–11
  and counternull value, 13–15
  and Hedges's g, 11–13
  and interpretation, 15–16
  and practical importance, 25–28
  and significance levels, 4–5
Equations, complete list, 185–190

Factorial designs
  comparing contrasts, 162–165
  counternull, 98–102, 116
  $F_{contrast}$, 73, 78–79, 109, 114–119
  Four-factor example, 88–102

nonsubstantive factors, 80–84, 117–119
$r_{alerting}$, 71–73, 102, 106–107, 110–112, 116, 120–121
r_{BESD}, 93–103, 106, 109–111, 116, 121
$r_{BESD\ counternull}$, 96, 98–102, 106, 110, 112, 116
$r_{contrast}$, 74–79, 109, 112, 116, 120
$r_{effect\ size}$, 79–91, 109, 112, 116, 121
$t_{contrast}$, 73, 115, 118–119
three-factor example, 84–88
zero λs, 102–112
$F_{contrast}$
  and factorial designs, 73, 78–79, 109, 114–119
  and $\bar{F}_{contrast}$, 64–68, 114–115, 118–120
  and one-dimensional designs, 37–41, 50–51, 61, 64–68
  and $r_{alerting}$, 40–41
  and $r_{contrast}$, 38–39
  and repeated-measures design, 130–131
Federighi, E. G., 196
Fisher, R. A., 5, 207
Fisher's z_r, 14
Focused questions, 1
Four-factor example, 88–102

Gaito, J., 4, 206
Gelman, A., 178, 205
Gigerenzer, G., 5, 29, 205, 206
Glass, G. V., 17, 27, 142, 206, 207
Guilford, J. P., 28, 206

Haase, R. F., 29, 206
Hall, J. A., 156, 206
Hallahan, M., 30, 206
Harmonic mean sample size (n_h)
  and power-loss index ($n_h/\bar{n}$), 30
  and repeated-measures, 141
  and transformations between Cohen's d and Hedges's g, 30–31
  and two-group comparison, 30
Hedges, L. V., 13, 206
Hedges's g, 11
  and counternull value, 13
  and Cohen's d, 12
  and Pearson r, 12
  and unequal sample sizes, 30–32
Hodgins, H. S., 4, 207
Huberty, C. J., x, 206
Hunter, J. S., 33, 205
Hunter, W. G., 33, 205

Intrinsically repeated measures
  more than two between-subjects factors, 128–133
  one between-subjects factor, 126–128
  two or more between-subjects factors, 133–136

Keren, G., 205
Kolata, G. B., 27, 206

L score, 37, 126–130, 138–141, 166–169
Lambda (λ) weights
  definition, 3
  set-aside conditions, 56–59, 102–112
Lewis, C., 205
Lindquist, E. F., 196, 203

McGaw, B., 142, 206
Meehl, P. E., 5, 206
Meta-analysis, 31
  computing the four rs, 61–63
Miller, R. G., Jr., 174, 178, 206
Morris, J. D., x, 206
Multiple contrasts
  adjusting effect sizes, 177–178
  adjusting p for planned contrasts, 176–177
  adjusting p for unplanned contrasts, 174–176
  comparing contrasts, 159–170
  nonorthogonal contrasts, 156–159
  nonsubstantive factors, 160–165
  orthogonal contrasts, 151–156
  $r_{alerting}$, 157, 159–162, 164–165, 171
  r_{BESD}, 158–161, 164–165, 169, 171, 178
  $r_{BESD\ counternull}$, 158–162, 164–165, 171
  $r_{contrast}$, 158–161, 164, 167–171, 174, 178
  $r_{effect\ size}$, 158–161, 164–165, 169, 171, 178
Murray, D. J., 205

National Heart, Lung, and Blood Institute, 27
Nelson, N., 4, 30, 206
Noncontrast noise into contrast signal, 51–52
Nonintrinsically repeated measures
  one factor, three or more levels, 137–138
  one factor, two levels, 137
  two or more factors, 138
Nonorthogonal contrasts, 156–159
Nonsubstantive factors, 80–84, 107–112, 117–119, 135–136, 160–165
Null-counternull interval, 13–14, 22

Odds ratio (OR), 23–25
Olkin, I., 13, 206
Omnibus questions, 1
Omnibus F test, limitations, 3
One-dimensional contrasts
  BESD, 47–49, 59–61
  counternull, 52–56, 59–61, 68
  $F_{contrast}$, 37–41, 50–51, 61, 64–68
  meta-analysis, 61–63
  noncontrast noise, 40, 51–52, 56–61
  $r_{alerting}$, 40, 44–46, 50–52, 57–63, 67
  r_{BESD}, 48–49, 51–56, 61–63, 67–68
  $r_{BESD\ counternull}$, 54–56, 59–61, 68
  $r_{contrast}$, 42–48, 50–52, 61–63, 67
  $r_{effect\ size}$, 44–47, 50–52, 61–63, 67
  set-aside conditions, 56–61, 67–68
  $t_{contrast}$, 40–41, 47, 61, 64

unequal sample sizes, 63–68
zero λs, 56
Orthogonal contrasts, 151–156
Ozer, D. J., 16, 206

Partial correlation, 42, 45
Pearson product-moment r
  and BESD, 17–19, 24
  and counternull value, 13–15
  and difference between success rates, 19
  and point-biserial r, 9–10, 14
Pi (π) statistic, 13–14
Point-biserial r, 9–10, 14, 17, 42
Power
  and sample size, 28–30
  and unequal sample sizes, 64
Power-loss index ($n_h/\bar{n}$), 30–32
Propranolol study (as example), 27
Psychotherapy outcome studies (as example), 27–28

r^2, 16–19
$r_{alerting}$. See Alerting correlation
r_{BESD}. See BESD correlation
$r_{BESD\ counternull}$
  and factorial designs, 96, 98–102, 106, 110, 112, 116
  and multiple contrasts, 158–162, 164–165, 171
  and one-way contrasts, 54–56, 59–61, 68
  and repeated-measures designs, 132–133, 136, 146
$r_{contrast}$. See Contrast correlation
$r_{counternull}$. See Counternull
$r_{effect\ size}$. See Correlation effect size
Relative risk (RR), 23–25
Repeated-measures designs
  BESD, 127–128
  comparing contrasts, 165–170
  counternull, 132, 136
  $F_{contrast}$, 130–131
  intrinsically repeated measures, 125–136
  nonintrinsically repeated measures, 136–147
  nonsubstantive factors, 135–136
  $r_{alerting}$, 135–137, 143–145
  r_{BESD}, 132–137, 146
  $r_{BESD\ counternull}$, 132–133, 136, 146
  $r_{contrast}$, 127, 131, 135–138, 141–142
  $r_{counternull}$, 127, 146
  $r_{effect\ size}$, 131–137, 145–146
  $t_{contrast}$, 126–127, 137, 139–141
  unequal sample sizes, 140–141
Replication, 64
Risk difference (RD), 23–25
Rogers, P. L., 156, 206
Rosenthal, R., 4–6, 13–14, 16–18, 24, 30, 156, 174, 176, 206, 207
Rosnow, R. L., 4–6, 16, 30, 174, 206, 207

Rubin, D. B., 6, 13–14, 16–18, 24, 175–176, 178, 205–207

Sample size, 28–30, 63–64
Satterthwaite's method, 34–35
Schmidt, F. L., 5, 207
Sedlmeier, P., 29, 207
Set-aside conditions, 56–61, 102–112
Siegel, S., 192
Significance levels
   and dichotomous outcome variables, 22–23
   and effect sizes, 4–5
   and factorial contrasts, 73
   and null-counternull intervals, 13
   and one-way contrasts, 37–41
   and planned contrasts, 176–177
   and power, 28–30
   and unequal sample sizes in three or more groups, 63–68
   and unplanned contrasts, 174–176
Size of effect, 25–28
Smith, M. L., 27, 142, 206–207
Snedecor, G. W., 34, 207
Solomon, G. S., 29, 206
Steering Committee of the Physicians' Health Study Research Group, 25, 207
Stern, H., 178, 205

$t_{contrast}$
   comparing contrasts, 167
   for $\bar{L}$, 139–141, 166–169
   in factorial designs, 73, 115, 118–119
   in one-dimensional designs, 40–41, 47, 61, 64
   in repeated-measures designs, 126–127, 137, 139–141
   intrinsic vs. nonintrinsic repeated measures, 170
Three or more groups. *See* One-dimensional contrasts
Three-factor example, 84–88
Tippett, L. H. C., 174, 207
Tolerance for implicit contrasts (T_{ic}), 176
Transformations
   and effect sizes, 12–13
   and Fisher's z_r, 13–14
   and power-loss index, 30–33
   and Satterthwaite's method, 34–35
   and unequal variances in two samples, 33
Tukey, J. W., 33, 178, 207
Two-sample comparison
   BESD, 17–25, 33
   Cohen's d, 11–13, 31–32
   Hedges's g, 11–12, 32
   odds ratio (OR), 23–25
   power, 28–30
   $r_{counternull}$, 13–15, 20–23
   $r_{effect\ size}$, 9–13, 15–16, 25–28, 32
   relative risk (RR), 23–25
   risk difference (RD), 23–25
   t statistic, 8, 30, 34
   unequal sample sizes, 30–35
   unequal variances, 33–35

Unequal sample sizes
   and BESD, 33
   and effect size transformations, 30–33
   and repeated-measures designs, 140–141
   and t test, 30
   and three or more groups, 63–68
Unequal variances, 33–35
Unplanned contrasts
   and "data snooping," 170
   and adjustments, 174–178

Video game study (as example), 1–3

Waechter, D. M., 29, 206
Weights for orthogonal polynomial-based contrasts, 153
Wolman, B. B., 205

Yates, F., 5, 207

Z statistic, 19–22
Zuckerman, A., 4, 207
Zuckerman, M., 4, 207